My People

In My Place

New News Out of Africa: Uncovering Africa's Renaissance

To the Mountaintop: My Journey Through the Civil Rights Movement

Corrective Rape: Discrimination, Assault, Sexual Violence, and Murder Against South Africa's L.G.B.T. Community

My People

Five Decades of Writing
About Black Lives

Charlayne Hunter-Gault

Foreword by Nikole Hannah-Jones

HARPER ● PERENNIAL

NEW YORK ● LONDON ● TORONTO ● SYDNEY ● NEW DELHI ● AUCKLAND

HARPER ● PERENNIAL

A hardcover edition of this book was published in 2022 by HarperCollins Publishers.

HarperCollins books may be purchased for educational, business, or sales promotional use. For information, please email the Special Markets Department at SPsales@harpercollins.com.

FIRST HARPER PERENNIAL EDITION PUBLISHED 2023.

Cover photographs: The author with Nelson Mandela courtesy of Jacqueline Farmer. The author on assignment in Africa courtesy of Jeff Goldman. The other photographs courtesy of the author.

Library of Congress Cataloging-in-Publication Data has been applied for.

ISBN 978-0-06-313540-6 (pbk.)

23 24 25 26 27 LBC 5 4 3 2 1

To the next generation of journalists who I hope will join me in fighting the good fight. And to the late Valerie Boyd, the Charlayne Hunter-Gault Distinguished Writer in Residence at the Grady College of Journalism and Mass Communication at the University of Georgia and a multitalented author, journalist, and friend who helped me choose students committed to giving voice to the voiceless. Long Live!

Contents

PART VI: Honoring the Ancestors   293

Foreword

I first met Charlayne Hunter-Gault in 2016 when I shared the stage with her in New York City during a panel on covering race held for the George Polk Awards. I am not a journalist who has ever cared about how my profession can give access to celebrity, but meeting Charlayne Hunter-Gault for the first time rendered me—for lack of a better word—starstruck. It is seldom that one gets an opportunity to sit in conversation with someone whose life, activism, and career quite literally made it possible for you to live yours as you have, but for me, Ms. Hunter-Gault embodies that rarest of people. I did not feel worthy of sharing the stage with an icon of the civil rights movement, someone who integrated the all-white University of Georgia—and therefore its all-white journalism program that would one day award us both the Peabody—someone who had helped integrate newsrooms, someone who had been cataloguing the beauty and triumphs, struggles and resistance, of Black people across the diaspora for longer than I had been alive. It's a scary and vulnerable thing to meet your heroes, and yet, Ms. Hunter-Gault treated me with the grace and generosity that she is known for even as I told her repeatedly how honored I was to meet her and talk with her. So when an email from her popped up in my inbox asking me to write the foreword for her new book, I took it as such a tremendous honor.

In the aptly named *My People*, the veteran journalist compiles decades of reporting from the various news organizations lucky enough to have employed her, reports that begin with her own experiences integrating the University of Georgia, stretching throughout the South—the ancestral land of Black Americans—to the urban North, where she established the Harlem Bureau for the *New York Times*, and crossing the Atlantic to chronicle the freedom struggles of Black people on the African continent. In each story, Ms. Hunter-Gault brings the determination to analyze the fruits of the racial caste system that she was born into while also documenting the humanity, the striving, the joy, and the creativity of her people—our people. As she writes in part 5, she wanted to focus on reporting she "didn't see much of in the magazine (or anywhere else) at the time—the experience of ordinary Black people in the segregated South, like my dear grandmother. And while it was a South that had been challenged and changed by mostly young civil rights activists, I thought it was important to tell a story that focused on the ongoing, day-to-day experiences of ordinary Black people. It was equally important to me to show readers where we got our own sense of commitment to family and community. So I embarked on a journey that shed some light on those realities."

Ms. Hunter-Gault provided a template for me and countless other Black journalists across the world. Like mine, her interest in journalism was piqued as a precocious preteen, and like me, she came to understand that for Black journalists in the United States, there could be no pretense of neutrality in a nation that actively legislated against and suppressed the rights of our people.

What does journalistic neutrality and objectivity look like when your career began with a fight for racial justice? When you spent your life being the first of your race to accomplish the things that you did because Black people had been either officially or unofficially barred from doing those things before? Where your very education and career were born out of activism and the generational Black rights struggles? Where you've always known that democracy in the United States was more an idea than a reality, one that has to constantly be fought for, and that America is not the free and just country it purported to be?

Through Ms. Hunter-Gault's reporting and personal biography we see that what has been treated as journalistic objectivity in nearly all-white newsrooms that produce a nearly all-white report has and remains to be the antithesis of objectivity; that newsrooms became richer, more accurate, and more democratic as reporters such as Ms. Hunter-Gault took their places in them.

In these chapters we see Ms. Hunter-Gault as a young woman becoming part of the movement, then cataloguing it, then we see her through the years watching new movements arise, watching them falter, and then ultimately eulogizing her contemporaries.

We get to witness the journalist as her writing and thinking evolves, as her reporting spans continents and yet tells for Black people across the diaspora an often-familiar story of resistance and resilience, and for white Americans reveals our often-overlooked humanity. We witness writing that is powerful and urgent and unflinching and, perhaps most of all, determined—determined, as my spiritual godmother Ida B. Wells said, to shine the light of truth upon our society. And we see through her reporting that the battles she waged for equality—starting as a college student determined to gain access to the state university that her own parents subsidized with their tax dollars—are never won for good, that the struggle is ongoing, that the legal barriers have fallen but the architecture of racial inequality remains. And as Ms. Hunter-Gault shows us, as long as the architecture of racial inequality remains, so does the journalists' mandate to investigate and report on it.

This volume is a clinic for other journalists, but especially for Black journalists, as it is clear from every story, every interview, every voice centered in the work, that Ms. Hunter-Gault centered her work among Black people and saw herself as a Black journalist.

Here lies the work of a woman whose destiny would be both to chronicle history and to make it.

—Nikole Hannah-Jones

PART I

Toward Justice and Equality, Then and Now

The civil rights movement in Atlanta, Georgia, put me on the path of reporting stories that focused on the promise of liberty and justice for *all*, a promise that had been so long denied to my people. The lie of separate but equal was still the law of the South, and while not on the books, it was alive and well even up north, commonly referred to as Up South at the time. My effort to make the promise of our democracy and my dream of becoming a journalist a reality at the University of Georgia, an all-white establishment for its 176 years of existence, was working its way through the resistant system, and I had temporarily enrolled at Wayne State University in Detroit, which offered some courses in journalism. But the civil rights movement that had begun on February 1, 1960, with young Black college students sitting in at a lunch counter in Nashville, Tennessee, had now reached Atlanta, and some of my closest friends from our high school days were among those who were taking to the streets demanding that "Dogwood City" fulfill the promise of equal rights to them and all who looked like them.

At the same time, the Atlanta student movement was just one of many protest movements taking place all over the South. And I kept my eye on those, albeit from a distance.

And so it was in Atlanta that I took my earliest steps on my journalistic journey, steps that led me into the basement of an upstart newspaper called the *Atlanta Inquirer*. The paper was started by one of the men whose approach to myself and Hamilton Holmes ended with us desegregating the University of Georgia, where I was by this time matriculating. M. Carl Holman was a professor of English at the all-Black Clark College in Atlanta. He was close to many of its students and those from the three other Black colleges—Morehouse, Spelman, and Morris Brown, many of whom were taking part in the civil rights protests. They had organized themselves into what they called the Committee on Appeal for Human Rights, and had created a document that laid out their demands for racial justice, insisting they "did not intend to wait placidly for those rights which are already legally and morally ours to be meted out one at a time. . . . [W]e want to state clearly and unequivocally that we cannot tolerate, in a nation professing democracy and among people professing Christianity, the discriminatory conditions under which the Negro is living today in Atlanta, Georgia, supposedly one of the most progressive cities in the South."

In the early days, I waited for the students to pile in with their stories. In the early days, they would demonstrate for part of the day, then get arrested so as to establish a case that could be argued at a later date in court and hopefully lead to a decision that would overthrow separate and not equal.

Within hours, they would then get bailed out and many would come straight to the Holman basement to tell their stories to Julian Bond, who was one of the writers of the Committee on Appeal document, as well as managing editor of the paper. He had been a student at Morehouse College but had put that on hold for the time being. I bided my time rambling around the basement, looking over textbooks belonging to Holman, who wrote under the pen name Vox.

In time, I felt the need to get out of the basement and into the streets myself—not as a participant but as an observing servant of the people. And in a few years I traveled from the streets of Atlanta to streets up and down the East Coast, where there may not have been Jim Crow laws, but the pattern and practice of racial discrimination had the same effect on my people. So, along with my clothes, I packed my racial consciousness. And while some of my clothes wore out from time, my people and their stories kept my consciousness fresh and responsive to their ongoing challenges. For while their consciousness kept them focused on how far they had come in many instances, it also helped them (and me) keep their eyes on what continued and continues to be an elusive prize: equality and justice for all. At one point in 1967, following four summers of riots protesting inequality around the country, a National Advisory Commission on Civil Disorders was created by President Lyndon B. Johnson to address the cause of the disturbances. The commission ultimately concluded that the country was "moving toward two societies, one white and privileged, one Black and unequal." It included in the blame the mostly white media. And while corrective steps were taken in all areas, including the media, all these years later, inequality persists, even in many well-funded and well-staffed and even prize-winning news organizations.

The protests sparked by police killings of Black people over the last few years have caused another period of soul-searching, a moment to dig deeper, as clearly the racist demons of our past still haunt us. Even as Georgia voters sent Raphael Warnock, its first-ever Black senator, to Congress in 2020, shortly thereafter the Georgia legislature passed numerous bills that will undoubtedly lead to voter suppression that will disproportionately affect Black turnout if not overturned. But if the past has any lesson for the present and the future, look no further than John Lewis, who was among the civil rights activists who led the fight that culminated in the Voting Rights Act of 1965, which removed legal barriers at the state and local levels that had prevented Blacks from exercising their right to vote—a right that had been guaranteed under the Fifteenth Amendment to the U.S. Constitution. Today his name is attached to a voting rights bill that would stifle yet another effort aimed at reducing the voice of Blacks at the ballot box, this one by a Supreme Court ruling in 2013. While the challenges keep on coming, Black history teaches us that the civil rights movement's anthem of keep on keepin' on yields positive results. Thus we learn from our history the value of insisting on our full rights as citizens, for as I have written before, we are "heirs to a legacy of struggle, but struggle that was, as Martin Luther King taught, ennobling, struggle that was enabling us to take control of our destiny." (*In My Place*, 1992.)

Dispute Center Opens in Harlem

The New York Times
MAY 28, 1975

A community-based mediation center for minor disputes that is designed to free policemen "for more serious crimes" and help unclog the
courts was opened yesterday in Harlem.

The center, which is under the auspices of the Institute for Mediation and Conflict Resolution, is the first of its kind in the country,
according to Basil A. Paterson, the institute's president.

Situated at 402 West 145th Street, the center will employ community residents who have undergone four months of training in arbitration and mediation to handle cases such as harassment, domestic
disputes, and other "lesser crimes between friends, relatives and neighbors," Mr. Paterson said.

The cases—which involve about 1,000 people a year, according to
police estimates—will be referred to the center by police officers either
directly from the scene or from the station house if the disputants agree
on such a course of action.

A three-person panel will then hear the case, and if the parties
themselves cannot agree on a resolution, the panel will impose one.

"A lot of these cases just get bogged down in the courts now," said
Eda Harris, a social worker and one of twenty-four persons so far

trained by the institute. "They really don't belong in the court system. These people are going back to the community, they'll see each other. They need a resolution they can live with."

A major incentive for going to arbitration or mediation is that the disputants are judged by people from their own community, Mr. Paterson said, and that they also avoid establishing a criminal record.

In praising the new center, Police Commissioner Michael C. Codd said that it made "very little sense" to handle disputes in courts and "keep our valuable police power tied up rather than being in the streets attending to more serious crimes."

District Attorney Robert M. Morgenthau, who promised "100 percent cooperation" in the new venture, criticized criminal law as "an imperfect way of solving criminal problems, but particularly imperfect when it is called in to family and community disputes."

The center, which received a $306,000 federal grant from the Law Enforcement Assistance Administration, through the Criminal Justice Coordinating Council, will initially serve the areas covered by the 30th and 34th Precincts—all of Manhattan north of 141st Street.

State Supreme Court Justice Edward R. Dudley, who described the center as "a deterrent at its source," encouraged the community to work with the police.

After-School School for Black Youngsters in Search of Heritage

The New York Times
APRIL 17, 1976

"In many ways, it's hard raising a black kid in New York City," said Millie Thunder in explaining why she had enrolled her six-year-old daughter in the Patterson School for Heritage and Learning, which opened March 11. "They're usually always tokens and that can be devastating."

"In private schools," said Fred Benjamin, "there are usually only about two or three blacks. And once a kid becomes aware that he's black, he gets confused because his background is pretty much left out in those situations."

Nestled in a quiet corner of Harlem's Sugar Hill, the Patterson School at 144th Street and Convent Avenue is an after-school school that is teaching their heritage to black youngsters, from kindergarten through twelfth grade.

In the process, it also seeks to strengthen their skills in such areas as mathematics, language arts, and reading.

For several years, John and Jamelle Patterson, parents of two black school-age children and founders of the school, had not only heard of difficulties in schooling from their predominantly middle-class black friends, but had lived them, as well.

The Pattersons, who had tried both private and public schools for their children, had both had been extremely active in educational circles in the city.

It was while struggling with the problem of what to do in their own home that they decided that something should be done for black youngsters in general.

As a result of informal discussions with teachers and others in both public and private schools, Mrs. Patterson came across what she considered a startling discovery.

"By fourth grade," she recalled the other day, "black youngsters start falling behind and staying behind. And even in private schools, the scores of black youngsters were collectively lower than those of whites."

This ultimately led her to the conclusion last May that there was a correlation between a student's ability to achieve and a positive self-concept.

"That's when we decided to start our own school."

In the next ten months, there was a flurry of late-night meetings and early-morning reading sessions, curriculum planning, hiring teachers, and an extensive search for the right facility.

Through it all, the Pattersons' experience in and contacts with the educational community facilitated their effort.

Mr. Patterson, a lawyer, had already established three other institutions—the first black brokerage firm on Wall Street, Patterson & Co.; the Interracial Council for Business Opportunity; and the South Bronx Over-all Economic Development Corporation, of which he is currently president.

To help make their dream a reality, the Pattersons assembled a board of advisers that included Mr. Patterson's brother, Raymond, an author and lecturer at City College; Dr. Beryl Banfield, president of the Council on Interracial Books for Children; Dr. Gloria Blackwell,

Mrs. Patterson's mother, who is chairman of the English department at Clark College in Atlanta; Lerone Bennette, senior editor of *Ebony* magazine; John Henrik Clarke, historian and professor at Hunter College; and Dr. Francis Roberts, president of the Bank Street College of Education.

"To my knowledge," said Mrs. Patterson, the twenty-nine-year-old president and director of the sixty-pupil institution, "it's the only school of its kind. There are lots of alternative schools, as well as Hebrew, Chinese, and Japanese schools that have been in existence for fifty years or more. But in the black community, there's nothing like it."

Dr. James P. Comer, professor of psychiatry and associate dean of the Yale Medical School, and also a member of the advisory board, agreed that the school was unusual.

"One of our problems has been that we have had no mechanism, except the black church—when we were immersed in the church—for transmitting our struggle or our tradition of excellence and hard work from generation to generation," he said.

"And each generation wakes up saying, 'Why are we in this condition?' And the mainstream culture isn't going to tell you because they're struggling with it. They don't know how to integrate it into theirs. So they've treated it marginally or negatively or not at all."

The school's emphasis is on African heritage and tradition and a major aspect is the role of the extended family. The school has taken the role of a surrogate family in many instances, providing the youngsters with background on their heritage that they are not receiving elsewhere, either in their homes or in their regular schools.

Integrating heritage into the curriculum is easy, once there is the commitment to do it, said Mrs. Patterson, whose educational experiences range from high school in Orangeburg, South Carolina, to Wesleyan, where she received her Master of Arts in teaching. (She did further postgraduate work at Harvard and the University of Strasbourg, in France.)

"In learning how to compute averages, for example," she explained,

"I learned by computing Babe Ruth's batting average. Here, at the Patterson School, we'll use Hank Aaron's."

A major point of departure in the school's historical emphasis, Mrs. Patterson said, is that black history is taught from the perspective that the African continent was one of the first to emerge as land, and that human life, and the first civilization, began there.

"It's not about being militant or separatist," Mrs. Patterson said in explaining the school's motivation. "It's about why we have not been able to get along in this pluralistic society. Only the dominant group's culture has been emphasized. The more you know about your culture and heritage, the more productive you are and the more confidence you have in dealing with others.

"Normally, our kids are taught that their heritage is in slavery, in chains," she went on, "instead of in the context of the continuum of history in which they are direct descendants of thousands of years of kings and queens.

"Every group has been enslaved, but they never allude to that part of their history. The Europeans, instead, dressed it up and called it serfdom and kept on going."

Mrs. Patterson said that the new school, which was established with the help of grants from the New York Urban Coalition, Bankers Trust, and Chemical Bank, expected to be self-supporting. The minimum tuition is $30 a month for one two-hour session a week, and the maximum is $80 a month for fifteen hours. There are adjustments in tuition for income levels, and limited scholarships available for low-income students.

Situated on the fifth floor of an educational building recently purchased by the Convent Avenue Baptist Church, the school can accommodate about two hundred students.

Bryan Derek Haley, a twelve-year-old junior high school student, said he was attending the Patterson School because he likes math a lot and because "the teachers are not always screaming and cussing at you."

Sitting in a room surrounded by portraits of such prominent black figures as Langston Hughes and John Henry, Bryan said that he had also learned a lot about such people.

"I knew it," he explained. "But I didn't know there was such a lot of them, just knew Frederick Douglass and Shirley Bassey."

Black Activist Sees New South

Lewis Seeks Funds to Help Enroll More Voters

The New York Times
NOVEMBER 18, 1973

The year that the Black Panther and black power emerged as the symbols of a new direction for black politics in the South—1966—was the year that whites were urged to leave the movement and work in their own communities.

It was also the year that Stokely Carmichael, the architect of that change, urged blacks to turn inward and concentrate on strategies for seizing political power as a means toward reversing the trend that always saw blacks bargaining with whites for small favors.

And it was the year that John Lewis, a disciple of nonviolent demonstrations and coalition politics, was replaced as the head of the Student Nonviolent Coordinating Committee by Mr. Carmichael.

Now, seven years and more than a million registered black voters later, John Lewis is beginning to see a meshing of the two philosophies of black power and coalition politics. Blacks in the South are gaining political strength—there are now more than 1,000 black elected officials in the eleven states of the Old Confederacy—but they are doing it in conjunction with whites.

Mr. Lewis, who now heads the nonprofit Voter Education Project in Atlanta, the major organization registering and educating black voters in the South, was interviewed here last week on his way to a conference of black mayors in Tuskegee, Alabama, this weekend.

Explaining his rather circuitous route, Mr. Lewis said: "I'm here trying to convince the people with the financial resources that we need that what's happening in the South is good for the rest of the country."

What is happening, he said, is "a revolution—not as dramatic as the sixties, but a registration of more than three and a half million black voters, larger numbers of black elected officials, and a new breed of white politician.

"Within the next eight to ten years," he continued, "blacks are going to be elected to some of the highest offices. Georgia, Mississippi, the Carolinas are going to be sending several blacks to Congress to join the few who are there now.

"Now, many of those congressional committees are dominated by Southerners. As blacks continue to register, they're going to have to go. And even if whites still head a few of those committees, they'll be responding in a different way. And the politics of the South will change the politics of the country."

Mr. Lewis, who picked cotton as a boy in Alabama and was jailed and constantly harassed on freedom rides and sit-ins as a young man, believes that it was that era, those experiences that make him hopeful.

Mr. Lewis said that in his travels for the Voter Education Project he was running into the people he knew as sharecroppers and tenant farmers in the early sixties.

"These people are forty and fifty years old now, and they're the ones who are getting ready to run for office. As they listen to the whites talk about the disgrace of national politics, these black people are saying they're sick of it. And it's almost like 'I told you so.'

"And the whites are losing interest because they've lost faith in the national scene, and they're turning to the blacks as a kind of last hope. They're saying, 'They're the ones who've been excluded from this system; maybe if they get in they'll be better.'"

Mr. Lewis went on to say that they were right.

Mr. Lewis also said that the South had "killed the politics of race."

Despite racial overtones in the Atlanta mayoral race, in which a black was elected, he said, blacks helped elect a white woman over a black man to the City Council.

The black candidate had sided with the white mayor to use revenue-sharing funds as tax rebates for landlords, and also supported the mayor in his attempts to stop a sanitation workers' strike.

And while blacks voted heavily for the black candidate, they provided the white candidate the margin of victory. Mr. Lewis attributed their support of her to her stand in favor of the sanitation workers and her position that the revenue-sharing funds should be used for things like day care centers.

But Mr. Lewis would not have been in New York if he thought the battle was over, he said. Many of the newly elected officials need help and guidance—the kind the Voter Education Project experience would help provide them, according to Mr. Lewis.

In addition, half of the total black population, he said, is in the South. Of that number, there are six million of voting age and three and a half million registered.

"There's been very little enforcement of the Voting Rights Act under this administration," Mr. Lewis charged. "So that we still have places where there is not a single polling place in the black community."

Blacks Are Developing Programs to Fight Crime in Communities

The New York Times
FEBRUARY 23, 1976

Black groups in many cities have embarked on a new effort to cope with crime in their communities through such widely varied programs as videotape education projects and "big brother" counseling.

While some of the programs can demonstrate concrete results, few have been able to get substantial funding from federal, state, or local sources.

One constant in all of them is an insistence that the black community define the problems and put forward its own solutions.

"Blacks resent the suggestion that either they have been covering up for criminals or that they have been afraid to look at the problem," said M. Carl Holman, president of the National Urban Coalition. "It has not been the minorities who have had control of the machinery to deal with crime."

The heightened concern about what one black official called "black-on-black genocide" has led to community efforts in such cities as New York, Philadelphia, New Orleans, Memphis, Buffalo, Washington, and Chicago.

A key element in these efforts is a new attitude toward and increased cooperation with black policemen—either individually or through local affiliates of national organizations like the Guardians, an association of black policemen.

In a recent interview, Deputy Commander George Sims, of the Fillmore police district on Chicago's tough West Side, waved a report that showed crime in the district had decreased. Both Mr. Sims and the district commander, Robert Williams, believe that part of the reason is that black police officers are working more closely with the community, respecting it and receiving greater cooperation.

The view that crime-fighting priorities should be established by the community rather than by the police is shared by many black policemen as well as residents of the black community. Yet, for the time being, their input into policy, the policemen contend, is minimal. "We cannot initiate policy or change anything," said one black officer in New York.

As a result, much of their fight is still internal, with blacks in some cities planning to follow the lead of Chicago's black police association, the Afro-American Patrolmen's League, whose suit held up millions of dollars in federal funds on the basis that the Police Department practiced job discrimination against blacks.

Community approaches to crime vary widely, with some programs being no more than a compact among tenants in public housing not to buy stolen goods, as in the Taylor Homes on the South Side of Chicago.

In Chicago's Woodlawn area the Woodlawn Organization has a "block watcher program" in which suspected or actual crimes are reported to the organization, which notifies the police. The group is also about to begin a program to aid victims of crime.

Another Chicago group, the Metropolitan Anti-Crime Coalition, uses videotape presentations on how to deal with crime, which are shown to community groups. It also is pressing for more assistant state's attorneys to speed processing of cases.

In Memphis, the National Association for the Advancement of Colored People is using its own funds, a few grants, and extensive help from the black policemen's association in working with two hundred young men from low-income areas where many families have no fathers living with them.

In New Orleans, the Dixon Research Center, a federally funded community agency, is trying to reduce "black-on-black" crime through education and research, including "consciousness-raising" workshops and audiovisual presentations.

"You're dealing with behavior and attitudes which are developed over the years," said Clarence Guillimet, the director of the center. "In order to eliminate those patterns we're approaching it from three ways—research, reality, and revelation."

Near the center, a group of about twelve teen-age boys—volunteers—working in shifts and wearing red hard hats, patrol the construction site of a new Treme Community Center, from 3:45 p.m. to 6:30 p.m. to prevent young vandals from breaking the windows. In little more than two months since new windows were installed, only one window has been reported broken. The Treme Community Center has $125,000 worth of glass in it, according to Mr. Guillimet.

The results of many of the newer community programs that have sprung up recently are less easy to document. A group called the We Care Committee has just been formed in Buffalo. It consists of fifty well-known blacks, representing twenty-two public and private social and government agencies. Their funding comes from individuals and from the agencies they represent. Each spends a few hours a week counseling black youths in a "big brother" program.

They also try to make sure that there are no incidents of police brutality or police misbehavior against blacks.

In Washington and Chicago the Reverend Jesse Jackson, president of the Chicago-based Operation PUSH, has begun a campaign that includes slogans such as "Get off dope, get on hope." The campaign expects to involve parents and children in the problem of discipline in the schools.

The *New York Amsterdam News*, a black weekly newspaper, has launched a "War on Crime" that so far lacks a battle plan but has emphasized maximum involvement by black citizens. A retired black deputy police inspector, Eldridge Waith, who had years of experience in New York's black communities, has been named to lead the "war."

Citizen patrols have sprung up in several cities within recent months, but have drawn mixed reactions from the community and law enforcement officials.

Lieutenant Paul Blaney, of the Chicago Police Department, said that the number of citizen patrols had increased there, "but not in the areas where it is basically needed.

"They have made the greatest strides in areas where there are single-family homes," he said. "Once you have a mortgage you have a vested interest in protecting that. But these are middle-class working areas."

Black policemen like Renault Robinson, head of the black policemen's group that led the fight against alleged discrimination in the Chicago Police Department, argue that citizens' patrols "are not a deterrent and provide the community with a false sense of security."

"The citizen patrols are a reaction to failure, to poor police services," said Mr. Robinson. "These citizens are crying out for better police protection."

Whatever the effectiveness of local groups, many blacks involved in the problem see a need for a national organized black effort to achieve policy changes toward more comprehensive solutions.

"[Mayor Frank] Rizzo won with black votes in Philadelphia because he was talking about short-term solutions—more cops, locking up the youths, restoring the death penalty," said Robert L. Woodson, director of the National Urban League's administration of justice division. "And the people are more afraid of crime in the streets than the racism of a Rizzo."

The black community would get behind more creative solutions, given the choice and exposure, Mr. Woodson believes. Toward that end, the league has raised $100,000 of a $200,000 proposal to pull together black local and national leaders and groups to use their experience, research, and sensitivity to find those solutions.

Mr. Woodson said that the league hoped to get the other $100,000 from community resources like the black church, because "the federal government in the past has turned a deaf ear to blacks attempting to deal with the problem.

"None of the current research on black crime is being done by blacks," Mr. Woodson asserted. "And part of that has to do with the fact that the Law Enforcement Assistance Administration has only one black in a policy-making position."

Mr. Woodson said the Urban League hoped to develop a plan that would "launch an organized attack on crime—not just to make the street safe, but that would speak to such areas as victim relief, penal reform, and various sociological and institutional dimensions of the problem.

"Since the federal government won't do it," Mr. Woodson said, "we hope to give our people direction from a national black fountainhead."

Economist Finds Widening in Black-White Income Gap

The New York Times
NOVEMBER 29, 1975

NEWARK, Nov. 28—Despite "temporary" gains made by blacks toward economic parity with whites in the 1960s, recent trends indicate that the gap is once again widening, and that it may be at least seventy-five years before blacks catch up, according to one economist.

"The movement of the 1960s toward greater equality seems to be broken," according to Lester S. Thurow, professor of economics at the Alfred P. Sloan School of Management in the Massachusetts Institute of Technology.

Speaking at a symposium marking the tenth anniversary of the United States Equal Employment Opportunity Commission held at the Newark campus of the Rutgers University Law School, Dr. Thurow said, "At all points in time—good or bad—black unemployment rates are twice as high as white."

At the moment, he said, that condition is exacerbated by the recession and a decline in the proportion of black families with two or more workers—a phenomenon that is the reverse in white families.

While current recession data are not yet available, Dr. Thurow, also the author of *Poverty and Discrimination*, predicted that the trend would continue and the gap would increasingly widen. The essential problem is "a long-run deeply embedded relationship in the economy," he said.

"The rapidly escalating black unemployment rates of this recession or depression are not a temporary phenomenon," he said. "They are exactly what would have been expected given the structure of the economy. Nothing has changed in the past thirty years. No progress has been made."

Dr. Thurow attributed the gain in relative earnings among blacks to the absorption of younger blacks into the post–World War II labor force—"the type of change that causes the least disruptions" in the labor force.

But, he said, in periods of recession, the process is reversed because of seniority provisions (formal and informal) in hiring and layoffs.

"The youngest workers are most apt to lose their jobs, and they are the workers where the ratio of black to white earnings is most likely to be near parity," he said. "Therefore a recession shifts the weight of those remaining fully employed toward older groups with larger relative earning differences."

Thus, while black earnings from 1955 to 1973 rose from 36 percent to 66 percent of those of white males, and black females from 56 percent to 86 percent, the rate of gains for blacks was just as fast in the 1950s as the 1960s.

In addition, according to Dr. Thurow, since 1970 there is "little evidence" of any advance in the relative earnings of black males and the same is true of black females since 1971.

Although black women are not far from parity with white women, according to Dr. Thurow, not only have white women lost ground but black women have also made virtually no progress in the higher-income, or top 5 percent jobs. "Whatever the feminist movement has done," he said, "it hasn't got anybody high-income jobs."

As for black families, he continued, from 1947 to 1952, black family incomes rose from 51 percent to 57 percent of white family earnings at the peak of the Korean War, declined to 51 percent with the recession of 1957–58, rose to 64 percent under the pressures of the Vietnam War and the civil rights movement, and then once again started to fall, reaching 60 percent in 1973.

At the same time, however, among one of the two other ethnic groups—there are only three ethnic groups with incomes below the average—blacks, American Indians, and persons of Spanish heritage, according to Dr. Thurow—between 1969 and 1973, Spanish heritage families—particularly Cubans, Central and South Americans—have gone from a position of inferiority relative to both black and white families to a position of economic superiority relative to black families.

A "substantial fraction" of that improvement, according to Dr. Thurow, comes from falling relative unemployment rates for male Spanish-heritage workers, along with an increase in the participation rate of Spanish-heritage females—a rate faster than that of black females.

Rejecting the Equal Employment Opportunity Commission as the mechanism for major changes in the distribution of earnings, Dr. Thurow urged "an all-out effort" by minority groups and others interested in such problems to push for a comprehensive job or real "right to work" program, one that is permanent and open ended.

Irma Vidal Santaella, chairman of the Appeals Board of the New York State Division of Human Rights, argued against Dr. Thurow's conclusions about the gains of Puerto Ricans, whose unemployment rates, particularly in New York City, she said, had soared to 22 to 23 percent as a result of the curtailment of poverty programs.

In addition, the group of about two hundred people were advised by lawyers among the panelists not to discount law and litigation as forces for social change. That issue, along with a forecast for the future of the Equal Employment Opportunity Commission, will be among the concluding topics of the two-day session.

Fighting Racism in Schools

The New York Times
NOVEMBER 27, 2019

To the Editor:

Re "Finding the Tools to Spot, and Fight, Intolerance in Schools" (news article, Nov. 24): Having examined this disturbing phenomenon in my *PBS NewsHour* series looking at solutions to racism, let me hasten to say that intolerance is a worrisome development that is germinating in the underbelly of our democracy. And like so many other troubling challenges, it needs to be called out every bit as much as interference in our electoral processes, if not more.

Our children are our future, and while in my reporting I have found that our history—that is, the history of all our people—is not being taught in most schools these days, the need to combat malicious memes that are trying to fill that gap needs all the attention it can get.

Our union may never be perfect, but we owe it to our children to educate them perfectly.

Charlayne Hunter-Gault, Sarasota, Fla.

More Negroes Vacation as Barriers Fall

The New York Times
SEPTEMBER 7, 1970

OAK BLUFFS, Mass.—Zaida Coles Edley, a black television actress, was lounging on the beach here on Martha's Vineyard with her husband and a couple of guests. "Watch what happens to this scene," she said. "In just about an hour you'll be in for a surprise."

It was high noon and time passed quickly as a blazing sun beat down on the long, sandy beach and a handful of other bathers and sun worshipers, mostly white.

Then one of Mrs. Edley's guests sensed something had changed, sat up, and looked around. The sun had moved, a few degrees to the west, but that wasn't it. What had changed were the faces around them: There were more of them and almost all were black.

The figures in this scene—prosperous black families languidly whiling away the hours of a summer vacation—would not have surprised anyone here but a stranger, for tiny Oak Bluffs has for generations been a favorite vacation place of middle-class blacks.

But the same scene, or something like it, is becoming increasingly common throughout the country at beaches and resorts that have never before had to accommodate large numbers of black guests. The reason is that more and more blacks are taking vacations.

Discrimination persists at some places, but formal racial barriers are down, the black middle class is growing, and, at least for white-collar blacks, income is up and there is more money to spend.

According to D. Parke Gibson, a black public relations adviser for black travel agents in several cities, black vacation expenditures have risen by 25 percent in four years. As a "conservative estimate" of this year's total at the close of the current season, Mr. Gibson gave $675 million.

Many of the new black vacationers apparently prefer such traditional black vacation areas as Oak Bluffs or Sag Harbor, Long Island, or Fernandina Beach, Florida. But some were breaking new ground, venturing into previously all-white resorts or taking off for black-dominated areas like the West Indies or certain countries in Africa.

Even the more adventurous ones, however, seemed to want to travel with other blacks. (As Mrs. Edley put it: "We do like to be together.") And some of them have had problems.

Karen Batchelor and Joyce Jeffersons, both college students from Detroit, were among black vacationers who along with their families and about fifty of their friends vacationed this summer at a predominantly white resort in the Catskills.

A Detroit travel agent had suggested the place, partly for its golf courses, which sold the men on the trip.

They say they won't go back.

"People came up to us and asked us, 'Are you Mexican? Entertainers? A convention?'" said Migs Jefferson, a sophomore at Tufts University in Medford, Massachusetts.

"My little brother, sixteen, was sitting in the snack lounge and heard this man say, 'Did you see that bunch of Mexicans they got here? They look just like niggers.'

"It was like they couldn't believe that we were just black people that could afford their resort," said Miss Batchelor, a sophomore at Fisk University in Nashville.

In the South, the experiences of at least some of the black vacationers have been a little different.

Jacob Henderson, who with his wife, Freddie, owns a travel agency in Atlanta that has grown since 1955 from a $25,000-a-year business to one with nearly $1 million a year, said there has been "a definite increase" in the number of blacks going to formerly all-white resort areas since the passage of public accommodations legislation in 1965.

Most such places, he said, have "honored the law," and blacks going there have been getting a "good reception."

"Usually two or three black couples will go together," he said.

West Coast travelers seem to be going to Mexico, Hawaii, and Las Vegas, he said.

The Hendersons offer an "Ebony tour" through several European countries, and their emphasis is on blacks traveling with other blacks.

"There used to be a time," Mrs. Henderson said, "when blacks were self-conscious about traveling with other blacks. Now, if they're traveling with a group that includes whites, after the day's activities are over, at night people get together based on congeniality and similar interests. That's when it's important for other blacks to be along."

Mrs. Henderson said that blacks traveling to Africa were not much interested in those East African countries where the traditional white tourist has gone to hunt wild animals. Their main interest, she said, was in West Africa.

There is a pride in the achievement of such countries as Tanzania, Ghana, and Nigeria, which were among the first of the African countries to gain independence, she said.

"This started the trek toward Africa and the independent spirit," she said. "As they came out of colonial domination, they began to take on a new focus—blacks from America began to want to watch the total development—politically, economically, as well as culturally."

Most of the travelers "fit into the white-collar class," Mr. Henderson went on, adding: "But now there is a much broader range of white-collar blacks—the young professionals, primarily, who follow the normal pattern of white-collar workers."

Today's black vacationers at Oak Bluffs—the closest stop by ferry from the mainland at Woods Hole—are sometimes the great-grandchildren of the first blacks to buy property there.

Mrs. Sadie Ashburn, who at eighty-five still does most of the cook-

ing at her cottage resort—one of the few black businesses in the area—
can remember coming to Martha's Vineyard when she was five years old.

And while many city residents prefer the quiet solitude of the small
"up island" settlements—the most remote of which is Gay Head, about
forty-five minutes away—the blacks for the most part seem to stay in
this bustling little town with its quaint and sometimes elegant ginger-
bread houses.

When asked to describe Oak Bluffs, the usual reply from those
who live farther out is: "It's urban."

And yet, paradoxically, it is a desire to get away from urban living
that seems to have attracted most of the blacks here. Mostly they are
the families of businessmen, lawyers, judges, politicians, doctors, and
artists from Boston to Atlanta.

"We live in the heart of Trenton," said Mrs. Audrian Hayling, wife
of Dr. Leslie Hayling, a dentist, and mother of fourteen-year-old
Leslie Jr.

"Les can't ride a bike or do any of the things that he has the freedom to do here," she said. "It's such a change here. I call it coming to
renew my soul."

The Haylings own one of the most beautiful homes on one of the
most spacious lots in the section of the Bluffs called East Chop. It
overlooks the boat basin and borders on the West Chop area, a section
a few blocks away in which only a handful of blacks live.

While the Haylings at one time considered buying a home at Sag
Harbor, they decided that the disadvantage of distance—five hours by
car, compared with two to Sag Harbor—was outweighed by the variety: more beaches, more golf courses, more of their friends.

Of course, Dr. Hayling, a World War II pilot, said he would
probably not have bought a house on the Vineyard "if I didn't have an
airplane"—a Beechcraft Bonanza that seats five.

Mrs. Hayling and their son drive up and stay for the entire summer, while Dr. Hayling flies up on Thursdays—about a forty-five-
minute trip—and returns to Trenton on Monday afternoons. The
house has been "winterized," and the family spends long winter holidays there as well.

"From Tuesday to Friday, it's a real matriarchy," said Teixeira Nash, a personable artist—known as "Tex" to her friends—who is chairman of the Council of the Arts in Washington.

Mrs. Nash's father was a Portuguese who came to Boston from the Cape Verde Islands, off the coast of West Africa, in the early 1900s, and she and her friends spent their summers here as children. Her best friend then is still coming and has a daughter, fourteen, who is Mrs. Nash's oldest daughter's best friend. They both spend a lot of time horseback riding.

At a get-together at her rented house one night—she and her husband, Robert, an architect, are building here—Mrs. Nash's cousin and his wife, Mr. and Mrs. Harold Johnson, told how they had fallen in love with the Vineyard. Now that they are retiring, they plan to maintain here all year round.

Mr. Johnson drives a taxi, dabbles in other businesses, and serves as president of the local Alcoholics Anonymous and also of the Martha's Vineyard NAACP, which has about seventy-five members, mostly white.

"We don't have any real issues here," he said. "Mostly we raise scholarship money for the local children." During the winter, he said, there are about thirty-five to forty black families here. Most of them, he said, are elderly and include the Portuguese as well.

Still, in addition to the Chop area, there are other places on the island where blacks do not own property.

The town circle, for instance, at one time had a restrictive covenant prohibiting anyone from owning property there other than members of the Town Meeting, a fundamentalist religious group.

No one seems to know what has happened to the covenant, but it is apparent that the tradition has not been broken.

Bruce Lewellyn, a New York businessman, who along with a Puerto Rican and Jewish partner, owns a multimillion-dollar chain of eleven supermarkets in Manhattan and the Bronx, owns a house that overlooks the Oak Bluffs beach.

While his family—which includes his wife, Jackie, whom he met here, their two children, his cousin, United States Customs Court

Judge James L. Watson, and his family—have come here out of tradition, he said, the houses for blacks have become available mostly as the result of the exodus of whites to the more remote parts of the island.

But property values, at one time low, seem to be rising.

Ten years ago, the Edleys (she acts in a soap opera now and he is an official of the Ford Foundation) joined with five other couples from Philadelphia, where they were living then, and purchased their twelve-bedroom house for $8,000.

This year, after a decade in which each couple contributed $25 a month, the six couples finally paid for it. They could sell it now, they say, for twice that. But they don't want to. One reason is that altogether they have fourteen children.

One of their neighbors is Senator Edward W. Brooke, Republican of Massachusetts, whose spacious lot includes a tennis court.

But despite their professional and economic attainments, the gap between them and their white counterparts vividly exists.

"For thirty years we've [blacks and whites] been living side by side up here," said one of the black professionals, "and there is hope—but only for a continuing peaceful coexistence. If you're talking about integration, if it hasn't happened in thirty years, it won't."

Still, the ability to get away from it all may also continue to touch a sore spot with those blacks who are left back in the hot cities to cope with the urban, asphalt summers.

When Mrs. Edley's sister and her husband, Alpha and Walter Blackburn, flew up from Indianapolis for a long weekend, Mrs. Blackburn came a day ahead with their three young children.

Mr. Blackburn received a call from a friend just before he left, and he told her that Mrs. Blackburn was in the Vineyard and that he was about to join her. There was a long pause, he said, and then the caller said:

"Martha's Vineyard in the summer. The Bahamas in the winter and Europe in the fall. Humpf."

Panthers Indoctrinate the Young

The New York Times
AUGUST 18, 1969

Early one morning last week, as women in housecoats sat perched in windows trying to escape the heat, and men casually gathered on stoops along a decaying street in the Brownsville section of Brooklyn, the sound of voices came floating out of a church, shattering the quiet, idle scene.

"Power to the people," a young man shouted.

A chorus of young voices replied, "Power to the people."

"What is the main thing we want to get rid of?" shouted the young man. "Pigs," answered a chorus of voices.

"And how we gonna do it?" the young man asked. "Kill him," said one small voice.

The young man remained silent.

"Leave him like he is," said another.

The young man continued to remain silent.

"Put the right thinking in him," said another small voice. "Right on," replied the young man.

"Right on," replied the chorus of young voices.

On the second floor of the Good Shepherd Mission at the corner of Hopkinson and Sutter Avenues, two young men stood at the front of a small room, while seventeen boys and girls, ranging in age from four to fourteen years old, sat at wooden armchair desks.

The two young men, Henry McIntyre and Roscoe Lee, both teen-agers, are Black Panthers and the children made up the first class here of students in a new Panther program—the Liberation School.

Within the last six months, the Panthers have been concentrating on programs for slum children. The first of these was a breakfast pro-gram that Panthers say feeds 10,000 youngsters in cities throughout the country.

At the beginning of the summer, however, a directive went out to all chapters from Panther headquarters in Oakland, California, stating that during the summer the breakfast program would be replaced by the Liberation Schools except where both programs could be run with-out difficulty.

The Brownsville chapter kept both programs and feeds more youngsters—fifty to sixty—than it teaches. All of the students receive breakfast and lunch.

Panthers are basically Marxist-Leninist and see as their enemy the capitalistic system and its exponents—known in the Panther circles as "Pigs."

"We take them on field trips to point out the contradictions," a Panther guide, Henry Mitchell, explained to a visitor.

"They see streets that are not clean and they see fire trucks speed-ing up the streets where they play but no fires. When there is a fire, the Pig Department is seldom around in time to save the property or the lives of the people.

"We take them out on Prospect Avenue—to a block of dilapidated houses—to check out the genocide. We show them exposed lead pipes where they can get lead poisoning and TB."

The children are shown the "contradictions" and are taught about the "pigs." One portion of the three-hour class was devoted to a discus-sion of the "pigs." Teacher: "What is a pig?"

Student: "A pig is a low-down person who can be any color who beats us up and tells lies."

Teacher: "How many types of pigs are there?" Student: "Four kinds."
Teacher: "Name them."

Student: "The avaricious businessman pig ["who may be a landlord or a store owner," the teacher interjected], the police pig, the president pig, and the National Guard pig."

The teacher then says that there is a fifth type of pig—the faceless pig. "You see him but you don't know him," he said. "He's the one who comes into the street and tells people to be cool. He gets paid for snooping around." There was mention of a "demagogic politician pig," but no discussion.

The curriculum could be described as freewheeling, provided the teachers remain within the scope of the ten-point Panther program. The daughter of a female Panther captain Brenda Hyson, a pretty six-year-old named Semele, was asked by her teacher to name one point of the program. Her eyes brightened and faultlessly she replied:

"We want freedom and the power to determine our destinies."

Of the seventeen youngsters in the class, fifteen are girls. When asked about the significance of that, the Panther guide replied:

"That's a good thing. We've got to eliminate male chauvinism. We've oppressed our women more than any of the pigs and we've got to make the point now that they are our other half rather than our inferior half."

Other points that Panthers connected with the Liberation School make include teaching family unity and obedience to party leaders. The children are taught chants like "Free Huey" (Huey P. Newton, a Panther founder and Minister of Defense, now in jail on a manslaughter conviction) and "Free All Political Prisoners," as well as the one about the fugitive Panther Minister of Information, Eldridge Cleaver.

"Where's Eldridge?" the teacher shouts.

"He's free, eating watermelon and the pigs can't touch him," came the reply, loudly and in unison.

The two teachers in the class dropped out of high school and do not plan to return. They say they "gave up on the pig's school," and now attend the "people's school"—sessions in political awareness—held at the Panther office a block away.

When asked if they would encourage their young summer pupils to give up regular school, the Panther guide said, "They'll be sent to school because there are laws. But there'll be a vast difference in their ability to learn."

Police Seek "Bridges" to Harlem

The New York Times
JULY 20, 1971

The new commanding officer of the Sixth Division in Central Harlem feels that his policemen should spend as much time "getting out and talking to people" as they do "flying around answering calls."

The officer, Inspector Donald F. Cawley, also said he was "not concerned with accumulating arrest statistics" in such situations as streetcorner dice games, for instance. He believes the uniformed force should "break up the games and send the participants on their way," arresting them only when they refuse to go.

With less than a month in the job of heading one of the smallest but toughest commands in the city, Inspector Cawley said recently that he was interested in "trying some new things," with an eye toward "trying to build a bigger bridge" between the area's black community of about 300,000 people and its police force of 850, of whom about 200 are black.

The forty-one-year-old inspector, a twenty-year veteran of the force, believes there is a "desperate need to establish good working rapport between the community and its police."

To that end, he said in an interview in his office at 250 West 135th Street, he is spending his first few weeks getting acquainted with community people.

"It is my firm conviction that it is not for me to sit here and establish the priorities myself," he said. "They must be in tune with community problems."

So far, he explained, he has not had an opportunity to set up any programs, but he said he was "in the process of establishing" some. And based on some of the discussions he has had, as well as on "reading six months of *The Amsterdam News*" on his vacation before taking the job, he has reached a few conclusions.

Although the inspector talks of "putting a dent" in the number of crimes—there were 11,000 major crimes in the first five months of this year in the area—he said that one of his goals was making the streets safe.

"We have now gotten to the point in time in the Harlem community where we have to take what means we can to cope with this street-crime problem," he said. "We've got to take hold of this situation."

One step, he said, is "a meaningful and coordinated enforcement effort" directed at the narcotics seller—"the most important guy to get.

"The extent of the narcotics problem spills over into and creates the street-crime situation," he said.

Although he stressed that arrest records were not his goal, he was critical of "people who try to take prisoners away from the police officer.

"I can't understand why people say, 'don't take the brother,' when he has just committed a crime against another brother," he said.

Responding to a suggestion made by many community residents that there be more black policemen who live in the area and who presumably would then understand their problems better, Inspector Cawley, who is white and lives in Floral Park, Queens, said he could "appreciate their concern."

Of the three commanders within his division—it consists of the 25th, the 28th, and the 32d Precincts—one, Captain William Bracey of the 32d, is black.

A black policeman, the inspector said, "has one or two advantages going for him immediately." But a police officer, "well trained, regardless of color or where he lives, can deliver the services needed," he said.

Having an officer with enough time so that he has the opportunity to meet with residents about their concerns is what the inspector considers the critical ingredient.

The inspector's plans include the assessment of the manpower needs of the division to insure that we are getting our fair share of the total resources, as well as to try and make more time for policemen to get out of their cars and speak to residents.

"A police service," Inspector Cawley said, "—that's how the police department has to be looked upon—not as a force, but as a service."

Talking to Young People About Trump

The New Yorker
November 18, 2016

Last week, the day after the election of Donald Trump, I found myself recalling the words of Rodney King, spoken during the 1992 Los Angeles riots: "Can we all get along?" A black former congressman had told me about waking up his nine-year-old daughter that morning. When she heard the news, she began crying, fearful in ways she couldn't exactly articulate, but fearful nevertheless. The following day, I traveled to Pennsylvania and met with two groups of young people, some her age and some a bit older, and, curious as to whether the nine-year-old's reaction was unique, I began by relaying the story and asking how many of them had felt the same way. Most of the young people, in both groups, raised their hands, eager to share their anxieties and their fears.

The meetings were very different in some respects. One took place at a charter school with an emphasis on art, with students dressed in uniforms in a setting designed to highlight their often amazing artistic talents. The other was at a Boys and Girls Club, populated by students who needed a place to hang out after school until their working parents could come and fetch them. But there was a common denominator: except, I believe, for one child at the charter school, all the students were African American.

I was initially taken aback by their reactions, even though some adults I know had told me that they were having a hard time dealing with the election. (A friend who is white told me, "I'm just numb.") I told the students a little about my generation's history confronting racism, and about the ways in which that history had shaped my career in journalism—one that aligns with my dear, now tragically departed friend Gwen Ifill.

Gwen and I had an instant bond on so many levels—both as "firsts" in several journalism jobs—and Gwen faced overt racial hostility. When she was interning at the *Boston Herald American* many years ago, a coworker wrote a note saying, "Nigger go home." But home she didn't go, a choice I relayed to the anxious and fearful students. Gwen and I were both the children of ministers, and growing up in an AME household we were taught our history from the moment of consciousness. It is a history that includes the pain and sacrifice of so many of our people in the past, from the slave ships to the lynching trees, to the separate and unequal schools and the places where our parents, though paying customers, could not sit down to eat, to Charleston, where massacre-surviving worshippers at Mother Emanuel (again, AME) expressed forgiveness for the shooter who murdered many of their own. Gwen and I both loved clothes, but we loved the armor we wore even before we put on a stitch, the armor we wore as we traversed roads not taken by women who looked like us; Gwen took that moral armor into her work as a professional journalist, just as she took her consciousness of race and racism into whatever newsroom she inhabited, unabashedly but gently providing good information that helped cause hateful words or hateful glances to fall to the ground and dry up.

Last year, when I spoke at a National Press Foundation event honoring Gwen, I recalled the words of Viola Davis when she became, just a few weeks earlier, the first black woman to be awarded an Emmy for best actress in a drama. She began by paraphrasing a quote from Harriet Tubman. "In my mind I see a line," Davis said. "And, over that line, I see green fields and lovely flowers and beautiful white women with their arms stretched out to me over that line. But I can't seem to get there no how. I can't seem to get over that line." She went on to say, "The only thing that separates women of color from anyone is opportunity." Gwen not only got over that line but added color to the outstretched arms waiting in the green fields of our profession, encouraging other women of color to follow in her footsteps. And sometimes, even when there is opportunity, those who seize it—gratefully and productively—still meet resistance.

I told the students that their history is their armor and that they should not be afraid. Not that there wouldn't be challenges. It might be hard for them to imagine the experience of fifteen-year-old Brenda Travis, who, in 1961, joined protesters in McComb County, Mississippi, over the objections of the civil rights leaders who were worried about the ethics of taking young activists out of school. She sat in a segregated bus station, where black travelers had to use the back door, and was arrested and incarcerated. But Brenda, and the other young people fighting at that time, eventually saw justice done. I told the students in Pennsylvania about the journey traveled by those young people and many before them. And I told the worried students of the need to know that history, so that now and as they age they can embrace and erase their fear and contribute in whatever way they choose, and, in the words of the song often called the black national anthem, they can march on "till victory is won."

I felt so lucky to be able to talk to these students. They need to know that history, but also that it included not only black sacrifice but the sacrifice of white Americans who believed in freedom and justice for all and worked with the black activists toward a more perfect union. When some of the students condemned the attitudes of "white people" in general, I responded first as a journalist, talking to them about the importance of precision in language, and also about the many white people who joined with black people in their quest for justice. I told them about Andrew Goodman and Michael Schwerner and Viola Liuzzo and the Reverend James Reeb and others who died or were brutalized. They lived ubuntu, without knowing that word, so often used by President Mandela: it means I am who I am because you are who you are. As Archbishop Desmond Tutu has explained, a person with ubuntu is open and available to others, affirming of others, does not feel threatened that others are able and good, and feels diminished when others are humiliated or oppressed.

The people in the country now who are spouting hate-filled words don't seem to know their own American history. There is enough blame to go around as to why. But when it comes to fixing what's wrong with America, one of our priorities should be making more of an effort to put our history into our classrooms in the earliest years, and to educate our teachers, too. I want all of our people—even the haters—to know why we have needed that armor and how we can, while wearing it, remain open to one another.

Teaching the Civil Rights Movement

Beccastone
JANUARY 2012

Although the American civil rights movement has been described as "one of the defining moments in U.S. history," a report by the Southern Poverty Law Center tells us that civil rights education in America "boils down to two people and four words: Rosa Parks, Dr. King, and 'I have a dream.'" The civil rights movement is especially relevant today as social justice protests rage in the streets.

Well, I am hoping that my book *To the Mountaintop: My Journey Through the Civil Rights Movement*, published by Roaring Brook Press and the *New York Times*, will help change how young people understand the movement. The book is designed, in part, to help young people understand that, indeed, "there can be no progress without struggle," as Frederick Douglass put it in words that surely emboldened that generation of high school and college students in the American South. Through their struggle, they changed the face of America as it brought the South and its racist, separate, and unequal laws in line with the rest of the country that guaranteed liberty and justice for all. And while Frantz Fanon, that other freedom fighter in another country, told us that each generation must find its own cause and embrace or deny it, the lesson of the U.S. civil rights movement is that young people can make a difference. Their struggle led to the election of the first Black president, who acknowledged that he stood "on the shoulders of giants." What is required, to be sure, is courage, commitment, and righteous human values, in the case of the students of the movement— values that were informed by the principles of freedom, justice, and equality. Values that my generation was prepared to die for, and far too many did, as I chronicle in the book. Far too many also paid a price of being beaten, tortured, and thrown into overcrowded and cold jail cells, with few amenities. And yet, when the first group of young Freedom Riders left Washington, D.C., to test the law forbidding segregation in travel across state lines, so dedicated were they to their cause, they were prepared to die and left their wills behind in the case of that dreadful eventuality.

And while many of them were exposed to physical acts of hatred and brutality by racist white mobs, they kept on keepin' on, in one of the lines they spoke or sang during that time.

They also sang, "Ain't gonna let nobody turn me 'roun'," and they meant it.

I tell their stories, as well as my own, as I took my place not on a Freedom Ride or sitting in at a lunch counter or registering Black people to vote for the first time in their lives, but walking through a hostile white mob to get the education at the state University of Georgia that as a citizen I was entitled to, but which I and thousands of Black students in Georgia had been denied, even though it violated the 1954 Supreme Court decision outlawing the lie of "separate but equal." In the book, I describe the reality of "separate but equal" in my own elementary school, which got the hand-me-down textbooks, often with pages missing, from the white schools. And many of the other indignities Blacks suffered because of separate and far from equal.

And while I hope that the young people for whom this book was written will be informed by this history and the value of fighting for what you believe in, I hope they will also appreciate the words of the philosopher George Santayana: "Those who cannot remember the past are condemned to repeat it."

Look around the United States today and listen to some of the virulent rhetoric of the immigration debate or at some of the not-so-veiled racism in politics and public discourse and think about what they are doing to a country that once identified with the words inscribed on the Statue of Liberty:

"Give me your tired, your poor, Your huddled masses yearning to breathe free, The wretched refuse of your teeming shore. Send these, the homeless, tempest-tossed to me, I lift my lamp beside the golden door!"

Are these words still relevant to the increasingly Black and brown homeless, tempest-tossed, huddled masses yearning to breathe free? And what will it take to make those words a reality for them, and to help all Americans realize the possibilities of the American Dream?

Whatever it takes, there are lessons from the civil rights movement that may inform a new generation. Not to sit in at lunch counters or to go on Freedom Rides, but to determine their own path, emboldened by the victories of young people like themselves at a different time.

It is my hope that *To the Mountaintop* will, in the words of the late Edward R. Murrow, "illuminate, educate, and inspire."

Today's Horrors Are Yesterday's Repeats

The Vineyard Gazette

JUNE 22, 2017

Sometimes I have to abandon my journalistic training and resort to cliches—such as what goes around, comes around. From a recent memorial service in the nation's troubled capital to a museum in Siena, Italy, there were messages that spoke to the cliche.

At the memorial service for Roger Wilkins, he was remembered for being a part of the prize-winning team at the *Washington Post* that covered the abuses of power by members of the Nixon administration, coverage that led to articles of impeachment and the resignation of Nixon. Now, decades later, there is talk of impeachment again, much of it arising from dogged reporting by the *Washington Post* (and of course my alma mater, the *New York Times*).

Roger was also remembered by Cecelie Counts for his support of her and those in the Free South Africa Movement who demonstrated in front of the South African Embassy in Washington, D.C., to end apartheid in South Africa, where the black majority were victims of an oppressive white regime. Roger also eventually played an important role in Nelson Mandela's leadership of the new, nonracial South Africa.

Now, decades later, South Africa's black president is under increasing pressure from his own people due to mounting accusations of corruption and failure to address the ongoing needs of the black majority, freed from apartheid but still not free from poverty.

During the memorial service, former colleague and longtime friend Robert Borosage had this to say about Roger:

"Few have provided greater insight into how racism has scarred this nation. Few have wrestled so fiercely with the contradiction between the nation's ideals and its flawed reality. Few have struggled directly with that contradiction at the highest levels of government, philanthropy, and journalism."

A contradiction, hiding in plain sight until now, and coming around again.

My husband, Ron, worked with Roger at the Justice Department, where Roger was the first black deputy attorney general. Ron remembered his stewardship of a case involving the police in a D.C. shooting of an unarmed black man thirty-two times. The case ended with an acquittal, citing justifiable homicide. Not long after that, a deranged black man shot and killed a policeman, and black activist Stokely Carmichael, in a pre–Black Lives Matter moment, called it "justifiable homicide." That was all in 1969—and here we are faced with far too many of the same kind of scenarios.

Moreover, even as I recalled Roger joining a lawsuit against the *New York Times* for discrimination against its black employees back in the 1970s, the *Times* is once again in the news due to a discrimination suit filed by its black employees.

And now other media organizations seem to have forgotten the blame the Kerner Commission placed on mainstream media in 1968, following the explosions that lit up inner cities around the country. To wit: The riots came as a surprise because there was no one in the newsrooms of America from those communities who could have written about the simmering rage there due to lack of attention to their basic needs. Media organizations like the *Times* responded for a while, but now there is the rapidly changing, constricting media landscape and African American journalists are being forced to get their hats, with almost no one seeming to remember the much-heralded truisms of the almost fifty-year-old Kerner Commission report. Still another case of coming around again.

Also, not long after Roger's memorial, a few days later and thousands of miles away, in Florence, Italy, I turned on the television to see the despicable carnage in Manchester, England, and to hear commentators decry not only terrorist attacks against innocent victims in general, but something indescribably worse given that the targets were deliberately children. Shortly thereafter, as I walked through Siena's breathtaking art museum, so rich in ancient history and its legends and realities, I was stopped by a vivid painting portraying in Bethlehem the murder of all babies two years old and under, ordered by King Herod, who was said to have been angered over the escape of baby Jesus and obsessed by any threat to destroy him and his kingdom.

Soon after I arrived back home in Oak Bluffs, another attack in London—this one, as my friend and now Vineyard summer regular, the screenwriter Misan Sagay wrote me from her winter home in London, "again targeting children." And of course others followed, most recently Paris.

One chilling moment after another—and alas, all coming around again.

Urban League Director Accuses the Press of Ignoring Blacks

The New York Times
MAY 5, 1975

Vernon E. Jordan Jr., executive director of the National Urban League, accused the nation's press last night of "settling back into the spirit of 'benign neglect' of black people."

In a speech before the Capital Press Club in Washington, a group of predominantly black people, Mr. Jordan lauded the press for its coverage of Watergate but contended that the press, "after a fling at tokenism and liberalism"—a reference to its coverage of the civil rights movement in the 1960s—"has Watergated black people in its treatment of us in the news columns."

"I thought there would be an outcry from the liberal press about the San Francisco stop-and-frisk dragnet aimed at blacks," Mr. Jordan said. "But I didn't hear a peep out of the big-city newspapers that used to be so concerned about the rights of black people in the South."

Mr. Jordan also cited coverage of the energy crisis, focusing on middle-class whites in gasoline lines and neglecting, he said, the 7 percent rise in unemployment among black male family heads—"the first time this group's unemployment went up while rates for teenagers and women were stable."

Mr. Jordan also criticized what he described as the low employment rate of blacks in the newspaper and broadcasting industries—"still on the order of two to four percent," he said—and the small number of blacks in policy-making positions.

"That's another story neglected by the media," he continued, "its own inability to reconcile its editorial liberalism with its employment policies."

In the speech, which was released here, Mr. Jordan praised the black press as "the great exception" for its coverage of events relating to black people.

"In a nation apparently devoted to keeping black people under the hammer, it's been the black organizations and the black press that has tried to tell their story and to relieve their suffering," he said.

On the Case in Resurrection City

Transaction
OCTOBER 1968

Resurrection City—where the poor had hoped to become visible and effective—is dead. And despite the contention of many people, both black and white, that it should never have been born, RC was, as its city fathers had been quick to point out, a moment in history that may yet have a telling effect on the future of this country. For although Resurrection City was never really a city, per se, it functioned as a city, with all the elements of conflict that arise when public issues and private troubles come together.

The public issues were clear and could be articulated—at least in a general way—by most of the people who lived there. Handbills had helped residents formulate their statement of purpose. "What will the Poor People's Campaign do in Washington?" read one handbill. "We will build powerful nonviolent demonstrations on the issues of jobs, income, welfare, health, housing, human rights. These massive demonstrations will be aimed at government centers of power and they will be expanded if necessary. We must make the government face up to poverty and racism." If such a statement was not specific enough, residents—who in all probability found it difficult to always know just what the leaders had in mind (as did the leaders themselves)—would simply fend off the question with a statement like, "We know what the demands are." If pressed further, they would glare accusingly at the questioner, as if to further confirm his ignorance. (This technique of bluffing one's way into the offensive was initiated by the leader of the Poor People's Campaign, the Reverend Ralph Abernathy. The press was relentless in its efforts to get Mr. Abernathy to give out more specifics about his demands, but this was impossible for a long while simply because none had been formulated.)

The private troubles of those who came to live in RC were less clear, at least in the beginning. And as these troubles emerged—sometimes in the form of fights, rapes, thefts, and harassment—they became far more prominent than the cause or the individuals who came to fight for it. The outside world concerned itself with the disorganization and lack of leadership in the camp. And while this was certainly a valid concern, critics seemed to be missing one essential point—that the lifestyles of the poor vary, from individual to individual and from region to region. Long before coming to Resurrection City, leaders and followers had been conditioned by their backgrounds and the lifestyles they had established. That is why, for example, the first city manager of RC, Jesse Jackson—a twenty-six-year-old Chicagoan and an official of the Southern Christian Leadership Conference (SCLC)—had more success with the Northern urban hustler than did Hosea Williams, the second city manager, who came out of the South and had much more success with diffident rural blacks.

Most of the conflicts at the camp were caused by the ghetto youths whose lives in the asphalt jungles of the North led them to view Resurrection City as a camp outing and an alfresco frolic. Surrounded by trees, grass, and open air, the Northern youths were among alien things, which (before the rain and mud) were hostile to them. The innocence of their Southern counterparts—for whom the trees, grass, open air, and mud are a way of life—was a challenge to the Northerners. With such easy, church-oriented prey, the hip cat from the North immediately went into his thing—taking advantage of the uninitiated. Southerners had the history of the movement behind them. They had produced the sit-ins, the Freedom Rides, the bus boycotts—the 1960s Direct Action Task Force. And yet much of the Southern mystique got beaten by the hard, hostile lifestyle of the urban ghetto-dweller.

No one is quite sure how many people moved into Resurrection City, although there was an attempt to register people as they came in. The registration count was 6,312, but the community was nothing if not mobile and there was no way to count the outflow.

The people came to the District from all sections of the country. They came in bus caravans and on trains. Some came from the South in the Mule Train (which was put into a regular train in Atlanta because the horses were giving out); some came from the nearby North in cars or on foot. They came representing the church. They came representing the community. They came representing street gangs—those that would fight and those that wouldn't. And many came representing themselves. Most came as followers. But, of necessity, a few emerged as leaders. Many came to participate in the campaign for as long as SCLC wanted them there, and then they planned to go home. Others came thinking of the North as a land of opportunity. And they came to stay forever.

Today, the site where Resurrection City stood is cleared. After the sun baked the mud dry, patches of growing grass were placed there, and although the land is not quite so green as it was before, it is just as it was when the architects began designing Resurrection City on paper back in April. Perhaps if they had it to do over, they would change a few things, because, by now, they would have learned about the differences in poverty—that poor people do not automatically respond positively to one another.

The design, on paper, had been impressive. Three architects (none of them Negroes), with the help of students of the Howard University School of Architecture (all of them Negroes), produced plans that called for modest A-frame structures, which could be built small enough for two and large enough for six or eight and which would house three thousand people for two to four months. The prefabricated units—25 percent of them A-frames and 75 percent of them dormitories—were to be assembled in Virginia by local white volunteers, then brought to Washington in trucks that would be unloaded next to the building sites, starting west and building eastward.

By the time the first stake for an A-frame was driven in by Mr. Abernathy, around a thousand people had already come into Washington and had been housed in coliseums and churches.

During the first week, morale and energy and activity levels were high. But one of the first indications that the paper plans might not succeed came when the New York delegation insisted upon setting up shop in the most easternward section of the site. New Yorkers, independent, fast-paced, and accustomed to protests (like rent strikes) that require organization, were going to do things their own way. Though this meant that they had to carry their own wood all the way from the front of the site to the back, they set up their structures with record-breaking speed. Where it sometimes took three men working together an hour to put up an A-frame, in the New York contingent three men produced an A-frame in fifteen minutes. There was, among everyone, a feeling of distrust for larger communities: Provincialism had reared its head.

After a week and a half of more or less organized endeavor, there followed a long stretch of bad weather. It rained every day, and rivers of thick, brown mud stood in doorways and flowed along the walkways from one end of the camp to the other. But although the mud and rain sapped some of the energy of some of the assemblers, it seemed to inspire creativity in others—the majority, in fact, since they were eager to get their houses built so that they could move in. More people came to RC than left. And although many had been evacuated to churches and schools—often long distances away—the Mexican-Americans and the Indians were the only contingents that chose to stay on high ground.

When the rains did not let up, the last vestiges of formal organization at RC slid unceremoniously into the mud. But those who had left returned, and others joined them, and all waded through. Wood that had been lost turned up as porches for the A-frame houses—luxuries not called for in the paper plans. "It was interesting to see this mass-produced, prefab stuff developing into color and rambunctiousness," one of the planners said.

By the time most of the A-frames had been filled, what existed on the site of the planned city was a camp rather than a community, with some areas so compounded with picket fences or solid fences that no outsider could get in. Walking or wading through the camp, one saw not only simple, unadorned A-frames, but split-levels and duplexes. Some were unpainted; others were painted simply (usually with yellows and burgundy); and still others were both mildly and wildly, reverently and irreverently, decorated with slogans. One house bore on its side a verse from the Bible: "And they said one to another, behold, this dreamer cometh. Come now therefore, and let us slay him, and cast him into some pit, and we will say, some evil beast hath devoured him: and we shall see what will become of his dreams. Genesis 37. Martin Luther King, Jr., 1929–1968." Others had such slogans as "Black Power on Time," "Soul Power," "United People Power, Toledo, Ohio," "Soul City, U.S.A.," and "The Dirty Dozen," on a building I figured was a dormitory. And, of course, the inevitable "Flower Power." "I Have a Dream" stickers appeared in most places, as well as pictures of Martin Luther King—usually enshrined beside the canvas-and-wood cots inside the houses.

Just as the slogans varied widely, so did the inside appearance of the houses. While many looked like the wreck of the *Hesperus*, in others, by 9 a.m. when the camp was opened to visitors, beds were made, clothes were hung, floors were swept, and—in several houses—plank coffee tables were adorned with greenery in tin-can vases.

The Coretta King Day Care Center was perhaps the most successful unit in the camp. A local church group contributed most of the materials, including books like *Alice in Wonderland*, *What Are You Looking At?*, *The Enormous Egg*, and *Bennett Cerf's Pop-Up Lyrics*. There were even toy cars and trucks, water colors, and jigsaw puzzles. And a hundred pairs of muddy boots. The children played games and sang songs such as "If You're Happy and You Know It, Clap Your Hands" and, of course, "We Shall Overcome." And they went on field trips—to the Smithsonian, the National Historical Wax Museum, and Georgetown University. Enrollment was about seventy-five.

Altogether, Resurrection City never contained more than the

average American city—the bare-bones necessities. Still, many people received more medical attention than ever before in their lives. A young mother left Marks, Mississippi, with a baby whose chances of survival, she had been told, were very slim. He was dying of malnutrition. After three weeks of medical care—vitamins, milk, food—he began gaining weight and life. For others, teeth were saved. Upper-respiratory infections—at one point a source of alarm to those outside the camp— were treated and curbed. And when one of the residents died while on a demonstration in the food line at the Agriculture Department, there was little doubt that it was not Resurrection City that killed him, but the lack of adequate medical attention back home. Most of the residents were also eating better. The menus were often a hodgepodge affair—sometimes consisting of beef stew, turnip greens, apple sauce, and an orange—but the food was nutritious. And you did not need food stamps to get it.

Residents of Resurrection City found it difficult to understand the outside world's reaction via the press to conditions within the camp. The stink from the toilets that filled one's nostrils whenever a breeze stirred was, as one observer put it, "the smell of poverty." Residents put it another way. "I appreciate the mud," a woman from Detroit said. "It might help get some of this disease out."

The mud of Resurrection City was seen by many as unifying, if not cleansing. Andy Young, an SCLC executive, trying to dispel rumors of disorganization in the camp, said one day: "We are a movement, not an organization. And we move when the spirit says move. Anything outside is God's business. We are incorporated by the Lord and baptized by all this rain."

While the camp was virtually leaderless from a formal, organizational standpoint (Mr. Abernathy was always off traveling with a large entourage of SCLC officials), it did not lack individual movers and doers. One day, a discussion of the mud revealed such a person. Standing attentively at a press conference on a sunny day, with an umbrella over her head, Mrs. Lila Mae Brooks of Sunflower County, Mississippi, said, to no one in particular, "We used to mud and us who have commodes are used to no sewers." A tall, thin, spirited woman, Mrs. Brooks talks with little or no prompting. Observing that I was interested, she went on: "We used to being sick, too. And we used to death. All my children [she has eight] born sickly. But in Sunflower County, sick folks sent from the hospital and told to come back in two months. They set up twenty-seven rent houses—rent for twenty-five dollars—and they put you out when you don't pay. People got the health department over 'bout the sewers, but Mayor said they couldn't put in sewers until 1972." She is forty-seven, and for years has worked in private homes, cotton fields, and churches. In 1964 she was fired from a job for helping Negroes register to vote. For a while, she was on the SCLC staff, teaching citizenship. When she had a sunstroke, and later a heart attack, she had to go on welfare. (She is also divorced.) For three years, she got $40-a-month child support, and finally $73. She left her children with her mother, who is eighty, and sister to come to the campaign.

"People in Sunflower asked my friends was I sick 'cause they hadn't seen me. Then they saw me on TV in Washington and said I'd better head back before the first or they'd cut off my welfare check. You go out the state overnight and they cut off your welfare check. But that's OK. I had to come. When SCLC chose me from Eastland's County, he met his match. I've seen so much. I've seen 'em selling food stamps and they tell you if you don't buy, they cut off your welfare check. And that stuff they sell there don't count—milk, tobacco, and washing powder. Well, how you gonna keep clean? All the welfare people know is what they need. I ain't raising no more white babies for them. Ain't goin' that road no more. I drug my own children through the cotton fields, now they talkin' 'bout not lettin' us go to Congress. Well, I'll stand on Eastland's toes. People from twelve months to twelve months without work. People with no money. Where the hell the money at? I say to myself, I'll go to Washington and find out. Talking about using it to build clinics. Then they make people pay so much at the clinics they get turned away. What the people gettin' ain't enough to say grace over. I done wrote to Washington so much they don't have to ask my name."

I asked Mrs. Brooks how long she planned to stay here. "I don't know, honey," she said as she put her sunglasses on. "They just might have to 'posit my body in Washington."

There were other women organizing welfare groups and working in the lunch halls, and still others, like Miss Muriel Johnson, a social worker on loan to SCLC from other organizations. This was her first movement and she was in charge of holding "sensitivity" sessions. When I asked her what a sensitivity session was, she said, "Well, you just can't take a bunch of people out and march them down Independence Avenue. All they know is that they're hungry and want something done about it. We got 150 to 200 people out a day into nonviolent demonstrations. We got to teach them to protect themselves and prepare for whatever. We have to explain situations to people. And we have to talk with them, not down to them. If they get something out of this training, they'll go home and do something."

Joining Mrs. Brooks and Miss Johnson were many other young men and women, among them college students who, like the students of the old movement (the early 1960s), believed that it was better for black boys and girls to give themselves immediately and fully to a worthwhile cause than to finish college. Many of them wore their hair natural and some wore buttons that said, "Doing it black." Young men like Leon and JT, both SCLC organizers in the South, held no place in the movement hierarchy, but were, as the residents were fond of saying of anybody plugged in to what was going on, "on the case."

Leon and JT led demonstrations and boosted morale by taking part in the day-to-day problems and activities of Resurrection City. The difference between them and many of the other SCLC officials was that when RC residents were tired and smelly from marching eight miles to a demonstration and back, so were Leon and JT. When residents went to bed wearing all their clothes and wrapped in blankets saturated with dampness, so did Leon and JT. And if Leon and JT could still sing freedom songs the next day, then so could they. There were not, however, enough Leons and JTs. Many weeks had been spent building the Abernathy compound—a large frame structure surrounded by A-frames for his aides. But despite a ceremonial gesture of walking in with a suitcase and announcing that he was moving in, Mr. Abernathy never lived in RC. Nor did his lieutenants.

One of the most effective communicators around Resurrection

City was a man of a different breed from that of Leon or JT: Lance Watson, better (and perhaps solely) known as Sweet Willie Wine. Sweet Willie, twenty-nine, is the leader of the Memphis Invaders, the group accused of starting the riots in Memphis after the assassination of Martin Luther King. (Sweet Willie denies this.) He spent most of his time walking around the camp, wrapped in a colorful serape, combing his heavy Afro. He condemns the Vietnam War as immoral, and of his own time in the army paratroops says, "In service I took the great white father's word. I thought it was all right to be half a man. Now it is time to question. We are questioning everything now."

When the campaign was over, most of the Invaders went home. Sweet Willie, however, is still walking the streets of Washington, occasionally plugging in to local militants, but more often holding down some corner in the black ghetto.

The Invaders bridged the gap between the diffident Southern blacks and the hustling ghetto youth from the North. Memphis, after all, is a kind of halfway place, with elements both of the Southern rural and the urban ghetto scenes. And it is perhaps because of this that they made it through to the end. The Blackstone Rangers, from Chicago, did not. Early on, they were sent home for causing trouble. Acting on the theory that if the tough guys were used as peace officers, they would be too busy keeping others out of trouble to get in trouble themselves, SCLC officials began using the Blackstone Rangers as marshals. It didn't work.

Yet most of the gangs there saw themselves more as protectors of the other black people in the camp than as participants in the campaign. The leader of St. Louis's Zulu 1200s, Clarence Guthrie, said that the Zulus did not pretend to be nonviolent, but "since this campaign concerns a lot of brothers and sisters who are working their thing, we'll use our resources to protect them."

With so many disparate elements in the camp, it only took a slight incident to cause a large group to assemble, with a great deal of fight potential. Most of the Southerners had come with an SCLC orientation, and as a result they were still singing "We Shall Overcome," including the verse "Black and white together." But few people from above the Mason-Dixon Line were singing "We Shall Overcome," let alone "Black and white together." They usually ignored the whites inside the camp, who for the most part were either kids who would do all the dirty work or hippies off somewhere by themselves with their flowers. Still, any altercation outside the camp usually involved some white person. Such was the case when a fight broke out just outside the grounds. Police—mostly whites—appeared in large numbers. The Tent City Rangers, a group of older men formed as security officers, broke up the fight, but some of the boys whose adrenaline had risen headed for a white man wearing Bermuda shorts and taking pictures. With dispatch, they relieved him of his camera and disappeared. The man wanted his camera back, he said, because it was expensive. But he added, "I think I understand. I come down here in my Bermuda shorts taking pictures. And I guess I understand how this would make them angry."

Laurice Barksdale, a twenty-four-year-old veteran from Atlanta, was angry, too. But he vented his frustrations in another way. From early in the morning to late in the afternoon, the sweet smell of baking bread joined the other scents in the air. In a small A-frame decorated with the motto "Unhung-up Bread," Barksdale spent every day baking bread for residents and visitors as well. The supplies had come from a white New Yorker who travels from community to community teaching people how to make bread. At RC he discovered Barksdale, who had learned to cook in his high school home economics class, and set him up in business. After four years in the Marines, Barksdale had come home to Atlanta and had not been able to find a job. His mother, who worked for SCLC, suggested that he go along on the Poor People's Campaign to see if he could help out. Barksdale says he's not really interested in making money. "I got a cause," he says. "And a lot of brothers and sisters around me."

The one SCLC higher-up always on the case was Hosea Williams, who early in the campaign became the city manager. One of Hosea's major assets was the gift of rap.

One Sunday morning he was stopped by three well-dressed white men, one of whom said he was running for Congress from Florida and had come to RC because he felt he and his people ought to know about it. Soon after the conversation began, the man asked Hosea about his background, and if he was a communist. Hosea was not offended by the question, but moved into it slowly. He denied being a communist.

"What is Resurrection City all about?" Hosea asked rhetorically. "This is what you have to know. We are asking for jobs. Not welfare. Check the cat on the welfare rolls and you'll find his mother and daddy were on welfare.

"What we've got to have is a redefinition of work. As Lillian Smith indicated in her book, I think *Killers of the Dream*, what we have is a conflicting ideology in our value system. The reason I loved Dr. King was that he made six hundred thousand dollars in one year and died a pauper. We have got to let scientists go to work and create jobs. I know it can be done. I was working as a research chemist for fourteen years trying to rid this country of insects. I was born in Attapulgus, Georgia. My father was a field hand and my mother worked in the white folks' house. I raised myself while she raised the white folks' children. And we got to get some help for the old. And we got to do something about this educational system. That's what produced the hippies. White colleges. I got more respect for the hippies than I have for the hypocrites.

"RC is just a place we have to sleep and get some food to fight a war—a nonviolent war. We are here for an economic bill of rights. Congress's job is to solve the problems. We are political analysts and psychiatrists and Congress is the patient."

On that Sunday morning there was a sense of movement and activity throughout the camp. This was true on any given day. Near the entrance to the camp, young boys played checkers and whist, and some were getting haircuts. Over the PA system in City Hall, someone was calling for attention. "Will Cornbread please report to City Hall immediately? Attention. Will Cornbread please report to City Hall immediately?" Like Leon and JT, most people didn't know any other name for Cornbread but Cornbread. But Cornbread was a household word because he was on the case.

Also on that morning, a tall, thin, white man looking like the church pictures of Jesus took up a position behind a table near the checkers game and began making predictions—that there would be a big snow in August; that there would be a Republican president in 1972; that people of America would one day eat one another.

"Are you open to question?" someone called out. He did not respond.

The thin man continued, saying that he had prophesied the burning in Washington. He was interrupted again, by another voice from what had become a building crowd. "Tell me what the number gon' be so I can be a rich man tomorrow." An elderly Negro man with a pair of crutches next to his chair called out, to no one in particular, "Hey, where are my cigars?"

I asked the crippled man where he came from. Coy, Alabama. How long had he been at RC? "Since they drove the first nail," he answered. "What have you been doing?" "Well, I can't do much. I've got arthritis. I usually get up about four a.m. and just sit here. But I tried to organize a men's Bible class like at my church back home. Not too much success, though. I had a lovely time yesterday. Seven of us went out to a church and we had services. Then we had a wonderful dinner there—fried chicken, candied potatoes, and wrinkle steaks. You know what those are, don't you?" He smiled. "If I can hop a ride, I want to go back."

Sitting behind him were two young men. One was saying, "I got to fly home to court tomorrow. Charge of marijuana. Ain't had none." The young man was from New York. It was not the kind of thing one was likely to hear from his Southern counterpart. Narcotics is the traditional way out for many of the frustrated young in the asphalt jungles of the North. Somehow, this syndrome never hit the South. A young Southern black, eager to escape the lot of his father, has one way out— the army. And many of them, once they enlist, choose to stay.

Soon another announcement came over the PA system asking all residents who planned to take part in the day's demonstrations to report to the front gate.

On Sundays, Resurrection City—with all its diversity—was opened up to even more diversity. Sunday was tourist day and visitors began arriving sometime after breakfast. One particular Sunday, as the residents drifted out of the front gate to a demonstration, among the tourists coming in were many well-dressed Negroes from the District on their way home from church or elsewhere (as remote as they seemed to be from things, it didn't seem likely that they would have dressed up to come to RC). Some whites came, too. Mainly the tourists drove by in cars, slowing down long enough to snap a picture and continue on. To the Negro visitors (who almost never wore boots to protect their shoes from the mud), most residents (who did wear boots and slept in them at night to keep warm) were cordial, sometimes condescending (something of a unique turnabout in the scheme of things)—"Yes, do come in and have a look around. We're right proud of what we have here." Later, at a Lou Rawls concert, which was inadvertently set up before the demonstration, but which Hosea decided to let go on, Hosea addressed the crowd and concluded with a few well-chosen words for the Negro tourists: "The police want to use those billy clubs. But they ain't gonna bother you today. Today is Uncle Tom Day, and they don't whip up on Uncle Tom heads."

Demonstrations were the one constant in RC. Each demonstration I attended was different from another, not so much because the body of demonstrators changed as because of their usual tendency to "do what the spirit say do."

Although RC residents had been there before—to present demands for changes in the welfare system—my first demonstration was at the Department of Health, Education, and Welfare. The two hundred demonstrators marched into the auditorium of the building and sent word that they wanted to see "Brother Cohen"—Wilbur J. Cohen, secretary of health, education, and welfare. An otherwise impressive delegation—including Assistant Secretary Ralph K. Huitt and Harold Howe II of HEW's Office of Education—was sent in, but was given short shrift. Led by Hosea, the demonstrators began to chant, "We want Cohen," and Hosea turned from the second-string officials and told the crowd: "You might as well get comfortable," and before he had finished a young boy in gray trousers and a green shirt had taken off his tennis shoes, rolled up his soiled brown jacket into a headrest, and stretched out on the floor. As he closed his eyes, the crowd, led by Hosea, began singing "Woke Up This Morning with My Mind Set on

Freedom." In between songs the crowd would chant "We want Cohen." An elderly lady from New Orleans, who after the march obviously had little strength left to stand and yell and chant, simply shook her head in time with whatever she happened to be hearing at the moment.

The more pressure the officials put upon Hosea to relent, the stronger the support from the crowd. Given the demonstrators' vote of confidence, he began to rap. "I never lived in a democracy until I moved to Resurrection City. But it looks like the stuff is all right."

"Sock soul, brother!" the people yelled.

"Out here," he continued, "they got the gray matter to discover a cure for cancer, but can't."

"Sock soul, brother!"

Then, to the tune of the song "Ain't Gonna Let Nobody Turn Me 'Round," Hosea led the group in singing, "Ain't Gonna Let the Lack of Health Facilities Turn Me 'Round." And at the end of the song— something like three hours after the demonstrators had demanded to see Cohen—the word spread through the auditorium: "Cohen's on the case."

Demonstrators who had spread throughout the building button-holing anybody and everybody who looked important, demanding that they "go downstairs and get Cohen," filed back into the auditorium. And as Cohen appeared, an exultant cheer rose from the demonstrators— not for Cohen but for the point that they had won.

Before Cohen spoke, Huitt came to the microphone. He looked relieved. "I'd just like to say, before introducing the secretary, that I haven't heard preaching and singing like that since I was a boy. Maybe that's what wrong with me." The crowd liked that and showed it. "Get on the case, brother," someone called. And as clenched black fists went into the air—a gesture that had come to stand for "Silence!" and succeeded in getting it—Cohen spoke:

"Welcome to your auditorium," he said, managing a smile. He proceeded to outline his response to the demonstrators' demands, which included changing the state-by-state system of welfare to a federally controlled one. When he had finished, he introduced a very polished, gray-haired, white matron sitting next to him as "our director of civil rights." A voice of a Negro woman in rags called out to her: "Get to work, baby."

The second demonstration I attended was at the Justice Department. Earlier in the day, as rumors grew of dissension between the Mexican-Americans and the blacks, Reies Tijerina, the leader of the Mexican-Americans, and Rodolfo "Corky" Gonzales, his fiery lieutenant, appeared for a press conference to be held jointly with Hosea and the Indian leader, Hank Adams. Accompanying Tijerina and Gonzales was a small contingent of Mexican-Americans with unmuddied feet (during the entire campaign, their group remained in the Hawthorne School, where there was not only hot food but hot showers as well), and a few Indians. Tijerina had one major concern: regaining the land in New Mexico that, he claims, was illegally taken away from his people some three hundred years ago in the Treaty of Guadalupe Hidalgo.

As the press conference broke up and the demonstrators made ready for the march, the Mexican-Americans boarded buses to take them to the Justice Department, while the preparations of the blacks consisted of a black demonstrator's shouting: "Get your feet in the street. We're marching today."

The Justice Department demonstration was officially under the direction of Corky Gonzales. His demands were that the attorney general speak with 100 of the demonstrators, with all ethnic groups represented equally—which turned out to be 25 Mexican-Americans, 15 Indians, 20 poor whites, and 40 blacks. The attorney general agreed to speak with only 20 of the demonstrators, and this proved totally unacceptable to Gonzales. (Tijerina was not there at the time.)

For several days, talk of getting arrested in some demonstration had become intense. Somehow, as the hours wore on during the Justice Department demonstration, it was decided that this might be the place. The question seemed to be, was it the time and was the cause broad enough?

There were some demonstrators who came prepared for any eventuality, regardless of the cause. As long as the order came from SCLC. Ben Owens, fifty-two, widely known as Sunshine, was prepared. The

crowd blocking the entrance to the Justice Department (a federal offense in itself), though led by Gonzales, was singing the SCLC songs:
To the tune of "No More Weepin', No More Mourning," they sang,
"No More Broken Treaties. . . ." Sunshine talked about his involvement
in the movement.

"In Birmingham, in 1963, friends from my church were picketing.
I went down. I didn't tote no signs, but my boss still told me when I got
back to work not to tote. Then next time I went and toted. The third
time I toted, I didn't have a job. But I'd heap more rather work for Dr.
King for $25 a week than for $125. My house has been threatened. My
mother has been threatened. But I registered a lot of people in Selma,
Green County, Sumter County, and many others. Sometime I be sick,
but I can't go home. I've gone too far now to turn 'round. I've been so
close to so many things. Jimmy Lee Jackson got killed. James Reed got
beat to death. Mrs. Liuzzo killed. September 15, 1963, six people were
killed—two boys and four girls. If I die for something I don't mind.
I've been in jail seventeen or eighteen times. But we really got to work
in this town."

The police, however, did not seem to be in an arresting mood. They
just stood in the street behind the demonstrators, more or less impassive. Suddenly Hosea took the bullhorn.

"Look at those cops!" he shouted.

The crowd turned. The cops shifted uneasily. "You see what they've
done," he continued, his voice rising. The crowd looked. "They don't
have on their badges, so that when they take you to jail and do whatever
they're gon' do to you, you won't be able to identify them." The crowd
was now facing the policemen and could see that not one of them was
wearing a badge. Hosea started to rap about police brutality and the
sickness of America. "Just look at that!" he cried, pointing an accusing
finger. And no one had to be told, this time, what they were looking
for. All could see that the shiny badges had been put back in their
places—on the chests of the entire cadre of policemen standing behind
them. But Hosea was now into his thing. "But look," he said, again
pointing. "Just to show you how sick this country is—the sickness of
America and racism—look." The crowd was baffled. What was he

talking about now? Hosea, virtually overcome with rage, now shouted, "You see how sick this country is? Otherwise how come all the white cops are lined up on one side and all the black cops lined up further down the street? Just look at it!" The division in the line was distinct. Immediately behind the demonstrators was a line of white policemen. To the extreme left of the demonstrators was a solid line of black faces in uniform. Hosea rapped a good long while.

As the evening wore on, and the attorney general did not show up and the demonstrators did not get arrested, there seemed to be some indecision among the demonstration's leaders. Hosea, at times, seemed at a loss. Corky had tired of leading the group in songs, and the demonstrators had never quite caught all the words. Corky and Hosea huddled often, only to return and lead more singing. Father James Groppi of Milwaukee showed up, received wide applause, made an impassioned speech, and joined in the singing. At one point, Hosea broke off to consult with his lawyer, and Tijerina showed up. "What's going on?" he asked innocently. Hosea explained that the attorney general had refused to see one hundred, but would see twenty. "That's fine. OK, isn't it? We send the twenty?"

Hosea looked confused. "Corky is holding out for a hundred." "I will talk to Corky," Tijerina said, and good-naturedly bounced off.

The evening grew longer. The demonstrators grew tired. Few complained, but many were curious. They were not getting the usual positive vibrations from Hosea, who looked haggard and weary. Then, suddenly, as if he'd blown in on a fresh breeze, there stood Jesse Jackson, who has been described as being closer than anyone else to Dr. King in charisma and in his acceptance of nonviolence as a way of life. Jackson was wearing a white turtleneck sweater, and he towered above the crowd. Reaching for the bullhorn, he began, "Brothers and sisters, we got business to take care of." "Sock soul, brother!" "We got a lot of work to do on this thing, and we gonna march now on over to the church where they're having the rally to help take care of this business." Corky looked stunned. Hosea looked relieved. And the crowd of demonstrators obediently lined up and marched away.

The conflict between the causes of the Mexican-Americans and those of the blacks had come to a head. The relationship had been strained all along, but the SCLC and Tijerina had kept it going in the interest of unity and solidarity. Tijerina's lieutenant, Corky Gonzales, had demanded that Hosea support the demonstration at the Justice Department, and really didn't seem interested in much else. Hosea didn't mind being arrested. In fact, he wanted to be arrested. But this cause—the release in California of a small group of Mexican-Americans charged with conspiracy—just didn't seem broad enough. Corky thought otherwise.

Jackson was not only fresher than Hosea that night—not having been on the demonstration in the hot sun all day—but he was better equipped to deal with Corky, whose orientation was closer to that of the urban hustlers Jesse Jackson was used to dealing with.

The around-the-clock demonstrations at the Agriculture Department were perhaps the most strenuous ordeals for the demonstrators. More people than usual were asleep during the day at RC because they had been up all night sitting on the steps of the department. And they remained there, regardless of the weather.

One morning, as a weary group stood waiting to be replaced, the sky grew gray and a slight cool wind began to blow. As a heavy downpour of cold rain began, most of the group huddled together under army blankets and started singing.

The last demonstration I attended was on Solidarity Day. In that great mass of fifty thousand or more people, I looked for the faces that I had come to know over the last few weeks. I saw only a few, and concluded that the veteran residents of RC just happened to be in places that I was not. Later, as the program dragged on and I became weary from the heat, I walked back into the city, expecting to find it empty. Instead I saw the people I had been looking for outside. JT and Leon and many others.

Harry Jackson, a cabinetmaker from Baltimore, sat in his usual place—inside the fenced-in compound of the Baltimore delegation. He was keeping watch over the two dormitories—women to the left, men to the right—and a frying pan of baked beans cooking on a small, portable grill. Since he was not out demonstrating, I asked him why he had come to RC in the first place. "We came because of the lack of association between the black man and the white man. If the system don't integrate itself, it will segregate itself all over again. Our group was integrated. We had one white fellow from the University of Massachusetts. But he hasn't been back."

This man, I thought, was probably typical of the majority of RC residents. They wanted things to get better, and felt that they would if people got together. The system didn't have to come down; it just needed overhauling. Still, the system had created the provincialism and distrust of larger communities that prompted Harry Jackson to remark as I was leaving, "I believe we should keep the people together who came together."

As I walked through Resurrection City, in the distance I could hear the sound of voices coming from the Lincoln Memorial—voices too distant to be understood. After a while, I ran across Leon and JT. Leon said he was on the way to his A-frame.

"Why aren't you out at the demonstration?" I asked. And barely able to keep his eyes open, he replied weakly, "My demonstration was all night last night. Up at the Agriculture Department. And I'll be there again, all night tonight. That's why I've just got to get some sleep."

A few days later, Jackson and Leon and JT and every other resident of Resurrection City were either arrested (for civil disobedience) or tear-gassed (for convenience) by policemen from the District of Columbia. The structures came down in less than half the time it took to put them up. And Resurrection City was dead. Up on the hill, spokesmen for SCLC said they had achieved some of the goals of the campaign and were making progress toward achieving more. But the people were all—or mostly all—gone.

So, in the end, what did Resurrection City do? It certainly made the poor visible. But did it make them effective? Mr. Abernathy would have them believe that it did. And the people who believed him were, by and large, the ones who had come out of the same area that he had come from. An observer once said that Mr. Abernathy lived for the few hours when he could escape back to his church in Atlanta for Sunday services. This was home. Those who came out of that background were the ones who would have stayed in Washington until their leader said the job was done, working diligently all the while. But they, too, would be glad to get back home.

The confrontations of rural Negroes, not only with officials and the police but with urban blacks as well, may have engendered in them a bit of cynicism—perhaps even a bit of militancy. But one suspects that the talk, for years to come, will be of how they went to Washington and, for all practical purposes, "stood on Eastland's toes."

For the urban-rural types, who were in a transitional position to begin with, the frustrations inherent in the system became only more apparent. Already leaning toward urban-type militancy, their inclinations were reenforced by the treatment that even the nonviolent received when those in control grew weary of them and their cause.

The urban people did not learn anything that they hadn't already known. Except, perhaps, about the differences that exist between them and their Southern brothers. They expected nothing, they gave little, and they got the same in return.

Resurrection City was not really supposed to succeed as a city. It was supposed to succeed in dramatizing the plight of the poor in this country. Instead, its greatest success was in dramatizing what the system has done to the black community in this country. And in doing so, it affirmed the view taken by black militants today—that before black people can make any meaningful progress in the United States of America, they have to, as the militants say, "get themselves together."

PART II

My Sisters

From my earliest years, Black women helped me on my journey into journalism. My first mentor in high school was Elsie Foster Evans, the advisor to the school paper, the *Green Light*.

Being Black, she was forced to leave the South to obtain a degree available in the South only to white educators. She obtained her master's degree at the University of Michigan but returned to Atlanta and worked for a brief time as a reporter for the local Black newspaper, the *Atlanta Daily World*, the oldest Black daily in the country. She shaped and molded me during those two years with her gentle guidance. And it was she who helped me along my path to realizing my dream. Part of that dream was finding women like those who had inspired me throughout my life, but who often didn't get the kind of attention they deserved from the mainstream—that is, white—media.

In 1972 this dream led me to persuade my *New York Times* editors to allow me to fly from New York, where I was based, to Chicago to cover a group of some two hundred Black women who traveled there from all over the country to "have dialogue" over the concerns that they felt distinguished their interests from those of the white women's liberation movement. I was particularly impressed with their understanding that while Black women had been trailblazers throughout their history, it was more often than not that their opinions were not sought nor their voices heard. It may have been meant as a joke, but when a group of women in the civil rights movement informed Stokely Carmichael, one of the men in charge, that they wanted to present him with a list of their positions, he is alleged to have said that the only position for women in the movement was prone. Even in the Black church, which otherwise fought over the years for Black liberation, women were rarely embraced in leadership positions or supported in the pulpit. Even my father, a man I thought of as a progressive minister, had not allowed women to speak from the pulpit until I came to speak as an adult. Knowing how much my father respected me and my professional life, my stepmother whispered that I should ask him if I could speak from the pulpit, which he obliged. But it was still, even in the 1970s, a rare occurrence. Having been excluded for the most part from the white women's suffragist movement, and on up to the modern-day liberation movements, Black women have walked alone, and often taken diverse paths among themselves. They've had different experiences, and I believed it was important to record this phase of their diverse history.

On a more personal note, I was happy to be in a position to focus once more on Constance Baker Motley, who had been the lead attorney (and a tough interrogator) in my court case, with my classmate Hamilton Holmes, that she and her team won and which led to our desegregation of the University of Georgia in 1961. This was now five years later and although in another incarnation, she was still on the case, fighting for her people.

While I hadn't had the same kind of personal connection to Shirley Chisholm, I also saw her as a trailblazer, another committed to helping people who looked like her. And while my first cause was in the segregated South, hers helped reveal that the North was not so different from the South concerning discrimination against Black people. So I made it a priority to get her story told in the *New York Times*.

On another occasion, I was able to make a successful argument to my editors at the *Times* to allow me to follow a story beyond New York's borders, all the way to Jackson, Mississippi. It was for an occasion marking the two hundredth birthday of one of the Black women whom I had been introduced to by my Black teachers down South as someone who refused to allow her station in life to get in the way of her God-given talents. That woman was Phillis Wheatley, who was born in Senegal/Gambia, West Africa, and when she was about seven years old was transported to America as a slave. Yet she pursued her dream, which manifested itself in some of the most beautiful poetry that would eventually achieve international acclaim.

When I wrote about a Black woman judge presiding over a challenging case of a famous white athlete accused of murdering his girlfriend, I didn't travel back to South Africa, where I had lived and worked for seventeen years. But I had learned enough about the country during that time to be able to observe from afar the ongoing changes aimed at correcting the country's history of racial, as well as sexual, discrimination, not least in the judiciary. And so from afar but up close through the contacts I had developed over the years, I was able to put together a piece about Thokozile Matilda Masipa, the sixty-six-year-old judge selected to preside over the case. In her early years, Masipa was a journalist and an activist on behalf of Black women in her country who for generations suffered from both apartheid and misogyny within the Black community.

To be sure, the days are opening wider, as Xoliswa Sitole, a pioneering young South African filmmaker told me, "but we cannot take progress for granted."

Her sisters and mine—at home and abroad—need to see women who look like them, taking their/our place with confidence and the kind of ownership that results in more than episodic or transitory progress.

While not all of my reporting was on Black women, I continued to be on the lookout for stories that helped spotlight their exclusion and the need and ways to change that, not least in the world of publishing. Despite the inclusion of amazingly talented Black women, it has, for the most part, been an uphill climb for them to the decision-making top.

But hopefully the example of Black women who have made it to the top or have gone before them in other arenas, some captured here, will inspire them to keep on movin' on up! For while the publishing world has only recently begun to be more expansive, the stories my sisters instinctively seek out or are naturally receptive to need to be told so that younger generations know whose shoulders they stand on and will be encouraged to leave their own legacies.

For while I was able to make some strides toward more inclusive coverage of my sisters, a *luta continua*. That is why it is so important for those who are now fighting for equality in the workplace and in coverage to have history that serves not only to create deeper understanding on the part of all people, but history that serves as the wind at the backs of those most affected, so they know they have armor shielding them as they fight on to realize their dreams and the dreams of their sisters and mine.

2 Black Women Combine Lives and Talent in Play

The New York Times
JULY 13, 1971

Two young black women whose backgrounds differ but who share the belief that black experiences overlap have combined their talents and experiences in their first Off-Broadway production, *Black Girl*.

The play, a story about the trials and tribulations of three generations of black women, was written by J. E. (Jenny) Franklin and directed by Shauneille Perry, and is now at the Theater de Lys.

"If you're black, you know about these people in any city," Miss Perry, a cousin of the late playwright Lorraine Hansberry, said recently. "We are all a part of each other."

Or, as Miss Franklin put it: "Black women have lived in such a way that we have collected a lot of the elements of the human experience that other people have been excluded from."

Miss Franklin, who stumbled into playwriting while teaching in a Freedom School in Mississippi during the summer of 1964 and has never studied it formally, believes that plays must serve a definite social purpose.

"I feel that plays should not mirror the condition, but be presented in such a way that they leave you with choices," she said. "*Black Girl* is a play about choices. And that's what black theater and the arts should be about."

The choices, however, were not always available—either to blacks or to black women.

Miss Perry, for instance, who received her master's degree in directing from Chicago's Goodman Theater at the Art Institute, found that as a Fulbright scholar at the Royal Academy of Dramatic Art in London she was "always doing Cleopatra.

"We never go too far from that," she said, ironically recollecting that they were also doing *Home of the Brave* for "the other black there at the time."

She also remembered an encounter in Paris in 1959 with Richard Wright.

"They still lynching people back in the States?" she remembered him asking.

"I remember telling him, 'They do it a little differently there today,' and the next day I picked up the paper and saw the story on Mack Charles Parker [a young black man accused of rape, who was removed by force from his cell in Poplarville, Mississippi, and later was found floating in the river]. I kept wondering to myself, 'What is that man saying about my analysis of things?'" And, she recalled, she "kept wondering what [she] was going to do back home."

Back in New York, Miss Perry found a couple of choices that had not existed before she left—the New Lafayette Theater and the Negro Ensemble Company. "I got the feeling that maybe there's a place for me," she said.

A year and a half later, she got to direct a play—the NEC's workshop production of Miss Franklin's *Mau Mau Room*.

Miss Franklin took a roundabout route to her craft. She was working with the Congress of Racial Equality in Mississippi during the first major voter registration and civil rights drive in the South in 1964. She had returned to the South—she is from Houston, but had been living in New York—"because I felt my roots were dying.

"The children there couldn't read because they had been taken out of their community to pick cotton," she recalled recently. "They were really integrated internally, but they needed to have it brought out."

To bring out this capacity for expression, Miss Franklin started writing down their sayings. "We'd sit under a tree on the grass and they'd tell me things. Like one said one day, 'Some of them crackers say if you step out of line, they'll take you up on such-and-such a hill and do so-and-so.'"

Later, she would show their statements to them, and they'd read them.

"They had learned to read their own ideas, rather than talking a word," she said. "Once they were able to recognize their own ideas, you could expand on that. Don't use books. But talk all of the words out of them. Reading is just talking on the outside."

While the reading lessons were going on, the workers and community folks were building a community center. In six weeks it was finished, and so was Miss Franklin's first, full-length play: *A First Step to Freedom*.

"It was the first play they'd seen," she recalled. "The place was packed, and they really enjoyed it because it was real to them. There wasn't a youngster in that community who didn't want to be in that play."

After that, the play began touring, and opened up some choices for the young actors. "Not only did they learn to read," Miss Franklin said, "but the play put them in contact with people outside their communities. Three students—all from one family—went to college."

And from that point on, Miss Franklin, whose college major at the University of Texas had been languages, began using the language of plays, as she put it, "to communicate—to unite wholly, with others."

200 Black Women "Have Dialogue"

The New York Times
JANUARY 10, 1972

CHICAGO, Jan. 9—More than two hundred black women from all over the country gathered here this weekend to "have dialogue" over the kinds of concerns that they feel distinguish their interests from those of the white women's liberation movement.

The two-day symposium, sponsored by the Black Women's Community Development Foundation, covered a variety of topics, including domestic workers and welfare recipients as well as prison movements and personal issues such as the relationship of Negro women to Negro men and that of Negro women of divergent backgrounds and opinions.

"We felt there was much need for black women to talk to each other without fear and without being under pressure to be something other than what they are," said Mrs. Jean Fairfax, president of the small foundation, which is based in Washington.

"And we recognize that this first experience would be difficult and painful because of broad ideological and class differences."

Accordingly, many of the sessions at the Roberts Motel were marked by heated discussion, particularly over the relationship of Negro women and Negro men.

"I want to get together with all the sisters in this room who are married to junkies," said one participant. "I'm married to one and we have got to do something about this."

While there was no resolution of the problem of male and female relationships, the attitudes of the women, who ranged from college age to the mid-sixties, were divided between those who felt that the issue was Negro men and Negro women fighting together for black liberation and a smaller but more vocal element that felt that black men had often been impediments in the struggle for liberation.

Also unresolved was the issue of class. However, Mrs. Dorothy Bolden, founder and president of the National Domestic Workers Union of America, based in Atlanta and representing 1,600 women, said she had come to the conference to make sure that they were represented.

"Low-income black women outnumber middle-income black women, and those women have been overshadowed and overlooked, not only by whites but by the black middle class," Mrs. Bolden said.

Dr. Jacquelyne Jackson, an associate professor of medical sociology in the department of psychiatry at Duke University Medical Center, discussed the issue of female-headed households. She pointed out that the ratio of black males to black females had continued to decline since 1850, and that in several states the Negro female population far outnumbered Negro males. "The problem isn't that the black men have abandoned their family," Dr. Jackson said in an interview. "In many places he just doesn't exist."

She also said that perhaps the most significant factor resulting from such information was that slavery could no longer be regarded as the prime determinant of mortality among blacks, but rather, looking to patterns since 1900, that factor might be the sex ratio.

"We therefore should not be surprised at how large our proportion of black female-headed households is—around twenty-nine percent—but at the smallness of its size," she said.

The Black Women's Community Development Foundation, created in 1968, operates through a grant from the Irwin Sweeney Miller Foundation. It makes small grants to Negro women community groups that it believes will have an impact on the black community at large, according to its executive director, Inez Smith Reid.

Black Women Getting Job Help

The New York Times
OCTOBER 13, 1974

For four years after she got her master's degree, Barbara Hall taught mathematics in an Atlanta high school. Her base salary was $9,500.

Then she became disillusioned.

"I realized," she said recently, "that I would have to work twenty years to get to be the head of a department."

Last September, with the help of a new program in Atlanta, Mrs. Hall got a job at the Southern Bell Telephone and Telegraph Company.

One year later, Mrs. Hall, now twenty-nine years old, has been promoted from an assistant to an administrator, her salary going from $12,900 to $14,400.

Mrs. Hall's success and that of other black women who have moved into managerial and professional posts is due in part to the two-year-old Atlanta-based Black Women's Employment Program, a pilot project aimed at increasing the number of minority women holding white-collar jobs.

In 1972, when Mrs. Hall went to the project seeking help, black women made up 4.6 percent of the total workforce in the country, compared with 33.4 percent white women.

Among all Americans in white-collar jobs, black women make up only 3.8 percent of the total compared with 44.6 percent white women, according to the latest Census Bureau figures. Most of the jobs are clerical.

While no figures are yet available for 1974, there was a slight upward change in 1973, and the Black Women's Employment Program is hopeful that its work will begin to have an impact on increasing that trend.

Since the program started in 1972 with a grant from the Labor Department, more than 1,600 black women have sought advice on professional advancement. Of that number, 200 have been placed in white-collar jobs that carry such opportunities.

In Atlanta and Houston, which were chosen for the project because of their expanding labor markets and the pool of untapped resources, only a few minority women were employed in white-collar positions, according to Alexis M. Herman, twenty-seven, and Paulette E. Norvel, twenty-eight, who are directing the project.

"White women were moving up," Miss Norvel said, "but black females were not moving beyond the clerical level."

Miss Norvel and Miss Herman visited companies in Atlanta and Houston to find out why.

"We encountered a lot of attitudinal problems," Miss Herman said, "things like 'Women can't supervise' or 'Black women are looking for a handout.'

"A lot of the companies had affirmative action programs. But for the most part, they were not in compliance, and their inevitable response was, 'Can't find anyone qualified.'"

It was a difficult answer to accept, particularly in Atlanta, where there are excellent opportunities for blacks as well as an influx of young people lured by the city's progressive image.

Of the 1,600 women with college degrees in the project's files, 60 percent have been unemployed and 30 percent underemployed. Many who were working, according to Miss Herman, were earning $6,000 or less with bachelor of arts degrees and $9,000 or less with master's degrees.

Deborah Conley, for example, was graduated from Clark College in Atlanta in 1969 and went to work for an antipoverty agency as an accountant for $8,000 a year.

"I began looking around," she said, "because federally funded programs are just not that secure. But I really didn't know where to start. Anything in the newspapers, I found, was not worth looking at. The jobs were valid, the salaries good. But I could tell they didn't want to hire me because I was black. I was having a hard time."

Last year, Mrs. Conley, twenty-six, heard about the Black Women's Employment Program and "got a job right away.

"People at other agencies are working for a commission and they just try to pawn you off," she said. "They'd send you anywhere, on anything. That didn't happen here."

Mrs. Conley has since been working as an auditor for the Southern Railway Company, where her starting salary was $10,000.

One of the services the Employment Project offers involves helping applicants learn to "tailor" résumés.

"Many of these women tend to underestimate their experience," Miss Herman said.

In addition, she said, many of those in underemployment situations were already performing the duties of a higher-level post, minus the title and the benefits.

Miss Herman and Miss Norvel depend heavily on pressure from the government and community groups to provide the wedge they need to get a foot in the door. They visit prospective employers and press for opportunities for their black woman applicants.

"They're not the folks who put on the pressure," says Robert Glover, a research assistant at the University of Texas working on black employment. "What they do is deliver."

One of those they delivered was Margaret Howell.

Pronounced "overqualified" for a number of situations, she sought help at the Employment Program and got a job as director of General Services for the Metropolitan Atlanta Rapid Transit Authority, the only female administrator in the organization.

As a result of their success in Houston and Atlanta, Miss Herman and Miss Norvel plan to extend the project to five other Southern cities that are in the process of being selected.

In addition, the women plan to merge soon with a New York–based group called the Recruitment and Training Program, which aims at increasing minority representation in the construction industry.

As to whether the merger means that the project might expand to include black men, Miss Herman said that there was a recognition that the unemployment situation also affected black men.

But, she said, "one out of three black women are heads of households."

In addition, she said, "the number of single black women under thirty-five has gone from forty-one percent in 1960 to fifty-four percent in 1973, which means that we've got to be out there taking care of ourselves."

Black Women MDs

The New York Times
NOVEMBER 16, 1977

When Dr. Lena F. Edwards leaves home each morning, she takes a pair of pajamas, a comb, and a brush because, she said, "I never know what's going to happen."

She said it cheerfully, but at seventy-seven she has had four heart attacks, and although she retired from medical practice in 1960 after almost forty years, she still sees patients, traveling many miles a week in her hometown of Lakewood, New Jersey, and by bus to Jersey City.

While she claims to have delivered "probably half" of the babies born in Jersey City—she has had six of her own—she now concentrates on the problems of the elderly, counseling them and planning government programs for them.

Despite her unpredictable health, Dr. Edwards is "determined to keep fighting—not with my fists, but with my brains and with my dignity."

It is that spirit and endurance that mark the handful of black women doctors in the New York–New Jersey area who in the mid-1920s pioneered in overcoming barriers of race and sex, not only in medical schools but also in their practices in hospitals and among blacks as well as whites.

According to the Census Bureau, there were sixty-five black women doctors in this country in 1920. By 1970, according to the bureau, there were 1,051.

On a recent Sunday, black women doctors in the metropolitan area, who now number over one hundred, honored Dr. Edwards and five other black physicians who began practicing in the 1920s, including Dr. Agnes Griffin, who at eighty-one is still practicing ophthalmology in the parlor floor office of her Brooklyn brownstone.

The six women were cited by the Susan Smith McKinney Steward Medical Society at a luncheon at the Fifth Avenue Hotel. Cumulatively, they have more than three hundred years' medical practice. The two-year-old society, according to Dr. Muriel Petioni, its president, is one of the first organizations of black women doctors in the country. Its aims are to aid young black women medical students and to document the achievements of black physicians.

Dr. Steward, for whom the society was named, was an 1870 graduate of the New York Medical College for Women, and, according to the society, was the third black woman in the United States to have formal medical training.

Only one of the honorees—Dr. E. Mae McCarroll, a 1925 graduate of the Women's Medical College in Pennsylvania—has left the area, and she could not attend the luncheon. The seventy-seven-year-old doctor, who in 1946 became the first black appointed to a Newark City Hospital, formally closed her Newark practice in 1973.

Dr. May E. Chinn, one of the society's founders, was one of those honored. She recalled that her father, who had been a slave, opposed her even going to college. But her mother, who "scrubbed floors and hired out as cook," became the driving force behind her educational effort.

She was the first black woman graduate of the University of Bellevue Medical Center—there were four in this year's graduating class—and the first to in 1926 intern at the then predominantly white Harlem Hospital. The hospital is now mostly black, and five of the thirty interns are black women.

Now eighty-one and somewhat incapacitated by an operation last year which caused her to give up her position as a doctor for day care centers with the Department of Health, Dr. Chinn spends most of her days writing her memoirs in her apartment on the western edge of Harlem—not far from where she conducted most of her medical practice.

Dr. Chinn said that one of the first obstacles she had to overcome was the attitude of blacks toward her.

Once a black woman patient wept when she approached because, as Dr. Chinn recalled, "she felt she had been denied the privilege of having a white doctor wait on her."

At the same time, she said, the black male doctors appeared divided into three groups—"those who acted as if I wasn't there; another who took the attitude 'what does she think she can do that I can't do?' and the group that called themselves supporting me by sending me their night calls after midnight."

Eventually, time and a growing familiarity that bred respect changed much of that, and black male doctors began sending their wives, children, and mothers to Dr. Chinn.

The major injustices of that day, she said, were those involving the denial of admission to postgraduate medical schools and hospitals. Most black women doctors ended up with "family practices," although Dr. Chinn later studied cancer detection and prevention.

"We were forced to practice medicine as doctors did one hundred years before in rural Appalachia," Dr. Chinn said.

"Minor operations like tonsillectomies, we did in the office. The major ones, including abdominal surgery, removal of tumors, setting bones, we did in the home."

Dr. Chinn recalled how the day prior to an operation she would go to the patient's home, wrap the surgical dressings in newspapers, and boil them on a hot coal stove for three or four hours in order to sterilize them.

"The next day, we'd come back for the operation," she said.

Dr. Louise Carter spoke at the luncheon about how Dr. Chinn had inspired her in her medical career in the 1940s.

Dr. Carter said that her mother once sold stockings door-to-door to earn enough money to buy her a microscope that she needed at Meharry Medical School in Nashville, Tennessee.

Once Dr. Chinn found out what the selling was all about, she not only bought the stockings but also picked out the newer of two microscopes she owned and gave it to Dr. Carter's mother to send to her daughter.

Dr. Myra Smith-Kearse, the only woman in her Howard University Medical School class of 1926, said that because she was black it took her fifteen years to get on the staff of a hospital in Newark. In the interim, she said, she "lost a great deal—in fees, work experience, and training."

It was the shortage of white doctors created by World War II and constant pressure from organizations like the National Association for the Advancement of Colored People, Dr. Smith-Kearse said, that caused the hospitals in Newark and elsewhere to start opening up.

Dr. Smith-Kearse by that time had moved to Vauxhall, New Jersey, established practice, married a man who eventually became postmaster there, and had two children.

By the time she retired in 1966, she had become such a force in the community that she began a second career as an official in the local poverty program.

Dr. Smith-Kearse said that her determination and that of the others like her was no doubt rooted in the intense race consciousness of the era in which she was born—a time that was characterized, she said, by mounting racial oppression and white resistance to black advancement.

"Our parents knew the history of race," she explained. "The denials. The struggles. And we didn't hear anything else from the time we were born but get yourself ready to serve the race."

Indeed, Dr. Agnes Griffin, who was the only black woman in the 1926 class at Columbia University's College of Physicians and Surgeons (there were eight in the class of 1977), said she never felt particularly "determined or strong-willed," but was "just doing what comes naturally."

Retirement does not seem to be one of those things that come naturally to Dr. Griffin. One day last week, after she had taken care of three emergencies, which had extended her day by two hours, she said that she worked only four and a half days a week and was "thinking about retiring just a little more."

But she is concerned about her patients who, she said, "just keep coming back from all over New York."

Dr. S. Evelyn Lewis (Howard, class of '27) is enjoying her retirement—traveling and living comfortably—although she said that few, if any of the doctors got rich from their practices.

"It was two dollars in and three dollars out," said the seventy-six-year-old physician, who practiced mostly in Brooklyn.

"You might get twenty-five dollars for a delivery, but you don't get rich that way."

Having watched the number of black women doctors grow—although neither she nor the others are satisfied that they have grown nearly enough—Dr. Lewis said she was "really surprised and almost overcome" that so many turned out for the luncheon to honor them.

At the same time, when asked how she felt about being such an inspiration to so many, she said:

"I see it as part of the service.

"I am determined to keep fighting, not with fists, but with brains and dignity."

Civil Rights Pioneer Ruby Bridges on Activism in the Modern Era

PBS NewsHour

JANUARY 14, 2021

Judy Woodruff:

Finally tonight, we turn to civil rights activist Ruby Bridges, who writes her own story in a new children's book, hoping adult ears will listen too in these fractured times.

Telling her story is special correspondent Charlayne Hunter-Gault, who followed in Bridges' footsteps when, sixty years ago this past weekend, Charlayne, along with Hamilton Holmes, desegregated the University of Georgia.

This is part of our Race Matters Solutions series and our arts and culture series, Canvas.

President Barack Obama:

If it hadn't been for you guys, I might not be here, and we wouldn't be looking at this together.

Charlayne Hunter-Gault:

Ruby Bridges' name is synonymous with civil rights trailblazing, immortalized in this Norman Rockwell painting entitled *The Problem We All Live With*.

Bridges' historic moment came when she became the first Black child to desegregate an all-white elementary school in New Orleans at six years old. She had to be escorted by federal marshals as she walked past loud and unruly protesters and into the William Frantz Elementary School.

Now, sixty years later, Bridges has written to and for children the same age of her younger self. She describes it as a call to action and contains historical photos of her pioneering time.

Pioneering history is still being made and remembered, including a photo illustration that went viral after the election of Vice President–elect Kamala Harris walking alongside the shadow of Ruby Bridges.

Ruby Bridges, first, on behalf of my generation of civil rights pioneers, let me just say thank you for paving our way.

Now, you have written other books, but this one is specifically aimed at readers who may be as young as you were when you first took those historic steps, when you were six years old, into the elementary school there.

Why did you do this book? And do you see similarities between then and now in some ways?

Ruby Bridges:

Absolutely.

You know, back in March [*sic*], I was sitting in front of my television on lockdown because of the virus, like everybody else, and witnessed this young man's brutal death, Mr. Floyd, right in front of my face, like so many people did.

And I was so disturbed by it and didn't know how to react or what to do. I felt like I'd been spending so many years talking to kids across the country. And I knew that they were watching this as well and probably wondering what was going on.

The majority of my time, I talked to kids and explained to them that racism has no place in the minds and hearts of our kids across the country. And yet they were witnessing this. I was very moved by what I saw after his death. I saw young people take to the streets. And I felt like the torch had been passed and that now they had a cause to get behind.

When Dr. King was assassinated, I felt like we should have picked that torch up and kept it moving. Even my own experience after going into the school, it was something that happened. No one talked about it in my community, in my neighborhood. It was swept under the rug, and life went on.

I'm happy now to see that, all of a sudden, activism is cool again. And it should have been from 1960 until today. We didn't do a very good job of passing those lessons on to that generation.

Charlayne Hunter-Gault:

Let's talk about teenagers and others in their twenties, the big demonstrations that are going on, multiracial, multigenerational, led by a lot of young people.

But there are deep divisions. From politics, even to wearing masks, there are divisions. How do you explain that?

Ruby Bridges:

We cannot be a hopeless people. We have to be hopeful.

And we do have a lot of work to do. I mean, we all saw that. This last election showed us just how divided this country really is. After President Obama was elected, it seemed that racism really raised its ugly head again.

I think having a Black man elected as president just riled that element up all over again. Probably, they felt like, oh, we cannot have this happen. And yet it did.

And so all we needed is for someone to come along and add fuel to that fire. And I think that that's why we are so divided today.

Charlayne Hunter-Gault:

One of the things that you say in the book is you believe that racism is—let me read this—"a grown-up disease."

You're talking to the children now, the young people. You say: "We adults must stop using you, our kids, to spread it. It's we adults who passed racism on in so many ways."

I hear people all the time saying, well, I want to do something about this, but I don't know what to do.

Ruby Bridges:

We all know that none of our kids are born knowing anything about disliking the child sitting next to them.

Our babies don't come into the world knowing anything about racism or disliking someone because of the color of their skin. It is learned behavior. And I believe that, if it can be taught, it can be taught not to—not to be that way.

Charlayne Hunter-Gault:

You mentioned your children. You had four Black boys, and your eldest was involved in an unsolved murder.

What is your advice to mothers like yourself and also to those protesting the murders of Black men especially, but also Black women?

Ruby Bridges:

That is a parent's worst nightmare. My son's murder was never solved. We do know that the people that actually took his life looked exactly like him.

You know, there are so many parents out there, like myself, who have lost children my son's age or even babies by gun violence, which is very—very disheartening. That is an issue that we have to deal with as well.

Whether it's the murders, like the murder that happened with my son, or murders like George Floyd, if you are passionate about that, then you need to do something about it.

Charlayne Hunter-Gault:

I'm very impressed with your passion and moved by it.

And I imagine there might be a part of your book that is a favorite of yours. Is there any place that you could share with us?

Ruby Bridges:

Yes, I have it right here. I will definitely do that.

"When I think about how great this country could be, America, land of the free, home of the brave, I think about what Dr. Martin Luther King Jr. said about being great. Everybody can be great because everybody can serve. You only need a heart full of grace. Really, it is that love and grace for one another that will heal this world."

Many Blacks Wary of "Women's Liberation" Movement in U.S.

The New York Times
NOVEMBER 17, 1970

Despite the fact that a black woman, Aileen Hernandez, heads one of the largest "women's liberation" groups in the country (the National Organization for Women), black women have been conspicuously absent from such groups. And while liberation is being discussed by black women—in workshops, liberation groups, and privately—it is usually in a context different from that of white women.

The kind of liberation that black women are talking about raises some of the same questions being posed by the white groups. They include such issues as a guaranteed adequate income, day-care centers controlled and administered by the community they serve, and the role of the woman in relation to her man. The differences are rooted in historical traditions that have placed black women—in terms of work, family life, education, and men—in a relationship quite apart from that of white women. To militant black women—such as Frances Beal, a member of the newly formed Third World Women's Alliance—the white women's liberation charge of "sexism" is irrelevant because blackness is more important than maleness.

"Often, as a way of escape," she said in an interview, "black men have turned their hostility toward their women. But this is what we have to understand about him. It is a long, slow, and sometimes painful process for the black man who has been oppressed. But as black women, we have a conciliatory attitude. Firm, but creating together."

Such different perspectives make it all but impossible for some black women to relate to the white "women's lib" movement.

Mrs. Hernandez, as head of the National Organization for Women, which has a membership of roughly ten thousand, said she was dismayed that "people are making a lot of generalizations about the movement and not getting an accurate portrayal.

"It is a predominantly white and middle-class movement—which all movements are," she asserted in a telephone interview from her San Francisco office. "But we feel an identity with all women."

Mrs. Hernandez, former commissioner of the Federal Equal Employment Opportunity Commission, said she felt that "many more young women and many more black and Chicano women" are becoming active in NOW, "particularly in the Southern chapters."

"I find it strange that people are having to make a decision about which to be involved in," she said.

Miss Dorothy I. Height, president of the National Council of Negro Women—a coalition of more than twenty-five black women's groups, representing about four million black women—said that she hoped eventually to have a "dialogue with women's liberation groups." But even though she participated as a speaker in the Women's Liberation Day Program last August, she felt the presence of a wide gulf between them.

"Fifty years ago all women got suffrage," Miss Height said she reminded the group, "but it took lynching, bombing, the civil rights movement, and then the Voting Rights Act of 1965 to get it for black women and black people."

Miss Height said she felt it absolutely essential that "special attention be paid" to black women.

"With all the advances that black women have made—and we are in every field occupied by women—it is still true that we are in predominantly household and related services, with a median income of $1,523," she said.

Eleanor Holmes Norton, chairman of New York City's Commission of Human Rights, supplied another economic statistic concerning the black female labor force.

Almost 70 percent of black women with children between the ages of six and eighteen work, she said.

"Black women feel resentful that white women are raising issues of oppressions even, because black women do not see white women in any kind of classic oppressed position," Mrs. Norton said.

Miss Beal recalled, for example, that the Third World Women's Alliance had been against marching in the women's "Liberation Day" parade last August. But "at the last minute," she said, they decided that marching might be a way of letting other minority-group women who might be standing on the sidelines know of their organization.

"We had signs reading 'Hands Off Angela Davis'—and one of the leaders of NOW ran up to us and said angrily, 'Angela Davis has nothing to do with women's liberation.' And that's really the difference right there.

"'It has nothing to do with the kind of liberation you're talking about,'" Miss Beal said she told the woman, "'but it has everything to do with the kind of liberation we're talking about.'"

The Third World group, which has a New York City membership of about two hundred, and is establishing chapters in other states, includes young women who were formerly in the Black Women's Alliance of the Student Nonviolent Coordinating Committee as well as a wide range of nonaffiliated women. They see themselves as "part of the national liberation struggle" and, as such, believe that "the struggle against racism and imperialism must be waged simultaneously with the struggle for women's liberation."

Miss Beal, who is the mother of two daughters, said: "When white women demand from men an equal part of the pie, we say, 'Equal to what? What makes us think that white women, given the positions of white men in the system, would not turn around and use their white skin for the same white privileges? This is an economy that favors whites. And white women would have the privilege of their class.'"

While class and sex distinction undoubtedly exist in the black community, there are those like Mrs. Norton who declare that the distinctions are minimized by the experience of slavery and of discrimination.

"The black woman already has a rough equality which came into existence of necessity and is now ingrained in the black lifestyle," said Mrs. Norton, a Yale law graduate, and mother of a three-month-old child. "Black women had to work with or beside their men, because work was necessary to survival. As a result, that gave the black family very much a head start on egalitarian family life."

What about black women's attitudes toward black men?

According to Mrs. Norton: "Black men are the one group accustomed to women who are able and assertive, because their mothers and sisters were that way. And I don't think they reject their mothers and sisters and wives. I don't think they want wives to be like the white suburban chocolate eaters who live in Larchmont."

Mrs. Shirley Lacy, director of training for the Scholarship Education and Defense Fund for Racial Equality—an integrated civil rights leadership training organization—has been called in by some black women's groups to hold workshops that include discussions on the black woman's role in the feminist movement.

Mrs. Lacy said that it is terribly important for black women to look at where they are in this time and say: "'Given what I've got, how can I best use that in the context of the black struggle?'

"And if it means that today I walk behind the black man," she said, "that's what I do today, but that may not be true tomorrow. It may be that tomorrow he's going to fall, and I'm going to have to jump in there and be the leader. And the black man is going to have to understand that kind of juxtaposition, too."

New NAACP Head

Margaret Bush Wilson

The New York Times
JANUARY 14, 1975

While Margaret Bush Wilson was working as acting director for Model Cities in St. Louis, she was puzzled when associates openly referred to her as Mary Poppins. "It was not until I left," the diminutive Mrs. Wilson recalled yesterday, "that I learned that the rest of it was '. . . with a razor blade.'"

The sixty-four-member board of directors of the National Association for the Advancement of Colored People, which elected her as its new chairman yesterday, may or may not have heard that story.

But that quality, according to many of them, was certainly among those taken into consideration when they chose her from among four contenders to succeed Bishop Stephen G. Spottswood, who died in December after serving as chairman since 1961.

Board members say the natures of both racial discrimination, which comes in many forms, and the 400,000-member civil rights organization itself demand a leader at the top who knows how to combine the persistent optimism and charm of a Mary Poppins with a tough pragmatism.

They said the board had felt comfortable in choosing the soft-spoken but firm lawyer to lead the organization and its employees because they had not only watched her grow up in the organization, but had tutored her as well.

"She's from one of the better-known middle-class black families in St. Louis," said one associate, "but, as a lawyer and a lifelong worker in the NAACP, she has worked with the problems of folks who represent a large part of the association's membership—working-class and poor people. She'll be terrific for the job."

Following the election, Roy Wilkins, who as executive director of the NAACP is an employee of the board, said Mrs. Wilson was an "excellent choice, smart, and has never given in under pressure." He added that he looked forward to working with her. "She's from my hometown, you know—St. Louis. We're both from the 'Show Me' state."

The fifty-five-year-old Mrs. Wilson's involvement as a leader in the association began at the local level, where in 1958, she was the first woman president of the six-thousand-member branch in St. Louis.

Following four years as president of the Missouri State Conference of Branches, she was elected in 1963 to the National Board of Directors, where she remained until her election as chairman yesterday.

Part of her tutoring occurred under the late William Ming, a Chicago lawyer, whom she succeeded two years ago as permanent chairman or chief parliamentarian of the organization's national conventions.

"I don't have any horror stories," Mrs. Wilson said yesterday in explaining her commitment to one of the country's leading organizations for racial justice.

"I consider myself an aristocrat. Character. Competence. Accomplishment," she said firmly. "That's my definition of aristocracy."

Sitting on the edge of her hotel bed and pounding her fist occasionally for emphasis, she continued:

"I am what I am because my parents were fine, spirited human beings who had a sense of family and were concerned about bringing us up in the best possible world." Mrs. Wilson has one brother and one sister.

Although both parents are now dead, it was their lifetime involvement in the NAACP that charted her own course, she said, adding that they had been involved "because it was the thing to do."

She said her father, the late James Bush Sr., a real estate broker, was the "spark plug" who organized black real estate brokers to bring a suit against restrictive covenants in housing.

That successful case, *Shelley v. Kramer*, was to housing discrimination what *Brown v. Board of Education* was to segregated education, as one NAACP official put it. And Mrs. Wilson proudly recalls that her first case following her graduation from Lincoln University Law School in 1943 was to incorporate the brokers who brought the suit.

Following her father's interest and encouragement to her to enter a career in nursing, teaching, or social work—"all those female things"—Mrs. Wilson majored in economics and mathematics at Talladega College. After law school, she began working in real estate law, and later, among other things, served as an assistant attorney general in Missouri.

Mrs. Wilson, who has a twenty-four-year-old son, Robert 3d, a junior at Harvard Law School, is no feminist; she feels that the fact she is a woman at the top of an organization that has made few concessions to the women's movement is "irrelevant and immaterial.

"Sex and race are accidents of birth," she said. "I take them for granted."

Although she hopes to broaden the involvement of young people in the NAACP, she said yesterday that she contemplated no major change in the sixty-five-year-old organization's direction.

"We have to have an integrated society," she said at her first news conference. "That's what this country is all about."

Poets Extol a Sister's Unfettered Soul

The New York Times
NOVEMBER 9, 1973

JACKSON, Miss.—To mark the two hundredth birthday of the first book published by a black living in America, twenty black women poets from all over the country gathered here this week to celebrate the legacy of its author, Phillis Wheatley, a "pretty little slave girl" who managed at seventeen to become a poet.

The four-day festival at Jackson State College here, on whose campus three years ago two students were killed during a fracas involving policemen, saw the unveiling of a bronze sculpture of Miss Wheatley by Elizabeth Catlett, panels on her work, poetry-reading sessions, and a drama by Vinie Burrows about aspects of the poet's life.

The festival ended Wednesday with the examination as a public policy issue of the exclusion of black women from the textbooks of America.

The poets raised many questions, among them the crucial one of whether they as black poets are as stymied in reaching their full potential as they felt Phillis Wheatley was.

Miss Wheatley, born in Senegal about 1754 and later brought to America and sold to John Wheatley, a Boston merchant, learned to read and write in eighteen months. In her lifetime, she gained recognition for her poems and broadsides on religion, on America, on death, and on politics and freedom.

Her only book, celebrated this week, is called *Poems on Various Subjects, Religious and Moral*, published first in England in 1773.

An excerpt from "To the Right Honorable William, of Dartmouth," goes:

> . . . *I, young in life, by seeming cruel fate*
> *Was snatch'd from Afric's fancy'd happy seat:*
> *What pangs excruciating must molest,*
> *What sorrows labour in my parent's breast?*
> *Steel'd was the soul and by no misery mov'd*
> *That from a father seiz'd this babe belov'd.*
> *Such, such my case. And can I then but pray*
> *Others may never feel tyrannic sway?*

The poets, whose themes range from a celebration of black liberation and the politics of confrontation, included such well-known younger poets as Nikki Giovanni and emerging ones such as Malaika Ayo Wangara (Joyce Whitsitt Lawrence), a Pan-Africanist from Detroit.

And there were the pioneering ones like Margaret Danner, Margaret G. Burroughs, and Margaret Walker, the festival organizer, whose volume of poetry, *For My People*, published in 1942, broke with tradition and presaged the development of black writing that was unabashedly for and about blacks.

They read from their works and discussed their thoughts not only with each other, but also with the students who flocked to see them on this ninety-six-year-old, predominantly black campus.

Carolyn Rodgers, a Chicago-based poet, said she was glad to be in Mississippi because she felt "as if I've touched home."

As a child I grew up terrified and afraid of Mississippi because it was a place where the Klan ran wild and you were brutalized and afraid, and if you were from Mississippi, people snickered and sneered. So you didn't tell people. But I really feel as if I have touched home. Some root. Because I expected to come to a place where if you go home you see blood flowing in the streets.

June Jordan from New York said, however, that she did not want anyone to forget the sight of bullet holes still on a dormitory from "that twenty-eight-second fusillade of unfettered murder" dating back to the disorder in May 1970, which left two students—Phillip L. Gibbs and James E. Green—dead.

Mississippi Highway patrolmen, brought that night to the campus to quell a disorder, were absolved of blame for the shooting.

Mari Evans read from her book of poems, *I Am a Black Woman*, and later talked in the lounge about controls on black writers.

"Since the name of oppression is control," she said, "I cannot bring myself to feel that Phillis's life, even as the prize exhibit, was free of controls. I am sure that [Miss Wheatley's] exercise of control in maintaining a careful image is the reason we have no work from the poet that deals with the controversial issues of her time."

Later, Dr. Margaret Walker, who heads the college's Institute for the Study of Life and Culture of Black People, told the poets that "all the terrible stuff wasn't just a myth. America is like this—the horror is here, the corruption is here, the evil is here. But there is also some love and some beauty, as we see in this festival atmosphere."

Then Nikki Giovanni read to a packed audience in the auditorium a poem about hands ". . . in fact / two brown butterflies fluttering / across the pleasure / they give my body." Though the students sat as if enthralled as she jubilantly read to the background music of the Tougal Gospel Choir they never tapped their feet or clapped their hands. And while they gave Miss Giovanni three standing ovations there was silence in between.

Later, poets and some of the students and townspeople talked about the atmosphere. "It's because we ain't about too much these days," volunteered George Willingham, a junior at the college in the bookstore during an autographing session. "I'm from out of state—Florida—and I decided to come here after the students were killed. I wanted to help black people, and I figured ain't no better place to start."

But there was festivity, much of it buzzing around Dr. Walker, a figure styled by Miss Giovanni as "the living personification of the spirit of Phillis Wheatley."

Dr. Walker has been at Jackson State for twenty years. She feels this festival is particularly significant, because she says she sees many parallels between what happened to Phillis Wheatley and what is continuing to happen to black women and black men who try to get published today.

In 1942, she recalled, she received the Yale Younger Poets Award for *For My People*. It was, she said, a steady seller for sixteen years, and then, she said, her friends at the press either left Yale or died and the book went out of print.

"In 1968, the young black students forced Yale to bring it back. They reissued it in the sixth printing. But now that it's selling better than ever, they've decided it should go out of print, after thirty-one years."

Black women, Dr. Walker said, have "always been tokens" in the publishing world. "The textbooks haven't included them, no matter how well received or critically acclaimed they were. And this is one of the reasons we're having this festival. Our young people have got to be educated to all that has been hidden."

Shirley Chisholm

Willing to Speak Out

The New York Times
MAY 22, 1970

Mrs. Shirley Chisholm, who went to Congress as the first black woman member of the House of Representatives sixteen months ago, sat forward in her office chair and succinctly assessed herself and her colleagues.

"The difference between me and most of them," she said, "is that I am not a politician, I'm a stateswoman.

"I never told anybody that I came into politics for life. Therefore I have nothing to lose for speaking out against the wrongs in the system. I am basically a fearless person, and everywhere people look to that kind of person for leadership."

In winning the seat for the 13th District, in Brooklyn, Mrs. Chisholm defeated James Farmer, former national director of the Congress of Racial Equality and now undersecretary of health, education, and welfare. In speaking of Mr. Farmer the other day she referred to him as "the national figure." Mrs. Chisholm not only has become something of a national figure herself, but is also an important figure in Democratic state and local politics.

The double role, she has learned, is a demanding one.

Mrs. Chisholm, a former member of the Assembly, led the recent party fight to designate State Senator Basil A. Paterson for lieutenant governor. But because she is in Washington four days a week, and spends a day with her constituents in Bedford-Stuyvesant, she said she cannot go on the road to campaign with Mr. Paterson.

"Mrs. Chisholm reaches a lot of people," she said, "because she is in demand as a speaker, and I think Basil will get tremendous support, perhaps even more than if I were traveling with him because of the audiences I reach."

She has endorsed Howard J. Samuels in preference to Arthur J. Goldberg in the Democratic primary for governor even though Mr. Goldberg is running on the same ticket with Mr. Paterson. But the argument that her support for Mr. Samuels suggests a lack of enthusiasm for Mr. Paterson, who is black, "is a lot of baloney," she said.

"This is a smokescreen people are using to becloud the whole gubernatorial election in New York," she said. "The point has to be made that this year, because of new legislation, voters of this state do not have to vote for a slate in the primary, but can vote for individuals. That is why Howard Samuels can win and why Basil can win, too.

"I'm not fighting Arthur Goldberg per se. He's a fine jurist, a distinguished American, but he allowed himself to be used by the bosses, and Basil almost didn't get on his ticket, as a result.

"They kept saying to me, 'Three Jews and a black man. That just won't go over upstate.' I told them, 'OK,' if that's your problem, take one of the Jews off."

Mrs. Chisholm's outspoken style has been evident since she arrived in Washington. Right off she asked that her committee assignment be changed from agriculture to something more relevant to her mostly black, mostly urban constituency.

Since then she has taken sides on a variety of controversial causes: women's rights, abortion reform, ending the war in Vietnam, and enfranchising eighteen-year-olds, all of which she favors.

Such high visibility has led to a few ticklish situations. Because there are so few blacks in Congress, black people from all over the country deluge her with more calls than she and her small staff can possibly handle, she said.

A delicate problem arose last week when she refused to appear at a "Shirley Chisholm Day," held at her own church in Brooklyn, the Janes United Methodist Church. One reason, she said, was that church officials had used her name to solicit funds from other House members.

"It was all very embarrassing," she remarked.

Within the time span that includes student demonstrations at New Haven and the deaths at Kent State University and Jackson State College, the number of students visiting her Washington office in the Longworth Building has doubled.

"She can't say no," said Mrs. Carolyn Smith, her administrative assistant. At thirty-one, Mrs. Smith is the oldest member of Mrs. Chisholm's Washington staff, which is largely female and also includes college "interns" (most of them white) who get credit from their schools for their work.

A small, all-white contingent from Drew University in Madison, New Jersey, originally scheduled for a fifteen-minute meeting, ended up by spending an hour as they listened to a few of Mrs. Chisholm's sharply worded opinions.

On the war: "Many gentlemen in the House of Representatives have sons eligible to serve in Vietnam who are in reserve units. I know one who has six sons, all in the reserves. He can afford to get up and talk about escalating the war. But I'm compiling a list, and as soon as the public sees what is going on, they may start asking a few questions."

On the lack of black involvement in war protest: "Black people have so many here-and-now problems, like being concerned with getting a better apartment. It's a philosophical thing, a white man's thing."

The environment: "I agree with an eighty-five-year-old black woman who said to me: 'Earth Day. Polluted water, polluted air. But I'm not going to get caught up in that. What we need is a campaign in America about polluted hearts.' That's what's worrying black people."

School busing: "For years, for years, in Southern schools, black children have been passing white schools in buses to get to the little one-, two-, and three-room shacks across town. Now, whites are screaming about busing.

"One the other hand, as an educator, I believe in the neighborhood school. I can't see four-, five-, and six-year-olds being exposed to bigots in other communities. It's enough for a black man and a black woman to withstand . . ."

As one of the nine blacks in the House, Mrs. Chisholm has joined with the others on several issues, including "the campaign to make General Motors responsible" by, among other things, electing a black man to the company's board.

But mostly she goes her own way, with the help of her two major advisers, Wesley (Mac) Holder, the seventy-one-year-old manager of her Brooklyn office who, as head of the local Democratic club, brought her into politics, and her husband, Conrad Chisholm, who has taken a leave from his job as a senior investigator with the Department of Social Services. Mr. Chisholm sometimes travels or appears for her, or, as she is fond of saying, "tells me when I've had enough."

After her House committee assignment was changed—not to the Education and Labor Committee, to which she feels she is best suited, as a specialist in early childhood education and welfare, but to the Veterans Affairs Committee—she has set up a research project to investigate discrimination in the veterans organizations.

She also waged a campaign against the preventive detention section of the District of Columbia crime bill, and has urged repeal of the emergency detention section as the Internal Security Act of 1950, which would confine possible spies or saboteurs in the event of invasion, declaration of war, or domestic insurrection in aid of a foreign enemy.

Addressing the House, she said:

> Although the emergency detention section has not been invoked since its enactment, its mere presence on the books is an offense, especially to Americans of color. As I said earlier in my testimony, it was not the Italians and Germans who

were rounded up in 1942, under a presidential order but the Japanese Americans who were easily identifiable because of the color of their skin.

Today, it is not the Ku Klux Klan or the [crime] Syndicate whose doors are being kicked in, it is the Black Panthers. Skin, skin, skin color, gentlemen, that's the criteria. It makes us special targets.

Despite her range of legislative interests and the zeal with which she pursues them, Mrs. Chisholm's political effectiveness is difficult to gauge.

"Two of the things she has going for her," said a political observer, "are also the two things that go against her the most—she's black and she's a woman.

"The effect this has on white politicians, particularly those who consider themselves liberal, is absolutely deadly. They don't want to be labeled bigots or ungentlemanly."

As for black politicians, particularly those in Brooklyn, a woman long active in Brooklyn politics said:

"The same black men who supported her publicly against Farmer but who worked for him and raised money for him behind her back are the same ones trying to crush her now."

In her district in Brooklyn, the women outnumber the men on the voting rolls, and many people say it is among the women that she gets most of her support.

Mrs. Lucille Rose, assistant commissioner of operations in the city's Manpower Career and Development Agency, recalled how Representative Chisholm had invited a group—"mostly housewives"—to the Democratic state convention at Grossinger last month.

"Shirley took them in to hear some speeches," Mrs. Rose said, "and they were also able to see what a caucus was like, with people going in and out of various rooms. When we left—after Shirley fed us at her own expense—we were all in accord: we had learned something about how the political machine works."

The Woman Who Will Judge Oscar Pistorius

The New Yorker
MAY 5, 2014

Thokozile Matilda Masipa, the sixty-six-year-old judge in the Oscar Pistorius trial, which resumed Monday morning in Pretoria, has been sending messages all of her professional life. Pistorius, who is accused of murdering his girlfriend, Reeva Steenkamp, addresses Masipa as "My Lady," as do the lawyers on both sides, and she will ultimately decide his guilt. (South Africa doesn't have jury trials.) In the mid-seventies, when she was known primarily as Matilda or Tilly, she went to jail herself, arrested after demonstrating in downtown Johannesburg against the apartheid regime's attempts to suppress a newspaper she worked on, as well as the arrests of other journalists. Masipa and other women journalists who marched that day were deeply invested in exposing the harshness of white-minority rule, and, in particular, its consequences for women.

"We dealt with women's issues—especially the women NGOs like the YWCA that were making a difference in their communities," Pearl Luthuli, one of Masipa's former colleagues, told me.

Another colleague, Nomavenda Mathiane, remembered, "After '76, it was really hell."

These were the days of the Soweto uprisings. In June 1976, the police killed Hector Pieterson, who was thirteen years old; Luthuli remembered the incident as "the boiling point," although it was also a turning point in the struggle against apartheid. Another defining moment came in September 1977, with the murder of Stephen Biko, a popular activist whose death ignited more protests in townships all over South Africa. "In those days, we didn't see our struggle as politics. Our very existence was being threatened," Luthuli said.

Luthuli was twenty-three, and Tilly, as she called Masipa then, was twenty-nine at the time of Biko's death, married with two children (she now has four grandchildren), and very focused. She had already earned a degree in social work, in 1974, and, for a while, had used what she learned working with women in the townships, including Soweto, where she was born. Many of the women were contending not just with the conditions of apartheid and poverty but with domestic violence.

Now Masipa was putting all that background into her career as a journalist, covering serious issues that involved but were not exclusive to women. "We were writing about what was going on in the townships— demonstrations, brutal police, and especially women who had been detained, leaving their children behind," Luthuli said. "Mothers whose sons had been detained. Another mother who was detained for months because the police couldn't find her son."

On the day of their arrest, Luthuli said, the women journalists were marching in downtown Johannesburg to protest the detention of several of their black male colleagues at the *Post*, and to hand over a memorandum to the authorities stating that they were journalists and needed to be granted the right to work freely without fear of jail. As they set off for the demonstration, Luthuli recalled, "We were very, very scared because they threatened us."

Luthuli remembered that a white policeman, speaking in Afrikaans, shouted at her and Masipa, "Vandag julle sal Steve Biko ont moet" ("Today you are going to meet Steve Biko").

Once five of the women, including Masipa, had been roughly transported to the jail cells, Luthuli recalled, they continued their defiance, refusing orders to clean toilets that she said were clogged with human waste from previous inmates. Luthuli told me the message they sent that day was, "We are not prisoners yet, so we will not follow the orders you give to prisoners."

All of them slept that night on the cold floor of the cell, she remembered, using as sheets the pages of newspapers that they had taken with them on their march. The following morning, the women objected to taking part in the court proceedings. The message the five were sending was clear, Luthuli said: "We are not going to participate in your sham trial." They were eventually transported in a separate bus after all the other prisoners had been taken to the courthouse, where they refused to enter a plea, sending still another message: "We don't recognize this government."

But, Luthuli told me, the women were released after the white editors of their white-owned newspaper published an editorial stating that the women were young and headstrong and should be released. "They just needed to get out their paper, so they paid a fine to get our release," Luthuli said.

Still, the women persisted in covering the growing anti-apartheid protests, and Masipa became women's-page editor of the *Post*—"No mean feat," Luthuli recalled. "That position was for a white woman." A previous editor, a white woman, had left for England, saying she couldn't raise her children in South Africa. "Tilly was steady and grounded," Luthuli said. "She would be leaving work to go home, tend her family. . . . She would leave work and go home and study."

Nomavenda Mathiane remembered that Masipa was "very thorough and didn't suffer fools gladly." (Masipa recently admonished attendees in an overflow courtroom, "It is not an entertainment place. . . . Please restrain yourself.") Mathiane added, "Sometimes the police would call up and say you are not supposed to write this and that. But Tilly would stand her ground. She's really a tough cookie. And I think her strength comes from being so laid-back." At the same time, "You could still joke with her."

Masipa began her legal studies at a time when Nelson Mandela was still in prison; she earned her degree in 1990, the year he was released, and, having qualified, began practicing law. At some point, like many South African blacks with Christian names, she began using her African name professionally, too—Thokozile, which, in Zulu, means "happy."

In 1998, Masipa was appointed as a judge in the High Court of South Africa—only the second black woman to the bench. Albie Sachs, a former Constitutional Court justice, told me, "It was part of a breakthrough. In a sense, she is a pioneer."

Even today, Masipa still belongs to a minority—only seventy-six of South Africa's two hundred and thirty-nine judges are women. Earlier this year, the Women's Legal Center and Tshwaranang Legal Advocacy Centre, nonprofit organizations promoting women's rights, stated, "With 51.3 percent females in the country, having only two female justices in the Constitutional Court, the highest court on Constitutional matters, is inexcusable."

Masipa's past experiences as a journalist appear to have informed her approach to the bench; she said in an interview before the Judicial Services Commission, in 2003, that judges should be more transparent, using the media to explain their decisions and helping the public understand the judicial process. (Her office indicated to me that she did not want to talk about any aspect of her life while the Pistorius trial is going on.)

Her life may help inform her actions on the bench in other ways, particularly as it relates to domestic abuse, rape, and the murder of women. (Statistics from the International Criminal Police Organization, released in 2009, indicate that a woman is raped in South Africa every seventeen seconds.) In one case before her, Masipa handed down a 252-year prison sentence to a man who raped three women in the course of home burglaries; in another, she gave a life sentence to a policeman who shot and killed his estranged wife in an argument over their divorce settlement. ("You deserve to go to jail for life because you are not a protector. You are a killer," Masipa told him.) Her perspective could prove crucial in the Pistorius case, in which the prosecution has told a story of a man, quick to anger and reckless with guns, shooting his girlfriend after a quarrel, while the defense has drawn a picture of a boyfriend who loved Steenkamp and so would never hurt her, and tragically mistook her for an intruder. Both might see something in a comment that Masipa made, according to South Africa's CTVNews, in the rape case: "The worst, in my view, is that he attacked and raped the victims in the sanctity of their own homes, where they thought they were safe."

In reaching her verdict, Masipa will have the help of two legal assessors whom she selected, who sit with her on the bench daily. But the focus, as the defense reaches the end of its case in the next few days, will be on her alone. South Africa and the rest of the world is now awaiting the message Masipa will send this time, in her judgment of Oscar Pistorius.

Unlimited Visibility

The New Yorker
SEPTEMBER 17, 1966

One day last week, we called on Constance Baker Motley, the tall, attractive borough president of Manhattan, a few days before she was sworn in as the first woman judge of the United States District Court in this area and the first Negro woman Federal District judge in the country. (There are only two other women federal judges.) We saw Mrs. Motley in her office, on the twentieth floor of the Municipal Building, to which she had just returned after attending the swearing-in ceremony for another new Federal District judge, in the United States Courthouse, across the street. "I'm a little winded," she told us as she walked in, still out of breath. "But I was happy to see that the ceremony is only about five minutes long. Also, it's a relief to know that I won't have to make a speech." Before becoming New York's first woman borough president, Mrs. Motley was a lawyer for the NAACP Legal Defense and Education Fund, from 1946 to 1965, and from 1964 to 1965 she was a New York State senator. As she seated herself at her desk, we asked her to tell us a bit about the job she was now leaving.

"Well," she said, clasping her hands together and rocking slightly in her chair, "being the borough president of Manhattan isn't all cutting ribbons at flower shows and proclaiming Curb Your Dog Day, although these things are a source of contact with your constituents. Three years ago, the city charter was revised, and control of the city street workers was transferred from the borough presidents to a new Department of Highways, under the jurisdiction of the mayor. I do not see this as weakening the office of the borough president, for now he has become more of a spokesman for the aspirations of the people of the borough, instead of being a man who fixes holes in the street."

Mrs. Motley's telephone rang, and she spoke quietly into it for a few seconds, then swiveled around gracefully in her chair. "We've had to stay in a motel for two nights, because the painters have completely wrecked our apartment," she said. "That was my husband, Joel, wanting to know where he and our son should meet me." (Joel Motley Jr. is a real estate man, and their son, Joel III, who is fourteen, is a student at Exeter.) Then, picking up where she had left off, she said that as borough president she had, among other things, drawn up a compromise that brought the plans for the Morningside Urban Renewal Project out of stalemate. Also, she said, she had helped to halt the proposed elevated expressway across Broome Street, in lower Manhattan. "The most exciting project I've been associated with, though, is the future revitalization of Harlem," she continued. "We must reclaim the inner city, rather than wipe it out." She told us that she had met with leaders from the Harlem community and that they were strongly in favor of bringing office buildings and light industry into Harlem. "What's important," she said, leaning forward, "is that there be more dialogue between Harlem and the world beyond its boundaries. As a starter, it has been proposed that a State Office Building and a City Police Academy be built in Harlem, and it is hoped that City College's Baruch School of Business, with ten thousand students, most of whom are white, will be rebuilt there. And the city has the plans and the money to start more building in Harlem tomorrow. This is bound to create some worthwhile exchange, especially in the areas immediately surrounding the new buildings. At last, the people in these neighborhoods will see concrete proof that Harlem can be a productive part of a well-integrated whole."

Mrs. Motley paused to read a note brought in by her secretary, then told us she had to keep an appointment to be fitted for her judge's robe, and invited us to come along. We accepted, and on the way uptown in the borough president's car we asked her if she thought the custom of having Negro borough presidents would continue.

She nodded. "Ideally, anyone who is qualified should be able to hold this office," she said. "But, to be politically realistic, forty-five percent of this borough's population is nonwhite. By 1970, unless we succeed in breaking up this pattern—and I trust we will—a great many of the city's elected officials will be chosen on the basis of race. In spite of all that, this office offers unlimited visibility. How well it's used is up to the individual who holds it."

By this time, the car had stopped in front of the tailor shop, on West Thirty-Sixth Street, and Mrs. Motley hurried out of the car and into the building. The tailor, a short, jovial man, was waiting at the door when she walked in, and, after introducing her to several members of his staff, he brought out two black robes for her to try on. "We have a couple here that are cool in summer," he said reassuringly as Mrs. Motley slipped her arms into the first one, with a long, deep sigh.

One of the tailor's assistants said he thought the first robe was too long, and reached for the other one, which he said was two inches shorter.

The room was warm, and before trying on the second robe Mrs. Motley removed the jacket of her suit. As she looked around for a place to put it, she spotted a white robe hanging from a rack in one corner. Her face brightened for a moment; then, turning back to the black robe that the tailor was holding for her, she said, "I think that innovation had better wait until we get another woman on the bench."

PART III

Community and Culture

When I look back on how I developed my approach to covering Harlem as a community, in a real sense I owe it to my upbringing during segregation, when my people in my neighborhood, my school, and my church especially refused to succumb to that cruel system of denial that shackled my people . . . And when I think back on the impact their defiance had on me, one of the things that no doubt explain my approach to community and culture comes from Proverbs: "Train up a child in the way she/he should grow and when she/he is old, she/he will never depart from you."

There were lessons well taught and learned at an early age, long before those in college journalism classes, and years later they would show up in print. For example, the piece I reported in Martha's Vineyard. I had heard of Martha's Vineyard from one of my classmates, Bobby Jackson. The South was still segregated and Bobby's father, a doctor, used to drive many hours, through several states where Blacks were not allowed on the various beaches along the way to get to a place where Black people could enjoy everything the place had to offer. That included all of its beaches, and especially the one most frequented by Blacks, known as the Inkwell. The origin of the name is disputed, but as one legend has it, the Inkwell was so named due to the color of the people most in evidence. Another, and the one I prefer, is that it was called the Inkwell because of all the famous Black literary figures who sunbathed and swam there, including Dorothy West, the author of short stories and novels and a member of the Harlem Renaissance. But I never got to go in those days. Many years later, my husband, Ronald, and I were invited to the Vineyard by one of his colleagues at the Ford Foundation who had a place on the twenty-six-mile island. That part was widely referred to as "Up Island," where people like Jacqueline Kennedy and other white celebrities vacationed. While we had a wonderful time Up Island, I had heard so much about Oak Bluffs from Bobby Jackson that at the end of our visit, we headed down to OB, as it is known. Once there, I realized I needed to tell the world about this wonderful Black oasis and update where it now fell in the ongoing racial history of the country. So I called Arthur Gelb, the *New York Times* metropolitan editor, and persuaded him to give me a few more vacation days to chronicle my "discovery." The article appeared in what in those days was the crème de la crème of the paper's sections—the Second Front, with a great picture of one of the dark-skinned Inkwell regulars. Years later, I would come to make OB my home away from home, for, like the woman in my *Times* story who originally came from one of the Cape Verde Islands, OB was a melting pot and a window into that and other cultures.

This cultural diversity was often on display at various events that, thankfully, included food, especially at the end of the summer, up and down the long sidewalk above the Inkwell.

Among those who saw to it that I was properly taught at an early age was my grandmother, Frances Wilson Layson Brown Jones. I developed my first appreciation for Harlem when she took me from our small-town home in Covington, Georgia, to Atlanta, where we boarded a train to New York City and headed straight to my great-uncle Henry's apartment in Harlem. Even at the young age of five, I was captivated by how the address was lyrically given as 115th-Street-Between-Lenox-and-Fifth. Not only were the streets identified differently from what I was used to back home, but there were both similarities and differences in the people I saw around me. For example, children my age played hopscotch, just as we did in Covington. But instead of the dirt playgrounds I was used to skipping around on, these children played on the paved streets, and I quickly learned how to treat my aching feet after jumping around on concrete. And even though I had a harder time learning to understand the girls and boys I played with—their lilting, musical, and rapid way of speaking a language I had never heard before—in time, I even managed to pick up a few Spanish words.

And while my great-uncle was no longer among the living by the time I went to Harlem as a reporter some twenty-two years later, what I had learned about Harlem early on did not depart from me as I returned armed with pen and notepad—the days before cell phones made them mostly obsolete.

In attempting to expand readers' views of the Black community, I continued to apply my well-learned lessons about My People's community and culture, including the music. Now I often went to places in Harlem, like the historic Apollo Theater, where some of the legends of Black music performed music that was right up my alley. But when I learned about a symphony orchestra in Harlem, well, that was surely not anything that had ever seen the light of day in any newspaper, other than, perhaps, the Harlem-based Black newspaper the *Amsterdam News*. So I immediately set out to find it, and when I met some of the musicians, what a surprise it was, as by day some were employed as postal workers or schoolteachers or held jobs totally unrelated to a symphony orchestra and had no place other than Harlem to display their classical talents.

To be sure, I was exposed to Harlem in all of its manifestations, not all nearly as benign as those from my young years on 115th-Street-Between-Lenox-and-Fifth. I never shied away from reporting its darker challenges. But even when I had to cover those, I often tried to give context, like some of the reasons so many young people turned to drugs—using, selling, or both and sometimes dying, like young Walter Vandermeer, whose family I got to know. I offered whatever support I could provide to a mother with five children and no man living in their cramped apartment.

My other approach to Harlem was through culture and individuals who were attracted by and contributed to its vibrancy, people like

Frank Hercules, the Trinidadian author, and Lewis Michaux, whose bookstore they and so many authors and others frequented because of its huge collection of books by and about Black people.

The history it contained was also reflected on the corner across the street, where for generations Black men from Marcus Garvey to Malcolm X stood on tall wooden ladders to speak. While the content of their various messages was often controversial, the common thread was Black pride—a pride that was manifest in ways that I would "discover," as I had the Inkwell, and go on to share with readers.

7,000 Books on Blacks Fill a Home

The New York Times
MARCH 18, 1972

By the time Clarence L. Holte retired after more than twenty years as an advertising specialist in ethnic markets, he had a $400,000 hobby to come home to.

"Honey, I wouldn't give anything for this hobby," the sixty-two-year-old bibliophile said as he talked recently about his collection of books of black literature and history.

With more than seven thousand titles, acquired from all over the world, Mr. Holte's collection is one of the largest and most valuable private collections.

Although the collection is available to scholars, Mr. Holte discourages most other inquiries, preferring to refer students and others to the Arthur A. Schomburg Collection, which is housed in the Countee Cullen Branch of the New York Public Library in Harlem.

Mr. Holte's facilities are also limited—the seven thousand books line most of the wall space in the modest five-room apartment he shares with his wife, Helen, overlooking what was once the site of the Polo Grounds.

Mr. Holte has earned the gratitude of several historians who have used his collection, including Eileen Southern, who wrote *The Music of*

Black America, published in 1970. Arna Bontemps, the black anthologist, poet, and historian, inscribed one edition of his book *They Seek a City* to Mr. Holte, calling him "Our No. 1 book collector."

Mr. Holte has also served as adviser to a major reprint corporation, utilizing titles from his collection as a basis for the reissuance of fifty-seven books.

Some of his books, many of which he has had rebound, date back to the sixteenth century, like *The Late Travels of S. Giacomo Baratti, an Italian Gentleman, into the Remote Countries of the Abissins or of Ethiopia Interior.*

Among his favorites are slave narratives, such as *The History of Prince Lee Boo, Josia: The Maimed Fugitive*, and *Twenty-Eight Years a Slave.*

He studied at Lincoln University in Pennsylvania and later became a pioneer in developing ethnic markets for Batten, Barton, Dustin & Osborn. Mr. Holte easily combined his hobby and his advertising work, making each complement the other.

"The Ingenious American" series featuring blacks who made major cultural and technological contributions to this country was developed for the company that makes Old Taylor bourbon, and has now been made available to schools in pocket-sized reprints. The subjects were drawn from Mr. Holte's collection.

One book he's "sure can't be found any place else" is a census of Liberia, with tables showing the number of free blacks and former slaves from the United States who had settled in Liberia prior to 1843. It was prepared by the United States government in 1845, and contains 2,390 names.

By studying bibliographies, and having somewhat of a reputation as a collector of books—particularly first editions—Mr. Holte has acquired such rare books as the first book reportedly written by a black man in English—*The Life of Gustavus Vassa*, published in 1789; the first known description of Africa by Leo Africanus, a Moor, translated from Arabic in 1600; and one of the first histories of blacks written by a black, James W. C. Pennington, published in 1841.

Mr. Holte's latest venture, published last week, is a baby book for black families to record their children's milestones in—the "Cadillac of baby books," he calls it.

Published by Nubian Press, a family-owned company he established for the venture, it features pictures of black babies and their families, along with African proverbs and poetry by blacks. Mr. Holte sees it "providing a guideline for parents of black children during the crucial preschool ages when their images are being formed."

He also sees it preventing the kind of embarrassment he suffered as a college freshman who knew nothing about his people.

Meanwhile, he is still learning. He says in a lifetime a man is expected to read around 1,500 books. "I have seven thousand, which means that I look forward to living several lives."

An Entrepreneur's Trucks Bring Southern Soul Food to Harlem

The New York Times
DECEMBER 20, 1971

It's a sure sign that winter has come when Grady C. Houston's big trucks make the one-thousand-mile run from Macon, Georgia, to Harlem with the kind of Southern soul food that's hard to come by in the North.

When a chill creeps into the air in the South it means that hog-killing time is close. And that's when the rear ends of trucks are transformed into artful displays of down-home soul food that reach out and titillate the palate of every Southern-born soul who passes by.

Parked at various spots in Harlem, mainly on Saturdays, the trucks attract dozens of shoppers all day who come to pick from the baskets of yams, sweet potatoes, collard and turnip greens, pecans, homemade hot green peppers, liver sausage, hog's head cheese and chow-chow—hot and mild—cane patch syrup, sage, sausage links, smoked hams and cracklin', the residues of fat used for cracklin' bread.

Grady Houston, who started the whole thing in 1948 when his father died, has three trucks and his nephews, cousins, and brothers have six more.

"My oldest brother was a Pullman porter based in New York," Mr. Houston explained to a visitor in the Georgia Farm Produce Market, a little store that he owns at 2643 Eighth Avenue, near 141st Street.

"When he came home to Georgia for the funeral, I was hauling watermelons to Atlanta, selling them for twenty cents apiece. He told me if I brought 'em to New York, I could get two dollars apiece for them. So, after the funeral, I brought a load.

"That was on the twenty-fifth of June," he continued. "On the Fourth of July, I brought two more loads. And I cleaned up from 1948 to 1957."

At that point, Mr. Houston decided to leave his one-thousand-acre farm for his relatives to tend, and expanding his market to include some of the other products produced on their farm, he said he "went to handlin'" the sweet potatoes, peanuts, and vegetables, and eventually the meat, which brought upwards of 75 percent more in New York than in Georgia.

Mr. Houston, a small, sturdy man who still speaks in slow, deliberate, and heavy Southern tones, chose his sites then in the still-unfamiliar city near where his relatives lived—125th Street and Amsterdam Avenue, where a sister lived in a housing project, and Seventh Avenue and Fiftieth Street, near a brother's apartment.

By 1962, Mr. Houston had done well. He won't say how well, or even give a clue.

But he tells a visitor that among other things he opened three stationary markets, flies to Georgia now rather than drives, and has "moved downtown." In his only comment on the mobile markets, he said: "It just growed into big business."

Church in Harlem Plays Vital Role in Community

The New York Times
DECEMBER 6, 1970

"When you're talking about St. Philip's Church in Harlem," said its pastor, Dr. M. Moran Weston, "you're talking about a grassroots organization. Everybody here is part of the community."

The prestigious Protestant Episcopal church and its $2.6 million Parish House–Community Center complex at 230 West 134th Street belies the traditional grassroots interpretation. But Dr. Weston recalled the tradition of protest of the black Episcopal church in New York—it broke away from Trinity, the white church, in 1810—and how it helped shape the present philosophy of the church he now heads.

The church, which started out in lower Manhattan and moved north with the movement of the black population, reached Harlem in 1911, Dr. Weston recalled, at a time when there were more whites than blacks living there.

But its social concerns were to be honed later—first by the Depression, when the church became involved in early work relief programs, and, still later, in 1944, when a child was killed in an accident in the schoolyard next door.

It was also in 1944, Dr. Weston recalled, that the church "became very aware that a new group of people were living in the community."

"The density had increased," he said, "and the community, by now, was one hundred percent black. The church began to see that the people had new kinds of needs and we were their neighbors."

The church quickly began new programs to meet the changing needs.

By the time Dr. Weston—the church's sixth pastor in its 152-year history—arrived in 1957, the needs were even greater. A census he conducted showed that there were more than two hundred children on 133d Street in the block between Seventh and Eighth Avenues.

"Physically we had nowhere else to go, and yet we knew we had to address ourselves to new services for those not able to meet their own needs," he said.

The new complex, he explained, is a part of a ten-year expansion plan and is a "new channel through which the community can develop its potential." It includes, for example, a preschool day-care center, which is subsidized, in part, by the Department of Social Services so mothers who cannot afford the $32-a-week fee can bring their children free.

The church also has an auditorium-gymnasium with lockers, showers, and dressing rooms, a cultural and performing arts program, several multipurpose activity rooms, and among other things, a kitchen where hot lunches are prepared for the children in the day-care center.

Housing has been identified as a major need in the area, and the church is in the process of developing two hundred units for senior citizens on 133d Street between Seventh and Eighth Avenues, and 242 "low and modest" income apartments on Eighth Avenue from 133d to 134th Street.

Dr. Weston also has the approval of the church to convert the old parish house into a nonresidential prevention and rehabilitation narcotics center. "This shows a new kind of awareness on the part of our church people, too," he said.

As one of the founders of the Carver Savings Bank, a black institution in Harlem, and recently elected chairman of its board, Dr.

Weston is optimistic about future development plans. But he feels that while there are public avenues for funds that should be utilized, "it is the private sector—not the public sector—which we have to look to for support.

"The grant system will never do it," he asserted. "One of my greatest disappointments was the ultimate consequence of the poverty program. I was involved in Haryou-Act [Harlem Youth Opportunities Unlimited] for two years in the hope that if we could get larger public funds from the federal level we could channel them into the black community into organizations where black people could control it. Then we could bring about meaningful change. But that didn't happen.

"Worship creates a power potential. We become a catalyst for community leadership, direction, and therefore control."

How *Black-ish* Unpacks Hard Topics with Humor and Nuance

PBS NewsHour
JANUARY 15, 2018

Judy Woodruff:

Now, as part of our ongoing Race Matters series focusing on solutions, special correspondent Charlayne Hunter-Gault has a second part of her conversation with Golden Globe–winning actress Tracee Ellis Ross.

Last week, they talked about the momentum behind the Time's Up movement supporting women.

Tonight, Charlayne examines the popular TV series *Black-ish*, starring Ellis Ross, and how it handles race. The daughter of singer Diana Ross, Ellis Ross plays Rainbow Johnson, or just plain Bow.

Charlayne Hunter-Gault:

Black-ish is a comedy, to be sure, but it doesn't shy away from controversial issues, especially racism, taking on the N-word, biracial Bow, confused about her identity, and going to extremes to fit in with both black and white friends. I want to take you way back to when *Black-ish* first started. It's now going into its fourth season. Was there a conscious decision to take on controversial issues, especially like race and racism?

Tracee Ellis Ross:

Our show is consciously authentic and consciously honest. And a lot of the subject matter that we courageously dive into does end up coming across that way. I think that they are topics that are uncomfortable for people. They are topics that are—need to be unpacked and discussed, and I think that's why they're uncomfortable for people.

Charlayne Hunter-Gault:

I just wonder why they think that these heady issues can be addressed through comedy.

Tracee Ellis Ross:

When one's heart is open through laughter, so much more information can be received. I think it's like giving people their medicine with a spoonful of sugar, you know, or giving your dog its antibiotics in peanut butter, you know?

Charlayne Hunter-Gault:

Right.

Tracee Ellis Ross:

So, you can think of our show as peanut butter. It makes things more receivable. There is an ability to have an open heart while receiving things. And it makes them digestible in a way that, when you're getting punched in the face, sometimes, it's not as easy, because you're busy defending yourself and protecting yourself.

Charlayne Hunter-Gault:

I read somewhere—I think it was an interview with Kenya Barris—he said, "Even when digging deeper means arguing among ourselves, this—especially after the 2016 election."

Tracee Ellis Ross:

Yes.

Charlayne Hunter-Gault:

And that was one of the episodes that I thought was so powerful.

Tracee Ellis Ross:

"Lemons," yes. I thought it was a really powerful episode. And it did what we often do on our show, which I think is a part of the DNA of our show, in that we don't answer a question.

Charlayne Hunter-Gault:

Exactly.

Tracee Ellis Ross:

One of the ways I like to look at it is, I feel like there's a lot of things that are on the wallpaper of our lives in this country that we don't really notice anymore, or we are not forced to think about. And then there's some of those things that we are forced to think about, but they're on the wallpaper of our lives, to the point that we don't always unpack them. We just keep it moving.

Charlayne Hunter-Gault:

It's comedy, and yet it's not always funny, but is that helping an audience to decide some of these complicated issues, you think?

Tracee Ellis Ross:

We all look at these things from very different points of view, but what we end up with is not division, but connection.

Charlayne Hunter-Gault:

I also read—and this was a—you may not even remember this, but it was in the *New York Times* some months ago. It was a feature on you. You were in New York, and you talked about how these young white boys come up to you and . . .

Tracee Ellis Ross:

Yes, and I find it so wonderful.

Charlayne Hunter-Gault:

And they're such big fans.

Tracee Ellis Ross:

You know, I think it's really interesting, because, again, I don't—I am not a fan of categorizing race in that way. But in the specificity of them watching our show, which is unpacking racial identity and cultural identity for this black family, the Johnsons, and when I think of the subject matter that we have addressed, both from the N-word, to police brutality, to being biracial, and then I think of a young white boy who already is immersed in a culture that has music using the N-word or whatever those different things are, but then to be able to watch our show and have, for example, the historical context and relevance of the N-word to be unpacked in a way that I don't think anywhere else in our culture is that something that is being unpacked. I'm very intrigued by my character and the expansive way that I am able to breathe my life into a wife on television, and that . . .

Charlayne Hunter-Gault:

A wife who's a professional.

Tracee Ellis Ross:

Yes, I mean, but that's not even what's interesting. It's she's more than that. The story is told traditionally the way a sitcom is told. It's told through the husband's eyes. But Bow is not wife wallpaper in her husband's world. I don't think it's current. I actually think it's timeless. I think it is about time that television and our industry and our world wake up to the actual balance that exists. I mean, for me, one of my experiences is, you know, I have many a black woman and woman in my life that is the lead in their life, that is living their own life, and doing it their own way, and who is a doctor and a mother and a wife and a friend and a daughter and a sister and all a—of those things, and a coworker and all of that. So I don't think that I'm playing something that's new or current. I actually think it might be new for television, but it's not new for life.

Charlayne Hunter-Gault:

And what do you hope people who are concerned about race and racism take away from this show?

Tracee Ellis Ross:

The humanity involved is actually what moves the scale, like, actually being able to see each other as human beings, beyond ideas and concepts.

And I think our show unpacks that really well.

Charlayne Hunter-Gault:

Do you ever encounter negative reactions from people when you're off the set and out in the public, or is it all positive?

Tracee Ellis Ross:

No, I mean, the one—you know, I have heard, very interestingly, people say things like, "I had no idea I would like your show."

And I always—because that's the kind of person I am, I'm always, like, "Why? Why didn't you think you would like it?"

"Well, you know, the title."

And I'm, like, "Oh, well, what did the title mean to you, that you wouldn't like it?"

"Well, I thought it was just going to be just about like black people" or something, like, that it was unidentifiable. Or, "I mean, it's so funny. You guys, I'm so—my family is so much like yours," you know, as if it's surprising.

And—but that's the beauty of it. I think that's the beauty of it. That is the beauty of comedy. And people seem to be moved and changed by it, and I love that. It's a very rewarding thing.

I mean, you can just make entertainment, you can make people laugh, and that in and of itself is a gift and a really joyful part of the job that I have. But to also make people think is also really cool, and to make people talk and have conversations about things that they wouldn't normally talk about.

New Museum Traces Black Stage History

The New York Times
JULY 9, 1975

A worn-down black shoe with wooden taps on the heel and toe that belonged to John Bubbles when he danced with Judy Garland at the Palace . . .

A check stub for eighty-six dollars—the take-home pay in 1952 for Flournoy Miller, the black writer who created the prototypes of Amos 'n' Andy . . .

Two cow bones—replicas of instruments played in minstrel shows by the "Mr. Bones" . . .

A letter from Edward Albee's father upbraiding a theater manager for referring to black vaudevillians as niggers . . .

These are some of the items of theater history that show the long and continuing impact and influence of blacks on the American stage.

And while at the moment Broadway is overflowing with black talent, the contributions of blacks in the past, toward making Broadway what it is, have not been so well established.

But Helen Armstead Johnson is trying to change that.

Dr. Johnson, a perky scholar in her fifties, is starting a Museum of Black Theater History, partly to demonstrate that it was the Afro-American who gave the American stage its first native form.

Blacks in the theater in New York go back at least as far as 1821 and the African Grove Theater for free blacks, which was at the corner of Bleecker and Mercer Streets.

"They had a garden there," Dr. Johnson recalled the other day, "and as whites went to Chatham Gardens to sip and drink, blacks went to sip and chat at the Grove. They did *Richard III* and *Othello* and original pantomimes."

It was minstrelsy, however—initially a kind of slave entertainment—that Dr. Johnson says was the first native American theater form.

To develop the point, Dr. Johnson, also an associate professor of English at York College, uses the techniques she developed while digging through dusty shelves of London libraries for material for her doctoral thesis on Edmund Burke.

Libraries, including the one at Lincoln Center, and obscure little village bookstores yield some of the information, pamphlets, playbills, librettos, and other artifacts that line even the bathroom walls of Dr. Johnson's modest but growing suite of living and display rooms at the Chelsea Hotel, where she plans to maintain the museum.

Her best sources, however, are entertainers themselves.

"Many of them are growing old," she said, "but they are growing old in New York. And they share their things with me because they are so grateful that someone is taking them seriously."

One of these is U. S. (Kid) Thompson, a dancer, comedian, and orchestra leader, who created the role of the dancing porter in the 1921 production of *Shuffle Along*. He has introduced Dr. Johnson to a number of old theatrical people and contributed to her collection.

"She's done so much for the people I love," Mr. Thompson said.

Leigh Whipper, an actor who is now ninety-nine years old, is another helping Dr. Johnson. His grandfather ran a station of the Underground Railroad in Columbia, Pennsylvania, where he was a planter, and Mr. Whipper has shared old stories and some of his artifacts, too.

"His memory is excellent," said Dr. Johnson, who has spent hours taping interviews with Mr. Whipper. In one, he recalled a childhood nurse who had been a "strut girl."

Strut girls are important to the history of theater because they created the dance known as the cakewalk, which was an integral part of minstrelsy.

The name cakewalk came from the days when dancers would go from one plantation to another to compete, with the best couple winning a cake, Dr. Johnson explained.

"The slaves adapted the grandiose posturing of the Grand March, a part of every ball, to their own Afro-American rhythms, thereby creating a dance, which swept not only this country, but Europe as well," Dr. Johnson wrote in a recent issue of *Encore American and World Wide News*.

"Cakewalkers such as the Due Eclatants, Olga Burgoyne, and Usher were in Russia in 1902. And La Olliette, partner of Happy Joe Williams in the Creole Duett, wrote from the Hotel du Nord in Odessa to Minnie Brown in Moscow in 1910," she added.

Yet New York remained a focal point, with cakewalk competitions at Madison Square Garden.

Dr. Johnson is critical of people who disdain minstrelsy. She says that the "persistent image of the buffoon created by white minstrels (especially amateur Elks) has obscured the real nature of black minstrelsy and the significant contributions of its performances."

Dr. Johnson said that *Shuffle Along*, the 1921 show based on a book by Flournoy Miller and Aubrey Lyles with music by Noble Sissle and Eubie Blake, introduced "hoofers" to Broadway.

"Prior to this," Dr. Johnson said, "white girls were prancers rather than dancers. But when the black girls came along with hoofing, it was earthshaking rather than stage-shaking.

"They showed Broadway something new. Whites had never danced that fast, and their speed and rhythm were always mentioned. And the fact that they could dance and sing at the same time was totally new.

"Ziegfeld hired black men to teach his dancers to dance," she said.

Her theater research is revealing "social, economic, and cultural history that no other research quite reveals," Dr. Johnson said, reporting that Flournoy Miller, the creator of the prototypes of Amos 'n' Andy, in 1952 was taking home only eighty-six dollars from CBS.

"It just represents the great irony that is characteristically true of the interrelationship of whites and blacks in the theater. So many of the whites learned from blacks, were taught by blacks and were written for by blacks, and yet made far more money than the originators of the material."

So far, Dr. Johnson has not had much luck with the covered silver vegetable dish she keeps prominently displayed on a table in her museum, next to a sign marked "Donations."

"People come and marvel about the collection, and in passing pick up the dish, look in it, and put it back down. Empty."

Nor have her long, detailed letters to foundations turned up anything so far, although the 21st Century Foundation, which is black controlled, has recently indicated some initial interest. So far she has put up most of the financing herself.

"The old-timers have been unbelievably generous," Dr. Johnson mused recently. "And I have been embarrassed that I could not even offer them modest sums. Most of them are living on fixed incomes, and I would like to be able to repay them—if even in just a small way."

Street Academy Program Sends School "Walk-Outs" to Colleges

The New York Times
JULY 15, 1971

Forty-two students who "walked out" of the public school system graduated yesterday from the New York Urban League Street Academy Program and are bound for colleges across the country.

Earlier this year, because of the program's financial problems, it was uncertain that this day would come.

The graduation, called an "exercise in innovation," was held in Morningside Park, where the students, ranging in age from sixteen to twenty-six, sat under a bright sun, surrounded by their families, friends, and teachers. Neighborhood children played nearby.

The audience included a former academy student, Yvonne Wright, now a sophomore at the University of Kentucky, where she reportedly scored so high on her English comprehension test when she first went there that officials could not believe she had taken the test herself.

"We are the students for social change," said Ylerilene Murphy, a sixteen-year-old student who is one of twenty-four academy graduates accepted as fully matriculated freshmen at the State University of Iowa. She was one of several speakers at the graduation.

Livingston L. Wingate, executive director of the New York Urban League, called the graduation "an incredible achievement."

In the last year, four of the ten street academies lost the support of four major corporations and were forced to close. The street academies, each of which had been getting $50,000 a year from the corporations, were roughly the equivalent of junior high schools. The next school level in the program is the "transition academy," followed by the prep school, the highest level.

Newark Preparatory School, which had absorbed many of the graduates of the two transition academies in the past, closed last year because of financial difficulties. Financial problems at Harlem Preparatory School—founded about the same time the street academies opened four years ago, but not connected—forced it to restrict its admissions.

"We didn't know exactly where we were going with our students," said Kwami A. Taha, director of the street-academy program. Students from the four closed academies had been worked into the remaining six, for a total of 1,278 students.

It was then that Dr. Susie O. Bryant, one of the program's founders, suggested creating "our own prep school," Mr. Taha said.

Thus, the Urban League's school was born—with no money, but with a staff borrowed from the other segments of the program who agreed to double up on their time, Mr. Taha explained.

Their salaries remained unchanged.

In April, as the outlook for the forty-two college candidates began to look its bleakest, a former Urban League employee became dean of admissions at the State University of Iowa and wrote asking Mr. Taha for students.

In addition to the forty-two college-bound graduates, twenty-nine graduated yesterday from the street academies into transition academies, and fourteen went from there into the new prep school.

The Corner

The New Yorker
JANUARY 7, 1967

Over the past forty years—give or take a few—there have been many
corners in Harlem where people have gathered for one reason or another, but the most popular by far has been the southwest corner of
125th Street and Seventh Avenue, a rallying place all day Saturday
for disaffected Negroes who live around there. On The Corner, as it
is known locally, there is nearly always someone orating, preaching,
exhorting, though the face of the speaker may change from time to
time. And people in the community stop to listen, and often to respond
aloud to what they hear. When one listener leaves, the gap is immediately filled by another. But if the crowd shifts, it does not change. Nor
does the theme. In one form or another, it has nearly always been black
nationalism—from the West Indian brand of Marcus Garvey and his
followers to the more militant brand of Charles (Morris) 37X Kenyatta, The Corner's chief present-day occupant, who is the spokesman
for Harlem's Mau Mau Society.

A street-corner speaker's identity can usually be determined by the
articles with which he surrounds himself. The standard equipment for
any Harlem street-corner speaker is a stepladder or a soapbox (or, on
very special occasions, a wooden platform), when he isn't standing on

a car hood; a flag or two (the Garveyites' was red, black, and green, and Kenyatta's is orange, black, and green); an assortment of placards; and a collection plate, bucket, or hat. Some of the speakers, including Kenyatta, do not take up a collection, on the ground that (in Kenyatta's words) "money makes a man sing a different song." In the old days, Garvey, before he was sent to prison (and later deported to Jamaica), established a spiritual legacy. The *Amsterdam News*, Harlem's durable weekly newspaper, commented in 1927, "In a world where black is despised, he taught them that black is beautiful. He taught them to admire and praise black things and black people. . . . They rallied to him because he heard and responded to the heartbeat of his race." In Garvey's absence, his followers extended both his word and his myth. The West Indians, who had come from societies in which class distinctions were more important than color, were hostile to the American Negroes, because—or so it is sometimes said—they could not understand how a black man allowed hatred based on color to keep him down. In exhorting their American listeners to abandon their docility, the West Indians who took to The Corner sometimes sounded a lot like the West Indian Ras the Exhorter (later Ras the Destroyer) in Ralph Ellison's *Invisible Man*. At one such rally, Ras could be heard for miles around shouting, "We gine chase 'em out! Out!" To which a hearty voice from the crowd responded, "Tell 'em about it, Ras, mahn!"

One day recently, as we were waiting on The Corner, with a number of other people, for Kenyatta to appear, we got into conversation with a slender West Indian in his sixties named James Thornhill, who used to speak on The Corner in the twenties and thirties but now mostly listens. We asked him how long he had lived in Harlem. Thornhill took us by the arm and walked with us a few steps away from the gathering. He told us that as a youth he had been a follower and bodyguard of Garvey's. (Nearly everyone who speaks on The Corner has a small retinue, which stands on each side of his perch and surveys the crowd.) "I left the Virgin Islands to become a seaman," Thornhill went on, in a voice that still had a slight lilt in it. "I traveled in Asia, Africa, the Caribbean, and Central and South America, and I learned four or five languages. When I came to Harlem, in the twenties, black people didn't even walk these streets. In 1932 and 1933, along with Adam Powell Jr. and other members of the Harlem Labor Union, I helped put Negro workers in all these stores." He waved a hand in the direction of the clothing and furniture stores on 125th Street. "The black people themselves have got to develop their own community," he continued. "I have said time and time again from this corner that we cannot depend on other communities to do what we must do for ourselves."

The campaign that Thornhill referred to had other advocates—Ira Kemp, Arthur Reid, and James R. Lawson, the last of whom was a Corner speaker on and off for twenty-five years. Lawson now works a few yards away from The Corner, at the Haryou-Act headquarters, in the Hotel Theresa.

On another Saturday when we were on The Corner, and Kenyatta, at the end of two and a half hours of speechmaking, had stopped for a coffee break, we took the opportunity to drop in on Lawson in the Theresa. A tall, heavyset man whose manner seemed dour at first, Lawson brightened when he talked about The Corner, which he called Harlem's Africa Square. He told us that during the Italian-Ethiopian conflict he was among the speakers who urged Harlem residents not to patronize the Italian businessmen there. "Don't even buy ice from them!" he would tell his listeners. He went on, to us, "No black man could, in good conscience, go into most Italian bars in Harlem. Mussolini's picture hung over almost every Italian cash register up there. At that time, black people owned only two bars in Harlem. When Mussolini's war was over, black people owned thirty-five. My voice was heard from this corner around the world." For his support of Ethiopia, Lawson received the Order of the Star of Ethiopia and was made a Knight Commander by Emperor Haile Selassie.

In the last thirty years, other speakers, on other topics, have sometimes used 125th Street and Seventh Avenue as their forum, Lawson continued. Negro communists, including Benjamin Davis, at one time a New York City councilman, were among them, but they are not recalled in the neighborhood with the same friendly nostalgia as are Alex Prempeh, Lewis Michaux, the late Carlos Cooks, Sufi Abdul Hamid, Mother Bessie Phillips, Nana Oba, and an elusive man named Eddie

Davis, widely known as Pork Chop, who all spoke on The Corner. Lawson said that these people's theme, and his, had not really changed but that it had often been necessary to change tactics. Many boycotts and picket lines had had their genesis on The Corner, he recalled, and during the Second World War some of the orators were pro-Japanese. "It was the whole color thing," he explained.

Probably the most dynamic speaker to come to 125th Street and Seventh Avenue in recent times was Malcolm X. One of the biggest rallies on The Corner was one that he held in 1960, when his purpose was to unify Negro leaders. According to his biographer Louis Lomax, fifteen "outstanding Negro leaders" were invited to participate but none came. Thirteen black nationalist groups took part, though, and for five hours thousands of people stood listening to various speakers, including Malcolm X himself, who then represented Elijah Muhammad's Black Muslims. "They call us racial extremists," Malcolm said that day. "They call Jomo Kenyatta [president of Kenya] also a racial extremist, and Tom Mboya a moderate. It is only the white man's fear of men like Kenyatta that makes him listen to men like Mboya. If it were not for the extremists, the white man would ignore the moderates. To be called a 'moderate' in this awakening dark world today, that is crying for freedom, is to receive the kiss of death as spokesmen or leaders of the masses . . . for the masses are ready to burst the shackles of slavery whether the 'moderates' will stand up or not. We have many black leaders who are unafraid, especially when they know the black masses stand behind them. Many of them are qualified to represent us . . . in this United States government . . . if we are given one hundred percent citizenship and the opportunity for first-class participation . . . or else we can get behind these same leaders in setting up an independent government of our own."

Charles 37X Kenyatta told us one Saturday, before he began his speaking stint, that he and Malcolm X had been close friends since 1961, when they met in Detroit. Kenyatta, a handsome thirty-five-year-old North Carolinian with a neatly trimmed goatee, said he had wanted to be a lawyer but fate had been against him. "Malcolm made me realize what I could do," he said. "He told me how hard it was to buck the forces opposed to revolution, but I decided that if Malcolm could, I could." Kenyatta explained that people interested in forming a program often meet with him on Sunday nights in the Old Garvey Hall, on Eighth Avenue near 128th Street.

On The Corner, Kenyatta, who stands on the top step of a ladder, is a fiery speaker and punctuates his words with a machete, slicing and jabbing the air with it when he is really fired up. Off The Corner, he is a quiet, gentle man who weighs every word. He speaks calmly of attempts that have been made on his life, and of "outside pressures" exerted to remove him from The Corner. "You're good if you keep your mouth shut," he said, smiling. "If not, you're bad and have to be wiped out."

We asked Kenyatta how he happened to start speaking on The Corner.

"Just took it," he replied. "When Malcolm died, no one dared speak here. You couldn't even get a conversation here. But time went on. I took my shotgun and told people to come on, not to be afraid. On my first appearance here, three carloads of Muslims drove up, and instead of getting weaker I got stronger. I had been a Muslim, but when I saw what that had done to Malcolm, I broke away. Malcolm's whole trouble was that he got caught up in that religious bag. A person who leads must be unwilling to compromise. He must be able to go into the alleys and byways and get those who are not in love with material things to bring about this revolution. I start here, on this corner, at the crossroads of the world."

That Saturday, Kenyatta, upon arriving on The Corner, began to shout without any warm-up, "This is your day! You livin' in your day! You got to band together and live as free men and women or die as damn fools! You got to voice your protest against the whole rotten system!"

"You tell 'em, brother!" a loud voice called out.

"Preach on, man!" several people adjured simultaneously.

"Man, the middle class tried to sleep through this," a well-dressed Negro in the crowd said to no one in particular. "Well, we didn't. We're awake now, and we're finding out that seventy percent of what this man is saying is true."

After a few minutes, three police cars and a banana cart rolled up. A young Negro policeman made his way through the crowd and stopped in front of Kenyatta. A blind man tapping a cane approached, and a few people looked around. The blind man stopped for a moment, then moved on. The tapping of his cane was the only thing to be heard as the policeman wrote out a summons and handed it to Kenyatta, who didn't have a permit to speak that day. When the policeman had left, several people in the crowd passed up dollar bills to help cover the fine. Kenyatta, smiling, leaped onto the hood of a blue Oldsmobile—his own. "This is the story of the day," he said. "These people want to hear the truth. I'm just someone here to voice their opinions." By then, all three police cars had moved on, and only the banana cart remained.

The Professor

The New Yorker
SEPTEMBER 3, 1966

For more than thirty years, in two crowded rooms that make up the National Memorial African Bookstore, on Seventh Avenue near 125th Street, or on a soapbox out front, the owner of the store, Lewis Michaux, a small, nimble, Virginia-born Negro of about seventy, has been dispensing the truth as he sees it ("telling it like i' tis") about the life and welfare of "the black man." (He disdains the word "Negro.") The other day, when we paid him the first of a couple of visits, he told us that before he came to New York he had a job picking huckleberries for nine cents a day on a white man's plantation. "That white man had so many sheeps and cows and pigs that I decided he didn't need me," he said. "So one day I sat down and ate all the huckleberries I had picked, and then I walked away, followed by three pigs. Later, I sold the pigs out of a croker sack for a dollar and a half apiece, and I never picked another huckleberry." When Mr. Michaux arrived in New York, he had with him one book, *Up from Slavery*, and a bust of Booker T. Washington. Now he has, by his own count, stacked on tabletops and under them, and along stretches of the walls from floor to ceiling, a hundred and five thousand volumes ("a few less or more"), mostly by or about Negroes—there are more abouts than bys—and, along the walls not covered by books, what he calls the world's only Afro-American Hall of Fame.

Michaux has been preaching Back to Africa long enough to have been influenced both by Marcus Garvey ("We do not desire what has belonged to others, though others have always sought to deprive us of that which belonged to us. . . . If Europe is for the Europeans, then Africa shall be for the black peoples of the world") and by Malcolm X ("America has a very serious problem: us. . . . Once we all realize that we have a common enemy, then we unite on the basis of what we have in common, and what we have foremost in common is that enemy—the white man. He's an enemy to all of us"), and he has not confined his words to Negro audiences in Harlem but has often spoken over the radio and on college campuses. ("I told them at Hunter College, 'You are the future. What your forefathers have laid down, you'd better bypass it.'") As the years have passed, he has had some unusual visitors at the bookstore. There is a picture of Nasser on one wall of the store, alongside pictures of Negro and African leaders, and he told us that Nasser had given it to him. "Yes, Nasser came to see me," he said, with obvious amusement. "While Castro was cooking chickens 'cross the street, in the Theresa Hotel, Nasser was over here seeing me."

Journalists, foreign and domestic, often stop by at the bookstore—whose subtitle is the House of Common Sense and the Home of Proper Propaganda—to ask Michaux questions about Harlem, and students, young and old, black and white, are always dropping in, to browse, to buy a book cheap, or just to see if Michaux is getting along all right. People in the community who have nowhere else to turn come to Michaux with their problems. In the course of a recent week, he counseled a young mother whose fourteen-year-old son was in jail on a narcotics charge, and listened sympathetically to the tale of an elderly woman from Brooklyn who was having trouble keeping her telephone. Some people come to the store only in order to say that they've been there, but they seldom go away empty-handed. ("This house is packed / With all the facts / About all the blacks / The world over," one of a number of signs on the exterior of the store states.) A young Nigerian student arrived while we were there, looking for a book on Olódùmarè, the

Yoruba god, and found Michaux holding forth in the store's narrow doorway, which is identified by a sign as "Harlem Square." Michaux, who was quoting one of his own compositions—a triplet, "The white man's dream / Of being supreme / Has turned to sour cream"—heard the student say that the book was too expensive, and found out by questioning him that he was over here to get a master's degree in engineering, that he planned to return to Nigeria to work, and that he would allow Michaux to come home to Africa with him. Michaux gave him the book and wished him well.

The next morning, shortly after Michaux had opened the store, a group of three Negroes and twenty-one whites, who said they were a class of teachers enrolled in a three-week graduate workshop in human relations at City College, came by to have a session with the Professor, as Michaux is often called. We asked one young woman what happens during a three-week course in human relations, and she said, "We've been on a lot of field trips in the last few days. Last week, we saw *The Pawnbroker*." Members of the class wandered around looking at the books, pamphlets, and magazines in the room: old books, like a fourth edition (1910) of the *Etymological Dictionary of the English Language*; hardbound copies of W. E. B. Du Bois's *Souls of Black Folk*, of *Black Manhattan*, by James Weldon Johnson, and of *Fine Clothes to the Jew*, by Langston Hughes; copies of *Jet*, *Ebony*, the *Liberator*, and *Challenge*; and such paperbacks as *My Arabic Alphabet Book*, *Negro Pioneers to Color*, *The Subterraneans*, *Pilgrim's Progress*, *Cannery Row*, *Literature and Western Man*, *Ice Palace*, *The Spirit of St. Louis*, and *The H. P. Dream Book*. The students also examined pictures of African leaders and distinguished Negroes, among which, for good measure, a picture of Dwight D. Eisenhower and a picture of Franklin D. Roosevelt were prominently displayed. One middle-aged female student, who was carrying a booklet titled *A Manual of Intergroup Relations*, called several of her classmates over to read a sign on one of the walls: "'dope knows no color line / What I like about dope / Is that it plays no joke / It knows no color line / That's why it's color blind / It does not discriminate / Nor does it segregate' . . . says Lewis Michaux, Executive Member, Human Rights Political Association." Michaux, who was wearing slacks and a crisp light blue short-sleeved sports shirt, seemed for a while to be everywhere at once, but soon he went into his office, a tiny, overstuffed back room, and prepared to hold court. He opened a copy of Edmund David Cronon's *Black Moses*, the story of Marcus Garvey and the Universal Negro Improvement Association, to a dog-eared page that contained a quotation from Garvey: "A race without authority and power is a race without respect." Then he called the students into his office.

"I'm sorry to say that I'm dissatisfied with this group today, because I don't see enough black power," Michaux began with a chuckle. "The black folks and the white folks are fighting every hour about the black man wanting power, but we've been neglected for three hundred years, and as much as I hate to see what's going to happen, I believe that when the Negro knocks this time and nobody opens the door, he's just going to knock it right in." He had stopped smiling, and his voice had risen in pitch. He turned to a book that he had marked, and read a few sentences by a white Southerner who, writing at the turn of the century, had used the Scriptures to justify slavery. This book described the Negro as a beast ("not an offspring of the Adamic Family"), and Michaux asserted that many white fathers and mothers still read such books to their children. "That's why we go to Vietnam and fight and die for this country, and then we're brought back in caskets and can't even be buried right," he said, getting up momentarily from his chair.

Michaux talked for nearly an hour, condemning the Vietnam War, the white man's treatment of the Negro, and also Negro leaders who talk about Harlem but whom Harlem never sees. "No one has yet come to take Malcolm's place, and in my estimation Malcolm X is the only one since Mr. Garvey who has meant anything to our people," he said.

At last, he asked for questions, and one young lady queried him about a statement he had made that the Negro would have to destroy this civilization before he got anything. "Doesn't this mean that he will destroy himself, too?" she asked.

"The so-called Negro needs power, girl, and I don't mean missiles," Michaux replied, slowly and deliberately. "I have been in Harlem for thirty-one years, and I can't get a bank loan, because 'they' don't approve of my store. And now I've told you."

"Well, what about the lethargy among Negroes who already have the vote?" a young Negro woman asked.

"They don't vote because when they vote, they always get a goat," Michaux replied, making use of one of his favorite oracular forms. "It's usually six of one and half a dozen of the other."

With these few questions, the class seemed to have exhausted its curiosity about human relations on this level. One student rose to thank Mr. Michaux for giving them his time and advice ("That's my business," he replied), and around noon the students began moving toward the street. Michaux walked outside with them, and when one of the young women asked if she might take his picture, he nodded. He waited agreeably while two white students posed beside him, each with an arm around his shoulders and each with a look of satisfaction on his face.

Woody Strode? He Wasn't the Star but He Stole the Movie

The New York Times
SEPTEMBER 19, 1971

"Woody Strode?" Silence. "You remember. That marvelous-looking black man—the one in *Sergeant Rutledge*. Wasn't the star, but stole the movie."

A bit of dialogue that usually unfolds when Woody Strode's name comes up. Nobody remembers the name—even though he actually portrayed Sergeant Rutledge in John Ford's 1960 western. But everybody remembers the presence, particularly when you mention that body—6'4½", 215 pounds—and those eyes, those large, expressive eyes.

"I'm a ghost," Strode said recently as he sat in the living room of his two-room suite at the Drake Hotel. In town to promote *Black Jesus*, a film he made in Italy patterned after the life of the slain Congolese leader, Patrice Lumumba, Strode is surrounded by people who want to transform that ghostly presence into something real, or at least box office.

Surprisingly, Strode did not become a star after *Sergeant Rutledge*, despite the critical acclaim he received for it. Perhaps he and the film, with its sympathies strongly on the side of the black man, were ahead of their time. In the decade since *Rutledge*, Strode has kept working but even in a film like *The Professionals*, where his role was virtually equal to those of Burt Lancaster, Lee Marvin, and Robert Ryan, he was denied top billing. During the last three years, he has made five "spaghetti westerns" in Italy. But he has never protested from public platforms about the injustice of it all.

In New York, Strode's present entourage includes Sig Shore, the American distributor who bought *Black Jesus*, publicity woman Myrna Post, and general kinds of people who move in and out with promotion designs. Strode feels that "if Sig Shore hadn't bought *Black Jesus*, Woody Strode would still be just a legend."

Among the films contributing to the legend are some that are mediocrities, offering the image of Strode as semi-savage, and a few that he recalls not without a certain satisfaction—like *Pork Chop Hill*, a story of the Korean War, in which he acted "a reluctant black soldier who didn't want to fight. At one point in it, I pretended to be crazy. 'Don't you move, I'm aiming straight at your body,' I said to my superior officer, Gregory Peck. He tells me, 'But all the boys are fighting,' and I said, 'But you ought to see where I live back home. You sonfabitch, I wouldn't die for that and I be goddam if I'm going to fight for Korea.' That was in 1958 and Sy Bartlett, who produced the movie, almost got killed for that. It was never a big hit in the States."

Strode cherishes the times when he could speak such lines in films—"dignified lines." *Black Jesus*, he feels, gives him dignity, too. During the interview, when we are alone, Strode is relaxed and easy to talk with—almost as if he had discovered a long-lost relative and was eager to reconstruct the past. He is wearing cowboy boots, tight-fitting blue slacks, and a blue, short-sleeved knit shirt that is complemented by his broad chest and large, muscular arms.

Eagerly, he sits forward in his chair as he talks, sometimes saying "Negro" but often correcting himself and changing it to "black," and excitement brightens his eyes. But later, when his business associates are in the room, Strode is cautious. He talks, but carefully.

A former athlete who played football at UCLA, was named all-pro end in the Canadian League in 1948, was a professional wrestler and used to do 1,000 sit-ups, 1,000 push-ups, and 1,000 knee-bends each morning, Strode is now fifty-seven—looks thirty-seven—and can still muster 500 of each daily.

He remembers that he could beat Glenn Morris, the 1936 Olympic Decathlon champion, in all sports except sprints. "I could throw over 50 feet in shot, go 6'5" in high jump, 11 feet pole vault, throw the javelin over 200 feet—I would stand flatfooted. I couldn't hop—I hadn't the finesse.

"And I could run the five-minute mile. Can you imagine a black man winning the Decathlon in 1936? Yes, Jesse Owens was in the Olympics but only in one area; I could do many things. When I got older, I realized I could have had immortality."

Instead, Strode saw Glenn Morris go to the Olympics in Berlin and believes that he was encouraged to enter UCLA to keep him from competing. So Woody Strode, son of a Los Angeles stonemason, who "never had it too rough" and who "ate a lot of beef," went to college. "I got a cultural education—majored in history and education," he says with a slightly mocking tone. "Never used it, but I could walk into the White House with it now."

The physical skills that Strode developed during his years as an athlete have enabled him to be his own stunt man in all of his movies. When he made the western *Shalako* in Spain in 1968 with Brigitte Bardot and Sean Connery, he was behind the scenes shooting all the fire arrows for the Indians who were supposed to be shooting them at *him*. ("I always take my bows with me. I have several seventy- and eighty-pound bows. I was a little embarrassed to bring them to New York.")

Strode's career as a professional athlete ended when he suffered the effects of the no-blocking rule in Canadian football—two broken ribs over the heart and a shoulder that had to be completely reconstructed. "It was like I had fought Joe Louis," he recalls.

In 1950, Strode was approached to play in a Tarzan movie. He balked when the producers asked him to shave his head—he felt it was too dehumanizing—but when they told him they'd pay him $500 a week, "I said, 'All right, where are the pluckers?'" Then, Strode found,

"I was out in the world market with a bald head. Trapped for life. Finally, it became a way of life."

Other movies followed. Despite the preponderance of cowboy-and-Indian sagas, they have included *Spartacus*, *The Ten Commandments*, *The Sins of Rachel Cade*, and *Che*. But among them all, "I've never gotten over *Sergeant Rutledge*," Strode says. "That was a classic. It had dignity. John Ford put classic words in my mouth."

Set in the Southwest in the post–Civil War years, the film cast Strode as a cavalryman on trial for a double murder and the rape of a white girl. Innocent of the charge and fearful of the prejudice surrounding his trial, Rutledge runs away from his all-black cavalry unit. "But the Indians were about to trap my men, and for me, it was either freedom for myself or save them from the trap. You never seen a Negro come off a mountain like John Wayne before," Strode says, standing to demonstrate how he rode down the side of a mountain with a nine-pound gun hoisted in the air. "I had the greatest Glory Hallelujah ride across the Pecos River that any black man ever had on the screen. And I did it myself. I carried the whole black race across that river."

Strode is excited now; his eyes and the quick movements of his body start to reveal his other self.

He is still standing but he leans into a crouch and quotes his dialogue from the movie as if it were still real: "The Ninth Cavalry is my home, my self-respect, and my real freedom, and the way I was deserting it, I weren't nothing but a swamp-running nigger. And I ain't that. I am a man!"

Strode snaps his fingers, slaps his hand on his knee, and his gentle eyes tell you all. "John Ford wanted to know if we could get away with saying 'nigger' on the screen, and I said why not? It would be the first time a black man ever called *himself* a nigger on the screen. And I wanted to hit home."

But it was not at home that Strode found the greatest appreciation. He talks often about "the Italians" and it was, in fact, the Italians who, impressed with his work in Spain in *Shalako*, offered him sixty thousand dollars to come to Rome. The movies were to be westerns Italian style but by that time Strode had developed what black folks call "an attitude." Although his agent was concerned about bad scripts, "Me. I didn't care. If the money was right, I'd play Mickey Mouse."

During the years in Hollywood, why hadn't he protested the lack of billing, the one-dimensional characters he was given to play? "In those years, where could I go? I didn't give a damn. They paid me my money. Why should I have a publicity agent? What was I gonna say?"

Yet, despite his working in Italy, Strode and his wife, a Hawaiian princess, Luukialuana Kalaeloa, whom he met in Hilo, Hawaii, in 1938 when he went there to play football, continued to keep California as home base. Their son, Woody Jr., now a candidate for a master's degree in Asian studies at the University of Hawaii, and their daughter, June, an actress in TV commercials, flew back and forth to Italy to be with their parents.

Earlier this year Strode came home to see his son and, while here, was offered *The Last Rebel*, a western in which he acts with Joe Namath. But although the film is opening shortly, Strode is not doing any stumping for it, as he is for *Black Jesus*. He won't discuss his reasons but those around him hint that it's the billing thing again, with Namath on the top. Strode simply says, "Namath'll carry the picture because he's a star and the kids love him. I do enough to protect myself."

One thing that nettled him was the way *The Last Rebel* was promoted in Birmingham, Alabama. "They served slices of watermelon," he said wryly.

But Strode will stay in this country to make *The Revengers*, a "regular knock-down, drag-out western" with William Holden. And he has a publicity agent now—now that he hopes *Black Jesus* will make him "a different kind of star." Sig Shore, who has come into Woody's suite, remarks, "Woody now has a chance to be a giant."

But the facts of all those years do not change overnight—even when the money is right. After Shore joined us, Woody started talking about "all the opportunities here in America now and the way the black man must fight to win.

"You don't fight him head-on," he was saying of the white man. "He's definitely going to knock you down that way. Like he did the

Cheyenne and the Sioux. We've got thirty million black people—and Old Uncle Tom saved the goddamn thirty million."

And just as he started to get into that and how the black people could learn from the Jews and their struggle for survival—"I know their history better than my own because it's printed"—Sig Shore interrupted.

"I hate actors in politics," he said with a wave of his hand. And Woody's eyes flashed a change. "Yeah, let's sell the picture," he said, slumping back in his chair. At about which time Myrna Post reminded him that it was almost noon.

"You've got to be in Union City," she said. "And time is running out."

Roots Getting a Grip on People Everywhere

The New York Times
JANUARY 28, 1977

"My children and I just sat there, crying," said a black public relations director in Nashville. "We couldn't talk. We just cried."

"It has made the brutality of slavery more vivid for me than anything I've seen or read," said a black economist in Philadelphia.

"It's so powerful," said a white secretary in New York. "It's so distressful, I just feel awful, but I'm glad my children are watching."

All across the country this week, millions of people have been drawn to the unfolding drama of *Roots*, the eight-part television adaptation of the book by Alex Haley, tracing his origins back to an African village. It has produced the third-largest audience in television history (only the two parts of *Gone with the Wind* in 1976 drew more).

Nearly 80 million people have sat before their television sets in penthouses and tenements, bars and brownstones, fraternity houses and dormitories as the saga of Kunta Kinte had flashed before them night after night since last Sunday.

Doubters and enthusiasts, whites as well as blacks, young and old, wealthy and poor had reactions they wanted to share.

Some laughed when a hungry Itunta Kinte, who was thought to have learned no English, suddenly thrust his plate toward the older slave, Fiddler, and said, "Grits, dummy."

Some cried as Kunta Kinte finally gave in to the whip's lash and accepted the slave name Toby. And some got angry at the long, deep scars on his back in a later episode.

But however different their reactions might have been, people everywhere, even those who had not seen it, were talking about *Roots*.

Doubleday reports that sales of *Roots*, now in its thirteenth printing since publication in October, have soared even higher since the television serial went on the air. The best-selling book is Mr. Haley's narrative account of his twelve-year search for his origins—a search that started with stories of family members and a handful of African words, including the name Kinte.

The search ended in Gambia, a tiny state in West Africa where, with the help of the griot—the oral historian—Mr. Haley went back in time to 1750, when Kunta Kinte, his ancestor, was born.

The story dovetailed with the one Mr. Haley had heard from his family.

The people of Gambia embraced "Meester Kinte" immediately, telling him, "Through our flesh, we are you, and you are us."

After a young black writer from the West Coast watched the first two-hour episode on Sunday, he shook his head and, referring respectively to the author of the book and the director of the television adaptation, said:

"Haley, yes. [David] Wolper, no."

The production, he said, was "too Hollywood," lacking in both depth and truth to the original narrative.

After Monday night's showing, which included the scene where Kunta Kinte is whipped by the white overseer to force him to give up his African ancestral name and accept the slave name Toby, the writer, smiling, said to his host:

"Haley, yes. Wolper, maybe."

A black man carrying an attaché case stepped into the elevator of the predominantly white company where he worked.

"Good morning, Kunta Kinte," said a white colleague, cheerfully. The black man lowered his head, smiled, and said, "Toby."

In one middle-class white Queens household, there was a lively debate over coffee and bagels after the second installment.

"It doesn't show any good white people," said the wife. "There must have been some decent white people and it should have been more balanced."

"No, the good whites had their day with *Gone with the Wind*," said the husband. "Anyhow, how good could any whites look to a slave? And that's whose eyes we're seeing it through. All the white bosses must have looked pretty bad, like Nazi Party members did to Jews."

"They were terrible," shouted the eighteen-year-old son. "Slavery was evil and this shows how bad it was, stealing those people from their homes and carrying them far away and buying and selling them."

A group of six young black men and women gathered at a counter as the short-order cook, her jaw set firmly, commented tersely about *Roots*.

"I had to cut the thing off about halfway through and go to bed," she said. "It was getting to me."

"I cried like a baby," said another of the women. "I just never thought it was so bad. I never thought they could treat you so bad."

"I tell you one thing," injected a somber young man in the group. "Those white folks better not mess with me today. I just might have to stomp one."

"Don't do that," another of the group snapped. "Things ain't changed that much. And jobs don't grow on trees."

It took a little while for the four- and five-year-olds in the kindergarten class at the Patterson School for Heritage and Education in Harlem to come alive, since most of them had stayed up way past their normal bedtime to watch *Roots*.

"I was having a hard time getting my four-year-old up," said one young mother, "but, at one point I said, 'Okay, Mandinka warrior. Time to go hunting in the forest.' He smiled, opened his eyes, and rolled out."

"It's just incredible," Mr. Haley, the author of *Roots*, said from

O'Hare Airport in Chicago yesterday during a stopover between lectures. "ABC has preserved the integrity of the thing as best they could. And I think they've done a fantastic job.

"A young white boy told me yesterday in Texas that his father had always hated my people, but after seeing *Roots*, he said, 'I watched my father cry for the first time in his life.'

"A black man saw me in the airport, and for a long time, didn't say anything. Finally, he turned to me and said, 'Look, man, I just can't be cool. I've just got to say thank you.'"

Jock's, a popular Harlem bar and restaurant with a TV, has been jammed all week with patrons like Ronald Guy, a lawyer who "wanted to watch it with other people around."

Joe Kirkpatrick, the owner, said that one night viewers got so angry over the treatment of Kunta Kinte that they would not allow the jukebox to be turned on even after the show had ended.

"They just wanted to talk it out," he said, "and it wasn't until they had talked and talked for a very long time that they finally remembered they were in a bar.

"That's when they started drinking up."

John Henrik Clarke, the black historian, said there were some "cultural inaccuracies" in the television series, "but those are minor.

"Overall," he said, "I think it has opened up a delicate situation that will probably cause some embarrassment on both the black and white sides. But it has paved the way for a much-needed, long-overdue discussion."

Harlem a Symphony for Orchestra

The New York Times
NOVEMBER 16, 1971

Harlem, he feels, is "a total symphony," and because of that, Karl Hampton Porter, a young black conductor, feels that Harlem is the place where his symphony orchestra will find a home.

"Black people have so many things going that basically this music is very easy for them to listen to," the thirty-two-year-old musician said. "The black man's head has been in so many places that we have the natural instinct; we just don't have the exposure."

With little more than instinct and feeling, Mr. Porter created the seventy-five-piece Harlem Philharmonic Orchestra, which celebrated its second season last weekend with a concert at the Horace Mann Auditorium at Columbia University.

Before the performance, Mr. Porter recalled that the first time he advertised for musicians was for a memorial concert following the assassination of the Reverend Dr. Martin Luther King Jr.

"They came from everywhere—schools, churches, the Post Office," he said. "They came out of the windows. Most of the bass players came from the jazz nightclubs."

The concert was a success in more ways than one, Mr. Porter said. Not only did the program receive encouraging critical notices, but also it brought together minority group musicians who had nowhere else to play.

"Every year music schools and conservatories accept black musicians," said Mr. Porter, who studied at the Peabody Conservatory, the Juilliard School of Music, and the Domaine School of Conductors. "They graduate and never go into symphony orchestras. They go into the Post Office."

For his first concert, more than 120 black musicians showed up. "Seven trumpet players and eleven flute players came and we could only use two," Mr. Porter said. "We had a real problem deciding who would play and who wouldn't."

The orchestra traces its origin to 1968 as the Harlem Youth Symphony Orchestra, but later changed its name to include a wider range of talent. "Now the ages span from sixteen to seventy-two," said Mr. Porter, a former jazz musician who plays saxophone and the bassoon.

While the group is sometimes referred to as a preprofessional training orchestra, Mr. Porter does not look on it in that way. Most of the musicians, he says, are professional enough. They simply do not have any place to play their classical repertory.

"One reason this group has to go on," Mr. Porter said, "is that white conductors tell black musicians who come to them to go out and get some experience. Where are they going to get it, if not in a group like this?"

Mr. Porter believes that his group can do something different with classical music.

"I once got into trouble for saying that black musicians were going to save music in this country," Mr. Porter declared. "I simply meant that we have a new approach—injecting soul into music."

Not all of Mr. Porter's musicians are black. "Harlem isn't an all-black community and the Brooklyn Philharmonic isn't all Jewish," Mr. Porter declared. "The problem that comes up is in finding a black oboist or violin player. They don't usually go into these things."

Mr. Porter said that economics was probably a factor, since a good bassoon costs about $2,500 and an oboe might range anywhere from $600 to $1,000.

It is Mr. Porter's hope that his players will eventually give up their other jobs—their main source of income now—and become full-time members of the Harlem Philharmonic.

The group has received about $30,000 in gifts and grants over the last two years from foundations, the Department of Parks, and the New York Council on the Arts. Columbia University donates space for rehearsals.

In recent months, to relieve Mr. Porter of some of the burdens of fund-raising, a board of directors has been organized. One of their first official acts was a twenty-dollar-a-plate champagne/soul-food buffet attended by more than two hundred invited guests at the Metropolitan Museum of Art.

"They may have saved me," Mr. Porter commented.

PART IV

A Single Garment of Destiny

A few weeks before I began my life in the professional world in 1963, I took time out from my studies and read Martin Luther King's "Letter from a Birmingham Jail." That was April 16, 1963. And while every word was memorable, the ones that I took with me into my professional journey were these:

"We are caught in an inescapable network of mutuality, tied in a single garment of destiny. Whatever affects one directly, affects all indirectly."

Though these words resonated deeply at the time, it would be some twenty-two years later before I was in a position to explore that idea firsthand, the result of witnessing friends and familiar strangers who were involved in the Free South Africa Movement, which started in the nation's capital in 1984. It was at a time when South Africans themselves were engaged in efforts to end apartheid—segregation based on race, so much like the system of Jim Crow in the American South, in which the white race saw itself as superior and, to maintain that belief, often went to extremes of viciousness against those who did not look like them. It was the system I grew up in during my early years.

As demonstrators of every color and social status started and kept up their protests outside the South African embassy, I began to look more closely at South Africa, a nation of fourteen different languages and cultures, including its white minority. And so it was I began to see it and its current struggle as possibly the last great experiment on earth in ending racism. At the University of Georgia's commemoration of ending its Jim Crow history of segregation some forty years earlier, I told the audience:

> I am once again hearing the siren call of history as I observe with a professional detachment that is informed by a history that is at least forty years old. Mine is more than an academic understanding of this Great Experiment, it is visceral, fueling my passion to tell the story. . . . One of the reasons, by the way, I have never liked the term *objective*, for we are all creatures of our environments and backgrounds. Rather, I prefer the words *fair* and *balanced* as a more accurate way of describing the work journalists are engaged in doing.

And so it was that I had gone to South Africa first in 1985, for the *PBS NewsHour* to get a firsthand look at the country I had come to know from a distance. Not only did that trip result in a five-part series, unique at the time, but it also solidified my belief in Dr. King's single garment of destiny. For in South Africa as in the United States, I found people not unlike My People. The series was appropriately called "Apartheid's People," but it also delved into those who believed that My People there, as one Afrikaner told me, were not ready to be full citizens, let alone take part in the governing of the country.

As was the case in the United States during segregation, Apartheid's People, who looked like My People in the United States, had refused to accept an inferior status and fought in many ways and over many years against domination and, yes, often extreme cruelty. During that time, I got to know South Africans of all colors, including one who served on our reporting team and gave us great insight into his country, whose laws he abhorred. His name was George De'Ath and he was known by all and sundry as Dr. Death. In time, he would meet his own while covering yet another protest of the system.

At the *NewsHour*, I continued to keep my eye on South Africa and returned in 1997, taking up residence as bureau chief and reporter first for NPR, then in the same capacity for CNN. My reporting took me all over the continent, where I carried with me the words of Dr. King, and enabled me to tell many stories that were different from the four Ds—death, disease, disaster, and despair—by which Africa and her people were more often than not portrayed in the media.

My travels and reporting offered me rare access to historical events, such as when Nelson Mandela was released from prison and the world's media descended on his small home in the Black township of Soweto. I was one of only two reporters to get a half hour with him while all the others got ten minutes. A few years later, when Mandela was about to become president, I traveled back to the country and was scheduled to interview him on that occasion. But shortly before the interview, I learned that our son Chuma's graduation from Emory University was scheduled for the same day that Mandela was going to be sworn in. When I sadly told Mandela why I regretfully would not be present for the country's most historic occasion, he didn't hesitate in assuming a fatherlike demeanor and quickly said, "Oh no, you have to be there for that. You can interview me anytime."

He remained true to his word over the many times I saw him during my seventeen years in his country, and also when he visited mine. Both countries, he acknowledged, were joined in a single garment of destiny.

I also traveled back for his funeral in 2013 as a special correspondent for NBC. My crew and I were stationed on a high, makeshift stand directly across from the little house in Soweto where I first met Mandela. We were set up at the home of a Black South African family and on breaks I spent time in the kitchen with the matriarch, who shared her life before, during, and after apartheid, a piece later printed in the *New Yorker*. It was an up close and personal look at the sacrifice and the victory of struggle in South Africa; it was the kind of story that still needed to be told.

Similarly, as I traveled the African continent—from Addis Ababa in the east to Lagos in the west and many points in between, including Zimbabwe—I sought out people whose struggles and, on occasion, victories had resonance with my own and whose stories I also felt needed to be told. For while they, like My People in the United States, continued to strive toward a more perfect union, I fundamentally believed that sharing their challenges, even the most personally painful ones, as well as their successes, echoed the lesson from Dr. King's words: "Whatever affects one directly, affects all indirectly."

A Rainy Day in Soweto

The New Yorker
DECEMBER 11, 2013

Unless you are a farmer, rain in America is more often than not metaphorically associated with trouble. Like: when it rains, it pours. But in South Africa, rain stands for blessings. "Rain is life," one South African said Tuesday, after the first of several mass memorials for Nelson Rolihlahla Mandela was drenched. Those who were near, in the FNB soccer stadium—also known as Soccer City—seemed to agree as they danced and sang joyfully, to the dismay of at least some of the speakers, Barack Obama excepted, who could tell that they didn't have the crowd's full attention.

But everywhere I went outside the stadium, South Africans like Selena Mkhabela were thankful for the rain; it signaled to them a happy transition for the man they call "Our Father." Mkhabela had given over her house, across the street from Mandela's former Soweto home, now a museum and landmark, to NBC. (I am a special correspondent for the network.) Cameras were set up in her front yard, with a platform high off the ground and open, except for a tarp on top that got expanded as the rain poured down harder. Most of the time, Mkhabela sat in her well-appointed living room, wrapped up to her chin in blankets, watching the service on her own TV. But as the four-hour memorial program was clearly drawing to a close, Mkhabela slowly threw off her blankets and walked past her dining room, filled with our computers and notes, and into her kitchen.

"I'm the Hoasi, you know," she said, joking, though for once there were other people in the house taking care of things. "That's the respectful way you address the help." Mkhabela is seventy-one, just a few months younger than me. In addition to my television colleagues, she was hosting her four grandchildren for the holidays, the youngest of whom, Sihle, age ten, sat with us in the kitchen, hanging on his grandmother's every word.

Soweto continues to be a mixed bag of progress and stagnation. A few blocks away, the few hours of driving rain, blessing or not, had already wiped out at least one bridge leading out of the township, and the water was threatening to engulf what looked like some of the same tin-roofed, cardboard shacks I saw when I first came to South Africa, in 1985. The white minority regime's ruthless scheme was then in force to relocate potentially restive black South African populations to areas far enough away from the main population centers that they could be cordoned off easily in case of trouble.

Although some who could afford it moved into previously white areas when apartheid ended, many stayed. Many of those who did have money used it instead to upgrade the places where they lived.

Mkhabela and her late husband had both worked at decent-paying jobs in Johannesburg during the apartheid era, she for forty-one years as a machinist in an industrial plant manufacturing canvases to prevent rocks from falling on miners, and her husband at a factory making license plates. She did well at her job, eventually being promoted to supervisor, she told me, as she straightened up her kitchen. It was good, she said, but paused—for emphasis, it seemed—as she went on to complete the sentence, saying with a grin, "except when we were striking for better wages."

During that time, she said, she and her husband lived in what she called *mkhumkhu*. She explained that the term referred to what was for the longest time their home—a shack. Over time, they made enough money to add on to the shack, until it became, room by room, the house she now lives in. They brought up four children there, all of whom completed high school and now have jobs of their own.

I asked if she was able to do this during apartheid. "Oh yes," she said. "But it wasn't easy. When you then go backwards, you don't even want to talk about it." She became more subdued. "I don't know how many times they"—the white authorities—"came into this house, asking questions like, 'Where did you get the money to build your house? How did [you] pay for this and that?' Once they came and spotted the fridge: 'What did you pay for that, and where did you get the money?'

"Before, you couldn't do anything without a permit. Not even be in town after dark."

Mkhabela went on to describe how, before Mandela was released, blacks had to move off the sidewalk and onto the pavement if a white person was approaching.

"We couldn't even go to the bottle store in town," she added. "We used to send someone colored"—the apartheid designation for multiracial people—"in there because they could go in and come out with it, and we would pay." After a few moments, she added, much quieter now, "It was never an easy life. Never."

I told her I'd come to the house across the street in 1990, a few days after Mandela got out of prison, to interview him. I asked about her neighbors, the Mandelas.

"Well, Mandela was in prison, and we were seeing [Winnie] every day before they took her to Brandfort." (From 1977 to 1985, the regime banished Winnie Mandela to a remote area miles from Johannesburg, with two young children, and confined them to a house with no electricity, running water, stove, or bathroom.) Then Mandela came home.

"Ohhhh," she said gleefully, stringing out the word. "When he came out of prison, he came to each and every house, greeting us. Honored. Oh, we didn't expect that. He told us all, 'I'm back.' We didn't expect that. 'I want to meet every neighbor of mine.' And we were invited when he made a speech. Oh, everybody loved it. He was a nice person. That's why today we say, 'Thank you, Mandela!'" Outside, it was still raining.

America and South Africa, Watching Each Other

The New Yorker
NOVEMBER 9, 2016

When I first went to South Africa, in 1985, during some of the darkest days of the country's violently repressive apartheid regime, one of the bright lights I found was the inspiration that protesters drew from the American civil rights revolution and its victory over apartheid-like discrimination. Even in the midst of torture and trials—black anti-apartheid opponents tossed from planes into the sea; the activist Stephen Biko murdered; Nelson Mandela and his comrades sentenced to life in prison—there was the example of Martin Luther King Jr. and the thousands who had demanded that America live up to its promise of freedom and justice for all. Once Mandela was released, in 1990, he told me that, in prison, he had thought often of King and his allies, and of the anti-apartheid movement in the United States.

In the years since, friendships and relationships continued. My husband, Ronald, and I moved to South Africa in the early years of its multiracial democracy and lived there for almost twenty years. And though we moved back to the United States in 2012, we have traveled back from time to time, and South African friends visit us here in America and otherwise keep in touch.

But in recent months the emails and Skype chats and talks with visiting friends have become intense and somber and worrying in a way that I haven't previously experienced. Sooner or later, the conversation turns to disturbing reports of the direction of South African's political culture, with accounts of ongoing corruption at the highest levels of the government of President Jacob Zuma. He is scheduled to remain in office until national elections in 2019, but is facing a revolt within his party. It is not of the same kind that drove his predecessor, Thabo Mbeki, prematurely from office. Mbeki was not accused of personal corruption; what put him in jeopardy was his alleged effort to undermine Zuma's chances of succeeding him. When the time came, Mbeki resigned rather than waiting to be removed, in part to avoid a political crisis ahead of the 2009 general election. (In South Africa, the president is chosen by Parliament immediately after an election.) At the time, Zuma had already fought off charges of corruption to win the leadership of his party, the African National Congress, and of the country.

But the stigma and stain of corruption never went away; instead, they grew as Zuma financed a lavish renovation of his kraal (or homestead) in his home base, Nkandla, in KwaZulu-Natal, with state money, and was subject to allegations of cronyism. Last week, South Africa's public protector, an ombudsman with constitutional powers, issued what has become known as the "state-capture report." It called for a full judicial inquiry into possible corruption and conflicts of interest involving Zuma, senior state officials, and members of the wealthy Gupta family.

Reports indicate that the Guptas plan to defend themselves against the charges at the upcoming inquiry.

Zuma has dismissed the report and seems ready to fight it in court.

Ahmed Kathrada, a revered eighty-seven-year-old anti-apartheid activist who served time in prison with Mandela, wrote an open letter earlier this year about what he called "a crisis of confidence" in the leadership of the country. He called for Zuma to step down. A few months later, Jackson Mthembu, the chief whip of the ANC, who was once one of the staunchest supporters of his party—often coming down hard on journalists who questioned anything the ANC did—called on the entire ANC executive leadership, including himself, to step down. Mthembu was quoted in the *City Press* as saying, of his fellow leaders, that, in certain respects, "We are not only equal to the apartheid state, we are worse." That may be an extreme statement, but it captures the frustration and disappointment of many in South Africa. And it reminded me of something F. W. de Klerk, the last apartheid-era president, told me when I interviewed him in Johannesburg shortly before Mandela and the ANC assumed power, in 1994. I had asked him how it was going to feel being out of power. He responded, almost jocularly, that his ruling party would likely not be out of power long, since a liberation movement had never successfully run a country. (I didn't bother to bring up our American Revolution, among other examples, not least because his reference was clearly to countries in Africa.)

As the unfolding political crisis grows, universities around the country have been engulfed with protests over proposed national tuition hikes. The University of the Witwatersrand, situated a few blocks from where I used to live in Johannesburg—I enjoyed walking my dog around its sprawling grounds—has been shut down, as violence has spread on the campus. In recent days, someone set a fire in the library; a shelf of books burned before it could be put out. Thirteen students have been suspended in the past four weeks, some arrested, others intimidated by a force of police officers brought onto the campus. As exam time approached and the protests continued, arrangements were made to extend the exam period for two weeks. At least one group of students took their finals in their professor's living room.

That professor, as it happens, is a friend of mine, and generally a big South Africa booster. When I wrote to ask him about the developments at Wits, as the university is known, and elsewhere, he responded, "South Africa these days is not for the fainthearted." When I asked another friend, a doctor and loyal ANC member, for his take on what on earth was going on in the country we both loved, he quickly replied, "We must continue to believe that we live in a constitutional democracy."

But the responses I got from other friends included questions about what seems to them like our challenges to our own constitutional democracy. I had just done a conversation for *PBS NewsHour* on the N-word, arising out of how it was recently used by a white man against an African American reporter, and it resonated in South Africa, which has its own N-word that starts with a *K*. My South African friends also wrote in disbelief of threats of revolt and possible violence in the United States if one party fails to win the presidency. The country that so inspired them during their struggle has them, as it has a lot of us here, deeply worried. The issue is not only the damaging optics of this campaign season but the impact those optics will have within our country, as well as in countries like South Africa, where our beacon light, albeit imperfect, nevertheless has helped to light their often treacherous path to inclusive democracy. As a South African journalist colleague wrote to me on Tuesday morning, "Just writing to wish you all the best with elections. We are watching with bated breath hoping that America will vote wisely. Things are bad enough as it is down here—the last thing we need is a bad role model for our African leaders."

Indeed, my work as a journalist has taken me to many other countries in Africa that are also continuing to struggle in their bumpy strides toward democratic freedom and the greater good. As I listened during the campaign to cacophonous debates in our media that have nothing to do with the substantive issues facing our democracy, I had a hard time telling my South African friends not to worry. That became harder still in the early morning hours of November 9, when it became clear that Donald Trump had won. A friend wrote to me, "South Africans are grief-stricken."

And yet—and yet. The road I've traveled, from a place in the Deep South, where I faced hatred up close and personal, and which only truly recognized my rights as a citizen some fifty-five years ago, when I was nineteen, to my recent conversations with people all over this country who've been working on and have found solutions to racism, causes me to live in hope. I believe that, once again, we shall overcome—and, in doing so, remain the inspiration the world has come to expect and depend on.

Ethiopia: Journalists Live in Fear of "Terror" Law

All Africa
JUNE 19, 2012

Nowhere across Africa is the message that its people want a way out of what I call "the four Ds"—death, disease, disaster, and despair—more resounding than among the continent's journalists.

In nation after nation, they are attempting to inform their people of their rights and encourage them to hold their governments accountable. For that, many of them are being held accountable in the most draconian ways.

I have seen this firsthand in Zimbabwe, where Robert Mugabe's regime has long attempted to conceal the repression of its people. Journalists have fought back and continue to yell truth to power, although they still face the prospect of jail as a consequence.

And most recently, I have seen it in Ethiopia, where Eskinder Nega, a journalist I visited seven years ago in Kalati Prison, along with his pregnant wife, Serkalem Fasil (who gave birth in prison), is back there on charges of terrorism. What appears to have been his crime is that he also continues to tell, if not yell, truth to power, although the government is actually prosecuting him for what they say is his membership in a terrorist network that advocates violence. As proof, during his trial they showed a video in which he questioned whether an Arab Spring–type uprising could ever happen in Ethiopia.

The government has empowered itself to prosecute what they see as dissent like this with a sweeping antiterrorism law that is, effectively, a weapon that can be used against anyone daring to criticize the government in a way the government doesn't like.

One journalist who published Eskinder's statement in court was also convicted, but got a suspended four-month sentence. Dozens of journalists have fled into exile and six have been charged with terrorism in absentia, according to the Committee to Protect Journalists (CPJ).

When I visited Ethiopia earlier this month with a colleague from the CPJ and the continent-wide project called the African Media Initiative, journalists we met with told us they all live in fear, calling the terrorism law a "game changer." One foreigner working in Ethiopia told me: "There is a red line. The problem is, we don't know where it is."

When we met Bereket Simon, Ethiopia's minister of information, he defended the incarceration of Eskinder and the seven other journalists locked up with him on the grounds that they were involved in terrorism. In a polite but firm dissent, he said neither Eskinder nor any of the other journalists were in prison for what they wrote.

When we asked to see Eskinder and the others in prison, we were told that it was not likely and that turned out to be the case. But his wife, Serkalem, who was recently in New York receiving on Eskinder's behalf a prestigious freedom of the press award from PEN America, told us when we met her in Addis that Eskinder had asked her to tell us that he was in no way connected with any terrorist group—there or in the United States.

She also told us that he said that if the price of telling the truth was imprisonment, he could live with that. Of course, when the verdict is handed down—which is scheduled to happen Thursday—Eskinder could be sentenced to life in prison or death.

Part of the reason for my involvement with journalists and their issues in Ethiopia and other parts of the continent is to try to present a much-maligned continent in a light different to that in which it is often portrayed elsewhere in the world: in a light that makes it clear that Africans want as much as anyone else to make choices about themselves and their children in an informed way, and that they have the same hopes and aspirations for themselves, their families, and their communities as do people in democracies the world over.

Imperfect as many democracies are, their governments do not put people in jail for words that come out of their mouths and the freedom-loving desires that live in their hearts. That's why, as an American, I hope that my countrymen and women who have that right should get on Ethiopia's case. They should insist that a U.S. government which is pledged to ensure those rights in America should also help ensure them in Ethiopia. And I hope they will be joined by freedom-loving people all over the world, including on the African continent.

But Ethiopia stands as a partner with the United States, in particular, in fighting *real* terrorists, including Al Qaeda, in a strategic part of the world. Surely the economic assistance the United States has provided Ethiopia in the past and the $350 million in assistance it is asking for in 2013 gives it some weight in pressing Addis Ababa to live up to the same principles enshrined in their constitution as in ours?

Freedom of speech is a crucial cornerstone of democracy. It should not be a death sentence.

New Party Urged for World Blacks

The New York Times
SEPTEMBER 5, 1970

ATLANTA, Sept. 4—More than 1,700 delegates to the International Congress of African People here were urged to create a World African party. The proposal, on the second day of the four-day parley, was made by Imamu Baraka, the poet playwright, widely known as LeRoi Jones.

The suggestion was greeted with enthusiasm by the conferees, for the most part youths, who represent a broad spectrum of black thought both in this country and in predominantly black countries abroad.

Many delegates here hailed the key role that Mr. Jones played in the election of Newark's first black mayor, Kenneth A. Gibson.

The slightly built bearded Mr. Jones has emerged, along with Haywood Henry, as a key strategist in this quiet, orderly conference that is attempting to bridge the gap between black and Third World people.

There are delegates here from twenty-seven African countries, the Caribbean nations, four South American countries, and Australia. Some of those from the United States include members of the Nation of Islam, and the Urban League.

Mr. Henry, the principal organizer of this meeting, is a twenty-seven-year-old lecturer in black studies at both Harvard University and the Massachusetts Institute of Technology.

"We are controlled largely by the ideas of our oppressors," Mr. Jones said in one of eleven workshop sessions being conducted throughout the conference. "The political party must build alternative systems, values, institutions that will move us and raise us. How we build alternative forms is what this congress is about."

Mr. Jones suggested that local community organizing would be the base for creating and developing "an international Pan-Africanist party capable of dealing not only with the international problems of Africans by means of international alliances and international exchanges of information and resources but also a party able to function on the smallest level.

"If you can't organize in a two-block area in your community," he asked, "what can you do to defeat Nixon?" He urged "getting into the homes of the black people, every day, organizing from strictly local to regional, to state, while the Congress of African People superstructure works to create the national and international cohesion and development."

In addition, Mr. Jones argued that the organization must also "run candidates in all elections." He maintained that local people respond more readily to "the goods and services that can accrue from even the smallest political office," than other more esthetic appeals.

"This is very important," he said, "because of the rush of revolutionary talk, it is not understood that whatever the level of the struggle, goods and services will be needed, and of course finance."

Local party people should not only set up programs such as free health care programs that would have a direct benefit to the people, but they should also control all monies to be used in the community—such as Model Cities and anti-poverty funds, he said.

Mr. Jones strongly urged coalitions and alliances with black organizations and Third World people, but he warned against coalitions with whites. This contradicts the positions taken by groups such as the Black Panther party.

"I would rather make a political alliance with Whitney Young

[Urban League leader]," he said, "than with Abbie Hoffman [the white yippie leader] because Whitney Young controls masses of black people's minds." The audience applauded heartily.

In a series of obvious allusions to the Black Panthers, who were not named specifically and who are not at this convention, Mr. Jones said:

"No so-called vanguard organization can bring a revolution. Only the people themselves can do this. An organization moving without the community or alienating the community will soon be isolated, and very soon eliminated."

Mr. Jones cautioned against being "co-opted by talk of instant revolution, and to being the peasant army, the first slaughtered wave for another people's rise to political power."

While he contended that disruption—"either the threatened use of violence, or the actual, is a means of achieving political power"—this was listed last on his suggested priorities.

School a Beacon of Hope in Nigeria

The Root
MAY 19, 2013

Whenever northern Nigeria has been in the news in recent months, the stories are usually about killings and kidnappings by Boko Haram—a radical Islamist insurgency group that has killed some two thousand people and kidnapped others in the region since its emergence in 2002. The slayings included several people killed during a bank robbery in Yola, a tiny village in the region.

The group's aim is to create an Islamic state. Nigeria's president, Goodluck Jonathan, has just declared a state of emergency there and in two other areas, and the Nigerian military has met violence with violence, drawing criticisms for what some see as unnecessary brutality. This week, U.S. secretary of state John Kerry said there were "credible allegations" of human rights violations committed by Nigerian security forces.

Boko Haram means "Western education is sacrilege," so when I was invited to come to Yola to give the graduation address at the American University of Nigeria, or AUN, it was with some trepidation that I considered whether or not to accept, even though there have been no attacks on Westerners or Western interests, except for one suicide bombing of the United Nations compound in Abuja, Nigeria's capital.

Although I had been to Nigeria many times over the years on various reporting assignments, I had never heard of Yola or the American University. I had heard of Boko Haram.

But the invitation came with a brief five-year history of the university and its goals: arming future leaders of Nigeria with the kind of education that will enable them to contribute to the development of the country. And it was the belief of the founder, Atiku Abubakar, a wealthy Nigerian who grew up in Yola, that the best preparation for achieving those goals was a Western-style education that grounded students in the liberal arts.

He has explained that his commitment to that kind of education arose from his own education under the British system at the dawn of Nigerian independence, when he had British teachers who always said, "Repeat after me," and slapped his hand when he didn't. Later he came in contact with U.S. Peace Corps teachers who asked his opinion and showed him the value of critical thinking. (The Peace Corps honored him in 2011 for starting AUN. The plaque says that he has done more than any other businessman to support higher education. He also just endowed a Peace Corps speakers series.)

The university board—whose members come from the United States, Nigeria, and other countries—helps guide the institution and its three schools: Arts and Sciences, Business and Entrepreneurship, and Information Technology & Communications.

In its five years of existence, AUN has graduated some 1,250 students from around the continent, most having been on some degree of financial aid, since many are from poor families and are the first in their families to go to college. Those under age thirty who graduate must do a year of community service.

The university has also launched other projects, including free secondary education and information technology instruction, as well as programs that teach teenagers how to farm—in order to stress the importance of preserving the environment—and teach local people how to recycle waste into useful economy bricks for building walls. They are literally building a new Nigeria. A new initiative involves a peace council aimed at fostering peace and harmony in the strife-torn region.

Margee Ensign, a diminutive, highly energetic American from California who is the president of AUN, sent me a few statements from this year's graduating class so that I could get some sense of the caliber of her students.

Malabo Williams wrote:

At AUN, I learned to believe in myself and the power of the idea. The endless readings and discussions with professors and students in class have ensured me that I can make my own story.

Chidi Francis Ahanonu wrote:

I remember my first day here, I was a shy person who could not open up to people and let my voice be heard. I could not stand in front of the crowd and give a speech or a presentation.

However, as I progressed, I learned how to efficiently and effectively get my message across in my presentation, in my services to the community, and in every leadership capacity I find myself.

What Manifah K. Arabi wrote was the final kicker for me because it reminded me of myself at an early age, when I dreamed of becoming a journalist in a segregated world where that possibility was far from being a reality. "I came to realize," he wrote, "that we only have a chance to achieve our dreams if we are confident and truly believe in them. AUN taught me to be innovative and courageous, never to be afraid of what others think about our dreams."

That did it for me, despite the fact that even longtime Nigerian friends whom I consulted about the trip always ended our conversation with "Well, just be careful."

Then the day came when my plane touched down in the tiny airport in Yola and I, along with U.S. ambassador Terence McCulley and Rwandan ambassador Joseph Habineza, was welcomed by officials from the university. Their warmth and ease helped dispel the little bit of concern that still occupied some space in a corner of my mind.

But there was no time to dwell on unease. As we rode the short distance from the airport, the reason for the university's emphasis on development unfolded before our eyes: a landscape filled with tumble-down shacks and littered with the detritus of poverty, scenes similar to ones I have witnessed all over the continent.

Within an hour of arriving at a newly built, university-sponsored hotel and with just barely time to change, we were in a gigantic hall filled with flowing thin, white cloth hanging from the ceiling in grace-ful waves and some two hundred tables set for dining. As is always the case in Nigeria, women and men turned out in some of the most beautiful long gowns and robes I've ever seen.

It was awards night for the graduating seniors. Local officials, par-ents, and students were joined by other ambassadors from the Euro-pean Union. It was here that I learned that half the student body is Muslim, the other half Christian, and that they live together on the grounds of this five-hundred-acre campus. It is a model of interfaith cooperation that the country sorely needs in the face of the ongoing religious and ethnic violence.

I was delighted to see that two of the main three speakers were young women, who also spoke of how they had grown since coming to AUN. One of them, Shalom Otuene, said that after years of respond-ing to every question with "I don't know," she has now permanently deleted the phrase from her vocabulary. Her major is internal and com-parative politics.

It seemed as if in no time, the following day dawned. Then I—along with members of the faculty from Africa, the United States, and other parts of the world—was outfitted in a long, bright red robe to march down the aisle of that same hall. The tables were now gone and replaced by four thousand chairs for the parents, loved ones, and sup-porters of the graduating class.

When I whispered to President Ensign how impressive the room looked, now filled with the 250 members of the graduating class who were also wearing red caps and gowns, she laughed quietly and told me of the 2011 graduation, which was supposed to be held in a huge tent, except that one of the area's frequent sandstorms had come roaring in just as the graduating seniors were assembling and had blown it down.

But that didn't stop the proceedings. Ensign told me, "We worked through the night to get our community hall ready and rented a few small tents from town—no one slept for twenty-four hours—and it ended up being a very beautiful graduation!"

Soon, in this cavernous new hall, the ceremony was opened with two prayers, one from an imam and one from a Protestant minister. In another part of this enormous country of some 160 million people, guests at an awards ceremony had recently protested the singing of the United States' national anthem before the Nigerian one, but there was no dissent in this hall, and the few who knew both joined in the singing. Then it was time for the top graduating seniors to speak—both of them young, composed women who spoke inspiringly, with confidence and humor.

Halima Olajumoke Sogbesan, whose major is communications and multimedia studies, was the valedictorian. She spoke of the impact that the university's motto—"Quality, integrity, and style"—had on her: It "made me dream of an AUN that would prepare me for a successful career in print journalism. I dreamt that from AUN, I would learn to write compelling leads, conduct intensive investigations, and grow to become an award-winning journalist. I also dreamt that in the process of getting my college degree, I was going to develop an American accent. I was a student of the American University of Nigeria, after all. As is quite evident, that didn't really work out the way I thought."

Then she spoke of the extracurricular activities that had broadened her understanding beyond AUN:

Through my experiences while serving as treasurer and secretary of the AUN Honors Society, vice president of the Women's Leadership Council, secretary of the Muslim Students Society of Nigeria, and a member of the AUN Academic Integrity Council, I have come to realize it is difficult to induce change in organizations, no matter how small they are. These experiences have honed my knowledge of the delicate intricacies of the world.

She concluded with words that further affirmed my decision to travel to Yola for this graduation:

It is very wonderful to know that the next time we check our banner records, our heartbeats will be regulated. We are free! About to go into the world, to be agents of change, to glow in the dark, and to stand up for what is right.

Then it was my turn to give the graduation address, although, as I told the students, I felt it was a little redundant after listening to their wise words. But my essential message was that I was there to affirm them and their important goals. I recalled the students of the American civil rights movement—who were their age—who did, in fact, achieve the change that they believed in and fought for, and I said that, having listened to and observed them over the past twenty-four hours, I believed they were capable of achieving this in their own countries.

Soon I was shaking 250 hands as the students walked across the stage to receive their diplomas. I heard their names and majors, which included petroleum engineering, economics, information systems, computer science, the arts, and, of course, journalism and communications.

Within a few more hours, I was on a plane for the long ride back to the United States. Despite all of Nigeria's, and the continent's, ongoing problems, I was returning more hopeful than ever about an African renaissance.

The Dangerous Case of Eskinder Nega

The New Yorker
JULY 17, 2012

The last time I saw Eskinder Nega was in 2006, on the outskirts of Addis Ababa, and what remains etched in my mind is the image of him gently rubbing his pregnant wife's stomach during a rare, brief encounter on a dirt path on the way back to their respective prison cells. Both had been arrested and put in Kaliti prison by the Ethiopian authorities for critical reporting of a violent crackdown on protests following disputed parliamentary elections, in which, according to some reports, security forces killed nearly two hundred people. Eskinder and his wife, Serkalem Fasil, a newspaper publisher, were acquitted in 2007, but their publications were banned and the Ethiopian government denied them licenses to launch new newspapers. But Eskinder persevered. He was educated in the United States, at American University in Washington, D.C., where he studied economics and continued to write on American-based Ethiopian diaspora news sites, pursuing what he saw as his duty as a journalist: holding the Ethiopian government accountable to its democratic promise.

The couple's son, the child who was born in that prison, is now seven years old; if the government has its way, he will be twenty-five years old when his father has his freedom again. Eskinder was arrested last September, a few days after publishing an online article criticizing the government's misuse of an antiterrorism law to arrest independent journalists and political dissidents. (One of those arrested was the seventy-two-year-old iconic Ethiopian actor Debebe Eshetu.)

And Eskinder is not alone. More than a hundred other Ethiopians, including nine journalists, were charged under the sweeping, not to mention vague—but let's do mention it—antiterrorism law. The law was passed in 2009 and was "a game changer," as one journalist told me when I was in Ethiopia recently.

The specific charge against Eskinder was that he conspired with a banned opposition party called Ginbot 7 to overthrow the government. At his trial, government prosecutors showed as evidence a fuzzy video, available on YouTube, of Eskinder at a public town-hall meeting, discussing the potential of an Arab Spring–type uprising in Ethiopia. State television labeled Eskinder and the other journalists as "spies for foreign forces." There were also allegations that he had accepted a terrorist mission—what the mission involved was never specified.

Even writing about Ginbot 7 and similar groups is apparently considered an offense. Al Jazeera was accused of "direct and indirect assistance to terrorist organizations" after an exclusive report on another organization that the Ethiopian government has formally designated as terrorist: the Ogaden National Liberation Front (ONLF), a violent separatist group in Somalia. And two Swedish journalists embedded with the ONLF were also found guilty on the same charge and sentenced to eleven years in the same prison as Eskinder. Five exiled journalists sentenced in absentia with Eskinder received in-absentia prison terms ranging from eight years to life. The leader of the opposition party, currently a professor at Bucknell University, in Pennsylvania, was sentenced to life. Many others have fled the country.

I traveled to Ethiopia recently and, with two colleagues, met with the minister of information in my capacity as a board member for the Committee to Protect Journalists, and asked for release of the journalists. We weren't alone. The U.S. government—which is at the top of the list of international donors that contributed an average of $3.56 billion a year in aid to Ethiopia between 2008 and 2010—according to the Organisation for Economic Co-operation and Development, condemned the sentences of Eskinder and the others. Victoria Nuland, a State Department spokeswoman, said that the United States was "deeply concerned" about Eskinder's conviction, and that it "raises serious questions and concerns about the intent of the law, and about the sanctity of Ethiopians' constitutionally guaranteed rights to freedom of the press and freedom of expression." The statement continued:

> The arrest of journalists has a chilling effect on the media and on the right to freedom of expression. We have made clear in our ongoing human rights dialogue with the Ethiopian government that freedom of expression and freedom of the media are fundamental elements of a democratic society.

While the American government has praised Ethiopia for cooperating in counterterrorism efforts in neighboring Somalia, its individual country reports on human rights found that Ethiopia had arrested "more than 100 persons between March and September [2011] including opposition political figures, activists journalists and bloggers," and that "the government charged several of those arrested with terrorist or seditious activity but observers found the evidence presented at trials to be either open to interpretation or indicative of acts of a political nature rather than linked to terrorism." So the U.S. government knows that there's a problem. There is no way of knowing whether the journalists' case was taken up quietly at the highest levels when Prime Minister Meles Zenawi visited the United States in May, as one of four African heads of state invited to attend a G-8 summit on food security. But the United States, in its new Africa strategy announced in June, has made the promotion of democracy a top priority. Here is a great test case.

What is baffling is that the ruling Ethiopian People's Revolutionary Democratic Front (EPRDF) remains the predominant political party by a wide margin. In 2010, it and affiliated parties won 545 of 547 seats, giving it a fourth consecutive five-year term. Electoral victories like that make one wonder what is really behind the repression. What, too, is to be made of countries like Ethiopia abandoning reform and reversing years of difficult struggle for democratization? Ethiopia's current rulers were once freedom fighters, not so different from South Africa's ANC. They promised to do things differently and to be accountable to their people. Now they risk turning into freedom's enemies, criminalizing peaceful means for Ethiopians to exercise their constitutional rights, such as freedom of expression or freedom of association. Ethiopia has grown a lot in twenty years, but it is on the verge of living out a favorite saying of one of my old journalism professors: we learn from history that we do not learn from history.

While in Ethiopia, I also met with Eskinder's wife, Serkalem. I had seen her for the first time since our prison meeting when she accepted the PEN American Center Freedom to Write award in New York this past May. She said, with her characteristic intensity, that she had recently visited Eskinder, taking food to him in prison, and told him of our pending visit. His one request, she said, was to assure us that he was in no way associated with any terrorist group.

Eskinder plans to appeal his sentence in the coming days.

The Third Man

The New Yorker
JUNE 28, 2010

On an unseasonably chilly morning in April, hundreds of South Africans, many wrapped in the country's traditional woolen blankets, turned up on the grounds of the Natalspruit Hospital, about half an hour southeast of Johannesburg. They had come to hear President Jacob Zuma describe a new AIDS initiative, whose goal is to have fifteen million of the country's forty-nine million people get HIV testing and counseling in the next year. Michel Sibidé, the United Nations AIDS program's executive director, called the initiative's ambitions "unprecedented."

Zuma has been president for a little over a year, and, as his country prepared to host the World Cup, he spent much of the spring opening new airports and stadiums. He was, as they say here, all over the show. But the event at the hospital was particularly important to Zuma, in part because it would demonstrate how much he differs from his predecessor Thabo Mbeki, who questioned the connection between HIV and AIDS, and whose health minister believed in treating the disease with garlic and beetroot. Even Nelson Mandela, Mbeki's predecessor, largely ignored the issue while in office. The UN estimates that about one in five South Africans between the ages of eighteen and forty-nine is HIV-positive, and that around a thousand people die from AIDS-related causes every day.

Zuma sat in a chair in the middle of a crowded stage and watched as Chomee, a stunning young singer of *kwaito*, urban-township music that sounds something like hip-hop, bounded up.

Dressed in a short red satin skirt and black fishnet stockings, and joined by a backup group of similarly sultry young women, Chomee was singing a song that was written for the campaign: "No blame, no shame / We need no stigma / You got to test in order to be treated."

Within a few minutes, Zuma, who is sixty-eight years old and was wearing a dark blue suit, a white shirt, and a red tie, had sprung out of his chair and joined the singers. He swayed back and forth, bending his knees and rhythmically dropping his body down, until you could see the shiny top of his clean-shaven head. He smiled broadly as he shimmied back up beside one of the young women. There was a blast of applause, and Zuma moved to a lectern and began to describe his new campaign. After a short while, he declared that he had recently taken an HIV test and wanted to make an announcement. The crowd grew quiet. "After careful consideration, I have decided to share my results with all South Africans," he said. Then he laughed and added, "I'm sure South Africans know I'm open about my life generally. No surprises."

The whole world knows quite a bit about Zuma's private life. In 2006, he was acquitted of raping an AIDS activist who was HIV-positive. He conceded that he had had unprotected sex with the woman, but he insisted that it had been consensual—and that taking a shower afterward was one way he had reduced the risk of contracting the disease. Zuma is a Zulu, and he made a debatable ethnic assertion at the trial to justify his behavior: "In Zulu culture, you cannot leave a woman if she is ready."

In 2008, Zuma, a polygamist who had already married three women (one of whom he divorced, and another of whom committed suicide), took a fourth wife. In January of this year, he took a fifth, and in February he admitted to fathering a daughter with yet a different woman, the daughter of a friend. This gave him, officially, twenty children. After the revelation, Zuma apologized to the nation and paid the traditional compensation to the woman's family. A survey taken after the announcement found that his approval had dropped to 43 percent, fifteen points lower than it had been a few months before.

Now, on the hospital grounds, the president paused and then said that the test results had been negative. Wild applause and ululating followed. Afterward, long lines formed as people sought HIV tests at stations that had been set up, and the event was widely publicized in the press. Speaking with wit and warmth, the president had done what he does best: confounded his critics and upended expectations. Jacob Zuma, the world's most famously nonmonogamous head of state, had launched a huge public campaign against AIDS.

On a recent Sunday morning, I went to interview Zuma at his official residence, an elegant Dutch-colonial-style mansion in Pretoria. It has spacious receiving rooms lined with generic African art and vases filled with king proteas, the national flower. While I waited in one of the rooms, I pulled the day's newspapers out of my tote bag. As is frequently the case, stories about the president's sex life filled the front pages.

Zuma rushed into the room and apologized for keeping me waiting. He was dressed casually, in a white linen African-style shirt, beige pants, and matching shoes. He sat on the sofa across from me, surrounded by pillows.

When I asked if he saw any conflict between his polygamy, his illegitimate child, and the message that he was trying to deliver at the Natalspruit Hospital, Zuma scowled, as if to say that he was tired of dealing with such questions, and replied, "The question is: How do you carry yourself? Many people have got one wife, but they've got many mistresses. What do you say to them? The only thing is that the mistresses are not talked about. At times, they're discovered, whatever." Why don't people "deal with an honest man who is transparent"? he added.

I asked whether young men, knowing that the president had not worn a condom, might be less likely to use one themselves. The president responded with a typical Zuma answer—it takes a second to process and it includes a joke.

"They don't know the reasons," Zuma began, clearing his throat as his smile faded. "They don't know the reasons for why people at a particular point do not condomize. They don't know the reasons. Otherwise you'd be saying, 'All human beings in the world should condomize,' and there's no birth. Or nothing."

Zuma scooted back among his pillows and laughed at the idea of a suddenly depopulated world.

He added, "I've just said to you I'm the only person at the moment who has stood up and said, 'I'm negative.' I've tested in public and I'm negative. If that's not a good model, I don't know what is."

At one point, I asked him to help me with the pronunciation of his middle name, Gedleyihlekisa, and he did so patiently, syllable by syllable. The name, he said, means "someone who laughs with you while actually endangering you." I told him that a Zulu prince had given me a slightly different definition, one that the prince said many Zulus find quite amusing: "a person who eats you up while he's smiling at you." Zuma laughed heartily.

Zuma's father, a policeman, died when Zuma was very young, and Jay Zed, as he is known, spent his days herding cattle to help his mother, a domestic servant. Although he had no time for formal schooling, he sought out other children and asked to see their books. A young woman in the village who had completed the fourth grade helped him study in the evenings.

Remembering her, he speaks of education with the passion of a man who believes that reading saved him from life as a cowherd or a criminal.

In 1962, when Zuma was twenty, he joined the guerrilla wing of the African National Congress, Umkhonto we Sizwe—or Spear of the Nation—formed by Nelson Mandela and others. The next year, he was arrested by the South African security police, briefly held in solitary confinement, and then sentenced to ten years in prison for conspiracy to overthrow the white regime. He spent his term incarcerated, with

Mandela, on Robben Island, where he got to know the future leader
and continued his academic and political education in what was known
informally as Mandela University. Athletic and tough, Zuma was captain of one of the soccer teams; when he wasn't playing, he served as a
referee.

After his release, in 1973, Zuma rejoined the resistance. He lived
in Swaziland and Mozambique and recruited comrades from home
for guerrilla training. While in exile, he established a friendship with
Thabo Mbeki, another activist who had fled the country. Zuma traveled to the Soviet Union for military training and worked in Mbokodo
("the stone that crushes")—the security department of the ANC,
which dealt with members charged with disobedience or disloyalty,
sometimes rather harshly. Zuma may not have been born into tribal
royalty, like Mandela, or political royalty, like Mbeki, the son of prominent ANC activists. But he was a skilled politician who easily made
alliances. He spent a decade and a half moving up the hierarchy of
the ANC, becoming close to the trade unions and communists on the
party's left. In 1990, Mandela was released, and Zuma returned to the
country. After he got back, he started an education trust to help young
people in rural areas escape poverty; this ongoing project is one of the
topics about which he speaks most passionately. "It took time for me to
educate myself," he said to me. "Because education empowers, I moved
forward and understood things. That's partly what made me what I am
today."

In 1994, just as the country was preparing to become a nonracial
democracy, serious violence broke out in Zuma's home region, now
called KwaZulu-Natal, where Zulus, the largest ethnic group in the
country, make up most of the population. Hundreds of people were
killed there in disputes between the ANC and the Inkatha Freedom
Party, which had taken up arms to demand a measure of self-rule for the
region. Zuma went there to help defuse the conflict. Frank Mdlalose,
who was the national chairman of the IFP, traveled throughout the
region with him. "We spoke to our different groups and told them
there is to be peace," Mdlalose recalled. Zuma "was charming, clear,
soft-spoken, and laughed quite easily."

By the end of the year, Zuma, who can get by in most of the country's eleven official languages, had earned a reputation as a conciliator and was elected national chair of the ANC, replacing Mbeki, who had moved up to become deputy president under Mandela. That year, I asked the outgoing president, F. W. de Klerk, whether he was going to miss the supremacy of the National Party. He responded that it would not be out of office for long. He wasn't the only one who believed that liberation movements often fail at governing.

Mandela sought to heal the social wounds of apartheid. Mbeki sought to transform an economy that had stalled and that he believed was designed to perpetuate inequality. In 1996, as deputy president, Mbeki, with Trevor Manuel, the finance minister, introduced a program for financial liberalization. By the time Mbeki took over the presidency, in 1999—he appointed Zuma as his deputy—the economy had started to improve, aided by increased international investment and a boom in commodity prices. The government reduced the national deficit from 3.8 percent of GDP in 1997–98 to 1.5 percent in 2004–05, and ushered in the longest period of uninterrupted growth in the country's history. A black middle and upper class soon appeared, with the more conspicuous consumers earning the nickname Black Diamonds. Only 8 percent of the seats on the Johannesburg stock exchange are owned by blacks, but the showrooms of Mercedes-Benz and BMW are fully integrated; so are the exclusive shops in the increasingly upscale malls, and so are the previously all-white neighborhoods, which are still gated, because criminals don't discriminate. "Everybody was anticipating a racial war in 1994," Adam Habib, a former activist who is now deputy vice chancellor of the University of Johannesburg, said. We were sitting on his back veranda in a prosperous, leafy neighborhood, overlooking a lovely swimming pool. "Sixteen years later, there's been no killing. There is no racial war. There are racial tensions surfacing every now and then, in part because of the nature of economic inequality." Habib then described his son's fully integrated and racially mixed public school. "These kids are growing up in a new environment," he said.

But Habib pointed out that, contrary to Mbeki's goals, the benefits of the boom have not been widespread. Jobs were created in South Africa's highly sophisticated financial services sector, but these were not jobs for the unskilled and uneducated. Although the country is by far the richest in sub-Saharan Africa, millions of blacks remain desperately poor—both the main victims and the perpetrators of crime. Mbeki's market-driven economic policies alienated the trade unionists and communists on the left wing of his party, and gradually the poor and uneducated turned on him. And while Mbeki has a graduate degree from the University of Sussex and a penchant for quoting *King Lear* that may have endeared him to the crowds at Davos, these qualities led many of his countrymen to feel that he was distant and too cerebral.

In 2005, a friend of Zuma's named Schabir Shaik was convicted of corruption for soliciting a bribe from a French arms manufacturer and sentenced to fifteen years in prison. Zuma, too, was accused of corruption in the deal, and Mbeki fired him. Zuma called the charges a politically motivated outrage; the left wing of the ANC sided with him and, two years later, helped him challenge Mbeki in an election for the presidency of the party. At the convention hall, hundreds of delegates held two fingers in the air to signify "Two terms is enough" (for Mbeki as president of the ANC) or rolled their fists over each other to signal "It's time for a change." Zuma won handily in a vote that seemed mainly anti-Mbeki.

A year and a half later, in April 2009, two weeks before national elections, the director of public prosecutions dismissed the corruption charges against Zuma, declaring that there had been political interference in the handling of the case. South Africa is a parliamentary democracy, and, after the ANC won the vote, Zuma became president, replacing Kgalema Motlanthe, a legislator who had served temporarily as president after Mbeki's resignation and before the new elections. (Shaik, meanwhile, was released from prison just before Zuma came to power, on the ground that his health was seriously deteriorating. When he was seen shopping in a Durban supermarket, he declared that his health was improving, thanks, in part, to a diet that included goji berries.)

Zuma's allies thought that he was a populist who would reverse Mbeki's policies. His enemies and other critics thought that power had been handed to a buffoon and a demagogue. What everyone seemed to agree on was that he would be able to connect with his least fortunate countrymen, and also that, in so turning the corruption investigation to his advantage, he had shown that he possessed remarkable political skills. "His opponents are lucky he's not educated," Aubrey Matshiqi, one of South Africa's most prominent political analysts, told me. Shortly after Zuma's election to the party leadership, Habib said, "You're going to have a president who jigs"—dances—"on the conference floor. He is not going to be quoting Shakespeare. He's going to strike it easy with poorer people."

Zuma's jigging, the traditional leopard-skin outfits he wears on ceremonial occasions, and his casual manner initially won the public over. He earned credit for appointing a diverse cabinet, comprising communists, trade unionists, and capitalists. It included competent men like Aaron Motsoaledi, the health minister, and Trevor Manuel, the head of a new National Planning Commission. Even de Klerk, who had long since given up hope of returning to power, praised Zuma. The enthusiasm, however, quickly waned as the unemployment rate climbed to 25.2 percent and manufacturing continued to decline. The nation produces about one-third less gold than it did in 1994. South Africa currently has the worst income inequality in the world.

The president didn't help matters with a lumbering State of the Nation speech in February, during which he seemed to lose his place at one point. Although Zuma hasn't substantially changed Mbeki's economic policies, the sex scandals have created the sense that he can no more control the economy than he can his libido. South Africa also continues to have one of the highest crime rates in the world and a police service woefully in need of professionalization.

There are close to fifty murders a day—about seven times the per-capita rate in the United States—along with some two hundred sexual offenses and three hundred armed robberies. Two out of five women say that rape was their first sexual experience.

The number of protests has surged since Zuma took office, many in response to the government's failure to deliver such basic services as water and electricity. In the first three months of 2010, there were more protests than at any point since 1994. Zuma's great political strength was supposed to be his ability to win the trust of the poor. Yet the unrest has been worst in the poorest areas, including Orange Farm, a sprawling informal settlement about forty-five miles from Johannesburg. In February, protesters there blocked a thoroughfare, burned tires, and threw stones to call attention to what they insisted were years of neglect and corruption on the part of local officials. Eventually, the protest turned chaotic, with hordes of young people looting foreign-owned stores.

I traveled to Orange Farm a day after the tumult—the smell of burning tires lingered in the air, causing my eyes to burn. A group of women gathered around me. Many spoke at once. "We don't have sewers and no lights in the streets or on the road," a woman named Dorothy Diphoko said. "We want Zuma to come here!" Amanda Sikhahleli shouted.

After a little while, the women started gently shoving me away and telling me that I should move—that it was no longer safe. Across the street, growing numbers of young men and some women were dancing the *toyi toyi*—the historic dance of protest, in which demonstrators move forward military-style. Other men and women were jabbing the air with tree branches, sticks, or long black whips known as *sjamboks*, which I had seen the apartheid police slam down on protesters in 1985. I then noticed police nearby preparing their riot gear and long rifles.

Eventually, a delegation of officials showed up, and the agitated crowd surrounded them. The crowd quieted down when the officials said that they had heard the grievances, and that work on resolving them would begin the following day.

I returned a few days later to see Pretty Methe, one of the women I had met on my earlier visit. When I reached the spot where the demonstration had occurred, all was quiet, and Methe—who is thirty-eight years old, tall, and highly self-composed—was sitting on a bench nursing her fourteen-month-old baby. She got in my car and we drove slowly through the neighborhood. "Look at this," she said, pointing to a tangled mound of wires and wooden slabs on the side of the street. "It's been left behind by contractors hired by the government who were supposed to fix the road. They say they left because they weren't getting paid. And we want to know why not. What happened to the money?"

Most of the streets were full of wide, deep ruts, but Methe took us on a route where the residents had piled bricks into the holes. We reached her house, secured the car behind an iron fence, and walked to a small yard, where she pointed to an orange plastic crate. "That used to be an open pit latrine, and that's where the child fell in," she said, explaining that a four-year-old girl had been playing with friends when her shoe came off. She attempted to retrieve the shoe from the latrine and slipped in. Her playmates kept running ahead, unaware that she had fallen into the slimy muck. Unable to scream, she suffocated and died.

We stepped on bricks arranged in a street overgrown with squishy grass and stopped at the tiny cement house of a friend of Methe's. She invited us inside, where I saw a tiny baby lying on top of a thick stack of blankets. They had been laid out to protect the child from water that seeps into the house because there are no pipes anywhere nearby. The baby's father, Peter Mvundla, was in a small kitchen that doubles as a living room. He is twenty-five years old and had been arrested during the demonstration. "I was protesting because this water is leaking down," he said, adding, "We are severely sick and tired."

"It's a place where you can't even get sick," Methe said. The roads are so bad, she said, that ambulances refuse to drive in. Anyone needing to get to the hospital has to be carried to a nearby highway to meet the ambulance. "It's a place for pigs, not people," she said.

"It's also a place that breeds criminals," Mvundla added. "That Jacob Zuma, he says he's going to create jobs. How many times we look for jobs but there's no jobs?"

Jacob Zuma didn't create the job crisis in Orange Farm, nor is he directly responsible for the uncovered pit latrines. He has been in power for a little over a year, and his term started just six months after the peak of the world financial crisis. But Zuma clearly knows that if he loses the trust of the poor he will lose any chance of governing effectively.

And so he has begun a campaign to improve the civil service, which he has denounced as the worst in the world. He told me that he is prepared to get tough on delinquent officials and that he has already started making unannounced visits to check on them. People who ignore his urgings to work harder, he proclaimed, will be fired. He told me about one community where he says that he found the mayor playing hooky. "When I went back for the second time, there was change," he said.

This story scarcely illustrates a national strategy, particularly since the second visit came only after a series of violent protests had shaken the town. All it showed was that the president could pop in on lazy officials and get them to shape up. But Zuma sees it in grander terms. "People were telling me, 'We now have water. The houses have been built,' et cetera." Then, referring to my encounter at Orange Farm, he said, "That's why those people are right. 'We want Zuma here.'

"Tomorrow, I'm going to be somewhere."

The lack of a broad strategy has earned the president widespread criticism. When he came into office, he reorganized government departments and gave them sophisticated new names.

Foreign Affairs, for example, became International Relations and Cooperation. Analysts complain that he has only created confusion, particularly in financial matters. Azar Jammine, the chief economist at the consulting firm Econometrix, points out that there are now several ministries in charge of economic policy, headed by people with different ideologies. Judith February, an analyst with the Institute for Democracy in South Africa, says that Zuma—who declared that 2010 would be a "year of action"—talks a lot and does nothing. "It's the nature of the presidency that he may be finding his feet, but, at the moment, there is a sense of drift," she said. Mbeki was criticized for deciding without listening; Zuma is called out for listening but not deciding.

Still, Zuma's position is secure for now. His term runs until 2013, and he does not have an obvious successor within the ANC, a political behemoth so dominant that South Africa is essentially a one-party state. Trevor Manuel, currently the head of the National Planning Commission, may be the most respected government official in the country, but he has a fatal political flaw. He comes from a mixed-race background and was classified as "colored" by the apartheid government, even though he identifies himself as black. When I asked people about the prospect that Manuel would himself become president, they often responded with a silent no, pointing a finger at their skin. Many other top officials are involved in claims and counterclaims about corruption, and that subject has become the second-favorite topic of the press. (The president's sex life continues its primacy; the latest scandal involved one of his wives and an alleged affair with a bodyguard who supposedly committed suicide when the affair was discovered.)

Much of the current political intrigue surrounds Julius Malema, the leader of the ANC Youth League, who, at twenty-nine, is too young to succeed Zuma directly but who could eventually be part of a coalition that tries to bring him down. In the past, he has declared that he would "kill for Zuma," but he has also criticized the president, and has caused no small amount of trouble for the party. In April, for example, Malema traveled to Zimbabwe, where he embraced President Robert Mugabe and his party, Zanu-PF. Malema declared support for Mugabe's land reform policy, which consisted of confiscating land from white farmers—leaving thousands of their black laborers jobless—and handing much of it over to political cronies who could neither care for the chickens nor fix the tractors. This policy is widely believed to have destroyed Zimbabwe's economy. At a press conference a few days later, Malema began vigorously criticizing Zimbabwe's opposition party, Movement for Democratic Change (MDC), noting that it has "air-conditioned offices" in Sandton, a wealthy part of Johannesburg. A British journalist interjected that Malema himself lived in Sandton. Malema erupted and threw the journalist out of the press conference, calling him a "bloody agent," a "bastard," and a "small boy." Just before that, Malema had been involved in an even more racially charged incident: he had led a large group of supporters at a rally in singing an old struggle song that includes the line "Shoot the Boer," referring to the Afrikaans word for "farmer." Soon thereafter, a right-wing extremist whom Malema has criticized in the past, Eugene Terre'Blanche, was killed. Though no one has proved a direct connection between the song and the murder, Zuma criticized Malema for continuing to sing it at other events after a court banned it. Malema responded by lashing out at Zuma. In May, the ANC sent Malema to classes on anger management.

All of this was seen as undermining Zuma, who is mediating peace talks between Zanu-PF and the MDC and is trying to position himself as a moderate on racial and social issues. Zuma has said that he will not confiscate farms, and he has been trying to assuage poor Afrikaners who insist that they are being discriminated against by the government's affirmative action policies. Zuma is, after all, far better at smiling at people than at eating them up.

"He's a communicator," Jesse Jackson said during a visit to South Africa this spring. "He's not difficult. He's a very down-to-earth person. He's as formal as required and informal as he needs to be." Unlike many other leaders, Zuma doesn't blame the apartheid past for all his country's problems. At a meeting of government officials in April that I attended, he began by talking about the government's successes during the sixteen years of black-led rule. But then his tone grew somber. Four years from now, South Africa will celebrate twenty years of freedom, he told the attentive audience. At that time, he said, "we will not be able to blame apartheid if some villages still have no water, no electricity, and no roads."

Since coming to power, Zuma has consistently countered expectations: he has defended his personal promiscuity while becoming an avowed AIDS activist; he is a populist who has maintained free-market economic policies and alienated the poor; he is a powerful leader in a dominant party who has a hard time taking action.

On the day he was rushing to prepare his response to critics of his budget vote in Parliament, the president and I sat down in his luxurious offices at Tuynhuys, a neoclassical structure that has been the seat of government in Cape Town for close to two and a half centuries.

A giant bronze sculpture of Louis Botha, an Afrikaner who was the country's first prime minister, still sits outside. I asked Zuma about the criticism that he is too much of a conciliator, and he responded wistfully by describing his rural home village, where men and women sit comfortably under trees and reason things through, for as long as it takes. Then he turned to the subject of his critics: "I don't think they know what they're talking about. The very people who say so, they would criticize the dictator who doesn't listen to anyone. One of the charges or allegations is that this Zuma is a friend to everybody else. But, if you are a leader, why should you hate some people and love others?"

When the World Cup games started, in early June, Zuma reveled in the attention. In a speech on June 16, marking the thirty-fourth anniversary of a historic anti-apartheid revolt, he praised South Africa's youth, along with the national soccer team, Bafana Bafana. He declared that the team had made the country proud in its "dazzling opening encounter" with Mexico, which ended in a 1–1 draw. Beaming, chest expanding, he told the highly energized crowd that South Africans had "displayed amazing patriotism and national pride" during the tournament. Zuma knows that such moments of shared national identity have been rare in the country's history—particularly as Mandela, known to his countrymen as Madiba, has stepped off-stage. But South Africans of all identities are flying their country's single flag on their BMWs, their bicycles, and their bakkies. A few days after the speech, Ferial Haffajee, the editor of the *City Press*, one of South Africa's largest newspapers, told me that the country now feels "as if somewhere in our tattered souls we had all found our inner Madibas."

Zuma's challenges, however, have not disappeared in the blare of the vuvuzelas. The day after his speech, I phoned Pretty Methe to find out how she and her neighbors were reacting to the World Cup. "It's bad now," she said, lamenting South Africa's 3–0 loss to Uruguay, which came shortly after Zuma's speech, and which eventually led to the team's elimination. But she added that she and her family "are not watching all the matches, because we don't have electricity.

"There is no electricity anywhere here since May."

Methe said that she doesn't think the hundreds of millions of dollars spent on the World Cup will make any difference in places like Orange Farm. "Those people are just keeping the money for themselves. I don't have hope." The sounds of screaming children almost drowned out Methe's voice. "They are playing soccer," she said.

Revolution in Tunisia and in the African Media

All Africa
NOVEMBER 16, 2011

Tunisia, the source and inspiration of the Arab Spring, witnessed a significant milestone in the growth of the African Media Initiative (AMI) and the maturity of African media last week.

When we chose Tunis as the fourth venue for our flagship program, the African Media Leaders Forum (AMLF), it was with the clear intention of positively exploiting their revolution to enhance our program of creating a revolution in the management of African media. Social media played a significant role in the extraordinary developments that launched the Arab Spring and it was with the idea of exploring the implications of social media for Africa that we titled our annual gathering "Empowering Citizens Through Social Media and Technology Adaptation: What Future for Traditional Media?"

As our CEO, Amadou Mahtar Ba, said: "Our meeting in Tunis was a way of paying tribute to ordinary citizens whose courage and hunger to have a say in how they are governed and by whom unleashed a revolution to restore justice and accountability. And that is at the core of media's responsibility: to ensure citizens have the kind of information they need to achieve those ends."

To be sure, revolutions in the past have happened without social or even traditional media. And, no doubt in time, Tunisians and the citizens of the other countries of the Arab Spring would have eventually thrown off the yoke of oppression. As the American civil rights martyr Martin Luther King Jr. often said: "No lie can live forever."

But there is no question that social media accelerated the Arab uprisings and, in most cases, limited the human toll that sometimes accompanies revolutions, as we are seeing, alas, in Syria. But that, thankfully, is the exception.

Since our last AMLF meeting in Cameroon, which concentrated on helping African media owners develop more effective business models, we have concentrated on concrete projects that would take AMLF closer to the goal of developing a media sector that would help citizens affect social, economic, and political change, not least holding their leaders accountable. Social media has become key in realizing those goals. So we held workshops that gave experts time to explore the possibilities of the new technologies. And the Tunis AMLF declaration emphasized the need to continue focusing on improving professionalism, management, content, and timeliness of reporting by harnessing the strengths of media technology.

The declaration acknowledges that "deficits in democracy and governance are inimical to the growth of Africa's media sector." But the body applauded and endorsed AMI's core principle of ethics and principled leadership. Our plan now is to get media associations around the continent to endorse the principles that promote ethics and best practice now being circulated among them. Already the Tanzania Media Owners Association has endorsed these principles.

What encourages our efforts to strengthen African media is that we are clearly growing from strength to strength. From an attendance of fifty at our first meeting in Dakar, Senegal, four years ago, we have grown to a record 350 from forty-eight African countries at our Tunis meeting.

We are committed to building on the solid foundation of action and innovation we have laid. And we intend to see that the ideas that drove the Arab Spring also create the kind of revolution in African media that will truly empower Africa's people, giving them the freedom, justice, prosperity, and equality they so richly deserve.

Violated Hopes

The New Yorker
MAY 21, 2012

On a recent Sunday morning in the black township of Kwa Thema, near Johannesburg, a young lesbian couple went to church. Kwa Thema is one of many settlements that were created by the apartheid regime to contain and control the black majority population, and it remains isolated today. The two women, Bontle Khalo and Ntsupe Mohapi, are leaders of a lesbian, gay, bisexual, and transgender organization called the Ekurhuleni Pride Organizing Committee, or EPOC. The couple formed the group three years ago, to combat rising violence against gays in Ekurhuleni, their municipality. They were concerned in particular about a gruesome crime known as "corrective rape"—an assault in which a man rapes a lesbian in an attempt to "cure" her sexual orientation. Another LGBT organization, in Cape Town, says that it deals with as many as ten such incidents every week. Since 1998, at least thirty-one lesbians have been killed in attacks that were motivated by their sexual orientation and many of which began with corrective rape. Few arrests have been made.

Khalo, twenty-seven, and Mohapi, thirty-nine, go to the Victory Fellowship World Outreach church every Sunday, accompanied by Xolile Dzanibe, a gay male friend who helped to found EPOC. Victory

Fellowship is one of many evangelical churches established in South Africa in the late 1970s. Its congregation is mostly black. Although few churches in the country welcome gays, Khalo, Mohapi, and Xolile told me that they were accepted here.

Members of South Africa's LGBT community encounter widespread discrimination, even though in some ways the country appears to promote tolerance—its constitution was the first in the world with a clause explicitly forbidding discrimination on the ground of sexual orientation. The language was included in the 1996 Bill of Rights, which was introduced two years after the transition from apartheid rule to democracy, and was intended to address South Africa's history of prejudice and legally enshrined segregation. But, in a country with high levels of poverty and inequality, and few policies in place to reduce them, hostility toward "difference" has barely slackened, and crimes against gays, and women, have increased. South Africa, with a population of fifty million, has one of the highest rates of violence in the world—more than forty murders a day, on average—and the highest rate of rape.

Statistics from the International Criminal Police Organization in 2009 indicated that a woman is raped in South Africa every seventeen seconds, and that nearly half the victims are under eighteen. One woman in two can expect to be raped at least once in her lifetime. A study by the South Africa Medical Research Council, also published in 2009, reported that one in four men admitted having committed rape at one time or another.

In South Africa, lesbians face assault twice as often as heterosexual women. Lesbian rape victims speak of verbal abuse by the perpetrators, including shouts of "We'll show you you're a woman," as though corrective rape were instruction in gender conventions. Unpublished research by the Johannesburg-based Forum for the Empowerment of Women suggests that black lesbians, especially those who are viewed as butch and live in isolated townships, are particularly vulnerable.

In recognition of male as well as female victims, the definition of "rape" in South Africa's penal code was recently widened to include not only vaginal penetration but "vaginal, oral, and anal penetration of a sexual nature by whatever means." Anti-rape activists are pushing for more legal reform: an amendment of the sexual offenses act to allow for heavier sentences, and the introduction of hate crimes legislation, which would address corrective rape. The 2006 trial of Jacob Zuma, the nation's president and the leader of the African National Congress, was a blow to their cause. Zuma, then sixty-four, stood accused of raping the thirty-one-year-old daughter of a family friend. He said that the woman in question had provoked him, by wearing a skirt and sitting with her legs uncrossed, and that it was his duty, as a Zulu man, to satisfy a sexually aroused woman. Such statements reflect the deeply embedded views of many South African men. After a two-month trial, Zuma was acquitted.

Aggression against gays is a clear illustration of the gap between the ideals of the constitution and the attitudes of the public. Only six years ago, Zuma called same-sex marriage "a disgrace to the nation and to God." (He later apologized.) At a ceremony in January marking the anniversary of a Zulu victory over British imperial forces, the Zulu leader King Goodwill Zwelithini created a firestorm when he reportedly called people in same-sex relationships "rotten." "Today, we are faced with different challenges," Zuma said in response. "Challenges of reconciliation and of building a nation that does not discriminate against other people because of their color or sexual orientation."

As Khalo and Mohapi walked into the church, they were embraced by some of the women who were setting up white plastic chairs on the cement floor. The service began with a congregation of about a hundred people, mainly women and children, singing hymns in several local dialects. After they settled into their seats, the church's deacon, a tall, brown-skinned man, walked to the altar to warm up the crowd before the sermon, which was to be delivered by a visiting pastor.

"I'd like to say, you are all so special," the deacon said. A younger man in jeans and a white T-shirt played a soft vamp on an electric keyboard. "I understand that some of you may not comprehend that, when you are hurt, God has nothing to do with that," the deacon continued. "Our God is an awesome God. He has never failed us!"

He began singing, "O Come, All Ye Faithful." Khalo and Mohapi rose along with the rest of the congregation and began waving their arms in the air, swaying back and forth, with a dip every few beats, and singing, until the deacon shouted, "Hallelujah!"

He went on, "The Scripture says, 'Fear not.' Fear can torture you. Fear can imprison you. . . .

"Whatever you are fearing this morning, chuck it out! If the Lord has good thoughts about you, he is on your side."

For Khalo and Mohapi, the deacon seemed to be speaking to the phenomenon of antigay violence, and bolstering the work of EPOC. The group had recently organized gay pride marches throughout the municipality, demanding justice for Eudy Simelane, an internationally renowned athlete, and Noxolo Nogwaza, a member of EPOC. Both were lesbians who were brutally murdered, in attacks that seem to have begun with corrective rape. EPOC is also investigating the death of Girlie Nkosi, a lesbian who, a relative told EPOC activists, was stabbed in the abdomen with a sharp instrument by a man she had rejected sexually, and died from internal bleeding.

The police, however, say that they have no reason to look into her death.

South Africans first became widely aware of the violence against lesbians when, in April, 2008, Simelane, a thirty-one-year-old former member of the national women's soccer team, was killed.

Simelane was one of the first openly gay women in Kwa Thema and was training to be the first female referee at the Men's World Cup, in 2010, in South Africa. Simelane was on her way home after a late night out with friends at a local bar when a group of men jumped her and stabbed her multiple times in the face, chest, and legs. Her body was found facedown in a drainage ditch. The entrance of her vagina was badly bruised, and some of the stab wounds, on the inside of her upper thighs, indicated to the doctor who performed the autopsy that the attackers had attempted to rape her.

"The whole community was outraged," Khalo told me later at EPOC's office, in Kwa Thema. The office is a cramped room in the back of the modest house that she and Mohapi share. The walls are covered with posters ("Just Let Us Be Happy People!") and pictures of

EPOC members marching in a gay pride parade. In one photograph, demonstrators are carrying banners that read "I Am Stabane," an appropriation of the otherwise derisive Zulu term for a homosexual person.

Soon after Simelane was murdered, four men were arrested in the case. Her celebrity undoubtedly made it easier for the police to find the killers. "A lot of people were there," Khalo said. "A lot of witnesses weren't afraid to speak out." At the trial, two of the suspects were released for lack of evidence. The other two were convicted. Thato Mhpithi, twenty-three, received a thirty-two-year prison sentence, and Themba Mvubu, a twenty-four-year-old who had had Simelane's blood on his clothing, was sentenced to life imprisonment. He smiled as he was walked from the courtroom. "I'm not sorry at all," he told reporters, as friends of Simelane's yelled that they wished he'd been sliced into pieces. It was a dramatic end to a contentious trial: Khalo recalled that the police had expressed disapproval of the way gay men in the courtroom were dressed, and had laughed at spectators in drag. At one point, the judge asked the prosecutor about the use of the term "lesbian": "Is there another word that you can use instead of that one?"

The majority of South Africans subscribe to some form of Christian belief. This coexists with the remnants of traditional religions, which are imbued with patriarchal systems and ancestral notions of evil embodied in witches and sorcerers. During the apartheid years, when most Afrikaner whites belonged to the conservative Dutch Reformed Church, which excluded gays, homosexuality was a crime. Traditional black churches also weren't welcoming to homosexuals. That began to change in 1994, after the African National Congress came to power. Leading clergymen, including Archbishop Desmond Tutu and the anti-apartheid crusader Rev. Allan Boesak, supported gay rights. Although the Dutch Reformed Church unsuccessfully opposed any mention of sexual orientation in the new constitution, it eventually began allowing gays to hold positions in the church.

In 1996, President Nelson Mandela's multiracial government adopted a constitution that emphasized civil and political rights. Encouraged by the legislation and the national mood of liberation and diversity, gays came out in large numbers. In the years that followed, equality laws were tested and upheld in the courts, leading to equal protection for gays in the workplace. Sodomy laws were overturned. LGBTs gained rights in adoption, immigration, inheritance, and medical aid. They were permitted to serve openly in the military, and to have their sex change recognized on identity documents. The constitution mandated the creation of several state institutions to protect equal rights, including the Commission for Gender Equality and the South African Human Rights Commission. In the fall of 2004, in response to an application brought by a lesbian couple, the Supreme Court of Appeal ruled that the common-law definition of marriage must include same-sex marriage. In December 2005, the Constitutional Court made any inferior status imposed on same-sex partners unconstitutional.

Most other African countries provide no legal protection for what many on the continent call "gayism." More than two-thirds of African countries have laws that criminalize consensual same-sex acts. Two men who held an engagement party in Malawi in 2010 were sentenced to fourteen years of prison and hard labor. (They have since been pardoned.) In Nigeria, the senate recently passed a bill that could impose a fourteen-year jail term on anyone who enters into a same-sex marriage, and a ten-year sentence on anyone who helps to arrange one. Vandals in Senegal, one of the more stable and progressive democracies in Africa, have dug up the corpses of gay men and desecrated them. Last year, a well-known Ugandan gay activist named David Kato was murdered. Earlier this year, one of Liberia's leading legislators introduced a bill that could impose the death penalty on homosexuals. And in Mozambique gays live under the threat posed by Article 71 of the penal code, which calls for "security measures" to be taken against anyone committing "vices against nature."

In recent years, South Africa—officially, at least—has stood in contrast to most of Africa. On June 17, 2011, South Africa introduced a resolution in the United Nations Human Rights Council calling for an end to "acts of violence and discrimination, in all regions of the world, committed against individuals because of their sexual orientation and gender identity." It was called the council's first gay rights resolution, and South Africa and Mauritius were the only African countries to vote in its favor.

In a speech in Geneva six months later, Secretary of State Hillary Clinton urged all African countries to respect gay rights, implicitly threatening to withhold American aid to countries that fail to do so. "Gay rights are human rights, and human rights are gay rights," Clinton said. "Gay people are born into and belong to every society in the world. Being gay is not a Western invention. It is a human reality." Clinton's statement was condemned by some leading African politicians.

This March, in a video message shown at a meeting of the Human Rights Council in Geneva, Secretary-General Ban Ki-moon called for an end to laws criminalizing homosexuality, citing seventy-six countries that have such laws. Leaning on a report presented by Navi Pillay, the UN High Commissioner for Human Rights, who is South African, he stated that the constant violence against lesbians, gays, bisexuals, and transgender people was "a monumental tragedy for those affected and a stain on our collective conscience."

Pakistan, in response, and on behalf of the Organization of Islamic Cooperation, led a walkout of Muslim states, arguing that the resolution would promote "licentious behavior" and lead to the "legitimatization of many deplorable acts, including pedophilia and incest." South Africa took a stand and prevented a walkout of African states during the debate.

South Africa's decisive move in the UN was praised by liberals as a moral and diplomatic victory, but it did not correspond seamlessly to the country's recent politics. In early May, the National House of Traditional Leaders—formed after the end of apartheid to advise the government on the interests and customs of various ethnic groups—asked Parliament to repeal the clause protecting citizens from discrimination on the ground of sexual orientation. The leaders were responding to the annual invitation of the constitutional review committee—a multiparty parliamentary group—to submit suggestions for amendments, and they insisted that the "great majority of South Africans do not want to give promotion and protection to these things."

Patekile Holomisa, a traditional leader and an ANC member of Parliament, who also chairs the constitutional review committee, said that homosexuality was "a condition that occurred when certain cultural rituals have not been performed," and that gays should be taken to spiritual healers so that they could start to behave like other people in society. He warned that the ANC could lose votes if it continued to ignore the values of its base by protecting gays.

The ANC caucus pushed back against Holomisa the following day. A statement issued by the chief whip, Mathole Motshekga, emphasized that the ANC "at no stage has considered debating this issue before Parliament."

For a historically conservative country like South Africa, regardless of its progressive laws, the shock of so many gays coming out of the closet at once was profound. Places like Kwa Thema and Cape Town developed a reputation for being friendly to gay men and women, with relatively little discrimination and lively nightlife. Still, gays who patronized the small bars known as shebeens often faced insults from straight men.

Dipika Nath is a former member of the Task Team on Sexual Offences and Gender-Based Violence, a group that the Department of Justice established after the murder of Eudy Simelane and several other gay women. Last December, Nath wrote an extensive study for Human Rights Watch, "We'll Show You You're a Woman," about violence and discrimination against black lesbians and transgendered men in South Africa. It was based on more than a hundred interviews, conducted in six of the country's nine provinces. "There are real gaps in just information of what sexual orientation is, what gender is, what gender identity is," Nath told me. "Coupled with that is a history of violence in the country." She cited a number of factors to explain the increase in violence, including mass migration of male laborers to cities, unsafe working conditions, and the legacy of segregation and apartheid policies that encouraged violent crime in townships by leaving them deliberately unpoliced. She pointed, too, to widespread firearm use, beginning during colonial rule and continuing through apartheid. Socioeconomic inequality has persisted in the post-apartheid era, as have alarming rates of unemployment, lack of educational and economic opportunity, uneven functioning of state institutions, and the devastating effect of HIV and AIDS.

I asked Saki Macozoma, a prominent businessman and a former employee of the South African Council of Churches, about this period of transition. "We live in an age that one Xhosa writer called 'the generation of doubt,' with one foot in traditional society and another in some form of modernity," he said. He theorized that the fading authority of the clan, the unit that once instilled order in the lives of many South Africans, had created a "sense of rootlessness," opening the road to criminality.

At the EPOC offices, a woman named Lungile Cleopatra Dladla, from a nearby township, told me of the night she was raped. Dladla, a stocky lesbian in her mid-twenties, was walking home one night with a female friend who was also gay. An armed man, wearing a hooded sweatshirt, came up behind them and directed them to a field. "Then he undressed us," she said. "He tied us, and then he was going, 'Ja, today I want to show you that you're girls.'" He raped them both. "And then, immediately after, he dressed and untied my friend's hands and then untied my feet and then he walked. You could hear the grass— like a snake is walking through the grass. From a distance, he shouted, 'Now you can dress and go.' My friend untied my hands, I untied her feet, and then we started dressing. He even wanted to take my clothes, because they're man clothes: my shoes and T-shirt. He says he will leave the pants."

The young women went to the local police station, where, Dladla said, she was "victimized" again; the police insisted that she was not a woman. "They said, 'He's not a girl. How can he be raped?'" Eventually, a former classmate who happened to work at the police station recognized her, and the officers finally took down information about the crime.

Dladla told me that she had been raped once before, when she was six or seven. The perpetrator was her father.

About two years after she was raped in the field, Dladla started having trouble breathing. She went to a doctor, who sent her to a hospital, where she was informed that she was HIV-positive and very ill. The HIV infection was so far advanced, she told me, that if she hadn't been put on antiretroviral drugs she would have died.

Dladla said her mother believes that she invited the rape, because of her homosexuality. Her mother has lost her job and has told Dladla she can no longer buy the healthy food that Dladla's doctor recommends. Dladla said her only solace is that her assailant was finally arrested and convicted.

According to the South African Medical Research Council, the number of sexual offenses that occur in a given year is nine times as high as the number reported. (The U.S. Department of Justice estimates that half of all rapes and violent crimes committed in the country go unreported.) In addition to shame, stigma, and fear of retaliation, victims of sexual crimes, like Dladla, have described experiencing indifferent, if not hostile, attitudes from authorities—a phenomenon referred to as secondary victimization. Dipika Nath's report indicates that South African policemen have also been commonly identified as perpetrators of sexual abuse.

Verdicts, too, tend to be lighter than advocates hope for. In 2007, a fourteen-year-old girl visiting from the United States was abducted while leaving a party and raped twice by the same man. The perpetrator could have received a life sentence but instead got eighteen years. This past February, four men were convicted of beating to death a nineteen-year-old lesbian, Zoliswa Nkonyana, after she left a bar in Khayelitsha, a township near Cape Town. It took almost six years to bring the case to court, and the men received sentences of eighteen years each. A news report on the South African Broadcasting Corporation's website called the sentences "heavy," but Nkonyana's stepfather said that he was disappointed.

On April 24, 2011, Noxolo Nogwaza, a twenty-four-year-old lesbian, was found dead in Tsakane, the township adjacent to Kwa Thema. Like Simelane, the soccer player, she had been at a bar in Tsakane and was on her way home with a friend in the early morning darkness. At some point, apparently, she and the friend separated. The following morning, at about 9 a.m., Nogwaza's body was found in a ditch. It appeared that she had been raped. Her eyes had been plucked out of their sockets, her brain had split, and patches of her skin and teeth were strewn about.

Although the neighborhood is densely populated, no one, including the security guards at nearby warehouses, came forward as a witness. Nogwaza's death, two years after the high-profile trial for Simelane's murder, brought greater attention to the increase in antigay violence, but there have been no arrests.

Captain Petros Mabuza, a rangy man with a genial manner, is the spokesman for the Tsakane police department. He said that at least five suspects had been taken in for forensic examinations but had been released. He speculated that the killer might have been drunk or on drugs.

I asked him if he thought that the case would ever be solved. One likely reason that no witnesses came forward at first, he said, was fear of revenge. Nevertheless, he told me, he was determined to find the murderers.

Mabuza admitted that his officers didn't have much experience with homosexuals, and that he was unprepared when, last November, LGBT activists marched on his police station, demanding action on Nogwaza's murder. He said that he was resolved to educate his officers about the trend of violence against lesbians, but that he knew of no other incidents of corrective rape in the area.

A few minutes away from the Tsakane police station, down a narrow alleyway, is the considerably smaller Kwa Thema police headquarters, an old brick building bustling with activity. The overseeing officer there is Colonel Matjie Johannes Manyathela. The colonel's manner is as genial as Captain Mabuza's, and he, too, insisted that he knew of no other incident of corrective rape in the area. He was moved, he told me, by a discussion that he and Mabuza attended with local officials and leaders of the LGBT community, who told them that they were children of the same God. After the meeting, Mabuza said, he proposed setting up workshops to help sensitize the police and avoid further secondary victimization of rape victims by skeptical or hostile authorities.

Months later, no workshops have been conducted. Manyathela said that he spoke to his policemen after the meeting with LGBT representatives, telling them that they needed to respect the rights of homosexuals—rights, he reminded them, that are protected by the law that they have sworn to uphold. But Khalo told me that although EPOC had invited Mabuza to several meetings—including a memorial for Nogwaza—he failed to come, or even to send regrets.

Dipika Nath's Human Rights Watch report, she says, provides meticulous evidence of "widespread, if not epidemic, hostility and violence against gay people—a far cry from the promise of equality and non-discrimination on the basis of 'sexual orientation' contained in the constitution." Despite a lingering cultural conservatism, gay pride parades are covered in the South African media, and gays have been featured in television soap operas. *Society*, a show on the SABC's public TV channel, had a story line in which a lesbian couple were attacked by men for behaving affectionately in public. The 2012 Mr. Gay World pageant was held in South Africa, and tickets sold out, although there was some controversy about the date, given that it would be held on Easter Sunday. (Mr. Gay South Africa came in second to the winner, Mr. Gay New Zealand.)

In daily conversations, however, many South Africans, especially men, maintain that same-sex relationships are "un-African." In a recent television special on corrective rape, the independent station ETV featured black men on the street saying things like "Sodom and Gomorrah were burned down because of this filth"; "It goes against nature"; and "We have lost our manhood because of these things." Another said, "These gay things ought to be killed."

Nath described the prevalence of gang rape in impoverished townships, a practice often referred to as "jackrolling" (after the Jackroller gang, which operated in Soweto in the late 1980s, and became notorious for abducting women and raping them). Not long after Nath and I met, a ten-minute jackrolling video went viral. The footage, taken and distributed by cell phone, shows a group of boys, between fourteen and twenty, raping a seventeen-year-old mentally disabled Sowetan girl. The girl, who doctors say has the mental capacity of a four-year-old, went missing for three weeks afterward. Her mother said that she had been raped several times before.

In Pretoria, I met with Juan Nel, a psychology professor and an LGBT activist who is also a member of the Task Team on Sexual Offences and Gender-Based Violence. Although Nel acknowledged that the recent cases of corrective rape "got the government to sit up straight," he told me that the national discussion about violence against women and gays should be broader. "The media have been very quiet when it's white men or black men who've been raped, sexually abused, assaulted, and subjected to grievous bodily harm," he said. Currently, the police are looking into a connection between the murders of eight gay men, all killed in similar fashion, in the small but populous Gauteng province, where Johannesburg and Kwa Thema are situated.

Tlali, the spokesman for the Department of Justice, has been involved with the Task Team since it was set up. He insists that the group is making progress, getting the government to act more quickly in making arrests in cases that might involve corrective rape and bringing them to trial. He told me that the government, in line with the demands of NGOs representing the LGBT community, has embarked on a campaign to make officials in the criminal justice system better aware of homophobic violence and to reduce the secondary victimization described by rape victims like Lungile Dladla. He said that the government is also determined to move faster on hate crime legislation, and to promote tolerance through school curricula. But he seemed to suggest that the South African leadership had few illusions. "Based on our violent history, it may not be easy for us to overcome some of these challenges," he said.

When the service I attended at the Victory Fellowship World Outreach church was over, I approached the visiting pastor, Benjamin Mooke. I asked him if other branches of the church were as accepting of gays as the Victory Fellowship Outreach seemed to be.

He said, "We believe that Jesus, when he came, he was even able to talk to that woman," referring to the woman at the well in Samaria. "Jesus, realizing that this woman needed help, he didn't chuck her out. He said to her, 'Go and buy food.' And then he was left with her, and then he talked to her about the food and the truth was revealed and then she changed. We cannot fight the sinner. We don't reject that person. If we send him out from the church, where do we expect that person to get help? That person is coming to the church to get help."

I asked him if this meant that the church intended to undertake its own version of "correcting" gays and lesbians, and he told me that it was important to understand "what causes a person to be gay. What causes them to be lesbian. What causes them to be like that."

Undistracted by the noise that the cleanup people were making as they put away the chairs, Pastor Mooke continued. "We believe God created men and women," he said, but he added, as though speaking to the gay and lesbian community, "We have not made a stand, really, that we are for or against you."

PART V

The Road Less Traveled

In my early days as the first Black female student at the University of Georgia, I was asked to write a piece for a magazine called the *Urbanite*, which was started by Byron Lewis, a young man I first met in Alaska, when he was serving in the army. He sang in the army base choir where my father, an officer, was the chaplain and also brought with him from his upbringing in a religious family and civilian life his love of hymns. When Byron returned to New York after his service, he saw the need for a magazine that would focus on Black people and their contributions in a way somewhat different from the other, however important, Black publications. He had read about my UGA experience and called and asked if I would write a piece about my experiences, so far, at the university for his fairly new magazine. I was focused on my studies but because of his relationship with my father, I agreed. I was a bit reluctant to do it since I was still being segregated to the extent the university could, without breaking the law that ordered my sole Black classmate, Hamilton Holmes, and me in.

Despite the court order, in the dorm I was still segregated, as I was put in a room on the first floor while all the other (white) girls lived on the second floor. But to honor my father and his relationship with his fellow Black soldiers, I agreed to write an article for the *Urbanite*. Once I finished, I asked for a first look over the finished piece so I could run it by M. Carl Holman. The *Urbanite* was published out of the Holman basement. I used to go back to Atlanta on weekends and help with preparing the paper in any way I could, even eventually getting out into Atlanta's streets and reporting on things that needed to change for My People. So, after I completed a few minor tweaks that Professor Holman suggested, he approved. That meant a lot to me. And, to be sure, the last paragraph of this piece was indeed prescient, for many Black students have since walked through that Georgia corridor, and while they are still in a minority on campus, and have their own challenges, none, thankfully, have had to walk through the university's corridors facing the same ones I faced.

Thanks to the kind of guidance I received from Professor Holman when I graduated from UGA with a degree labeled ABJ (bachelor of arts in journalism), I left with two degrees—one paper and the other of confidence. Also, thanks to William Shawn, the *New Yorker* editor who reached out to me in Georgia when he learned of my journalistic aspirations, I landed in a wonderful environment that in time helped me realize my dreams as a reporter. But that would take a little time, so with one exception—a small piece for the Comment section—I initially tried my hand at doing what many of the veteran journalists and writers were doing: writing a memoir. The magazine not only published it, it kept my title: "A Hundred-Fifteenth-Between-Lenox-and-Fifth." It was about the time I first encountered Harlem when I was about five years old, after traveling up on the train from Atlanta, Georgia, with my grandmother to visit my great-uncle. It was an eye-opening experience in so many ways and included meeting, for the first time, children my age who spoke in accents different from what I was used to hearing, and who played in a different way from how I was used to playing in Covington, the small South Georgia town where we lived. There were a few paved streets in our segregated Black neighborhood, but, like our segregated school playground, many of the grounds in our neighborhood were filled with red clay, hence no hopscotch when it rained. Moreover, the people who lived on that street—the street I named this piece after—identified it in a rhythmic way that stuck with me and shaped my view of the people in Harlem that would follow me many years later when I returned as a professional journalist.

To be sure, Harlem was different from Covington in many ways, not least how the streets were named. Our street in Covington was Brown Street and one in another Black neighborhood was Short Street. But hearing these descriptions in Harlem was like, well, music to my little Southern ears. That and the Spanish words and accents coming out of the mouths of my new friends playing hopscotch, not with the little pebbles we used to throw to the dirt squares in Covington, but with bottle caps that resonated differently in ears when they hit the Harlem concrete.

It would be a while before I tried another memoir, especially to focus on something I didn't see much of in the magazine (or anywhere else) at the time—the experience of ordinary Black people in the segregated South, like my dear grandmother. And while it was a South that had been challenged and changed by mostly young civil rights activists, I thought it was important to tell a story that focused on the ongoing, day-to-day experiences of ordinary Black people. It was equally important to me to show readers where we got our own sense of commitment to family and community. So I embarked on a journey that shed some light on those realities. But it was still a time when there could be unhappy consequences for Black people in places where the civil rights movement had not reached, so I submitted the piece as fiction, changing the name of the town I was writing about. But that was where the fiction ended.

This story, about the small injustices faced by Black people in Covington, reflected an ongoing reality my family and many other Black families knew all too well . . . some that, alas, remain to this day.

A Walk Through a Georgia Corridor

The Urbanite
1961

On one hot day early in July of 1959, Hamp (Hamilton Holmes) and I went down to the Court House in Atlanta to have our application forms certified, a routine but necessary step in our attempt to enroll as students at the University of Georgia. We went to one judge and presented the papers. Though the papers were in order he flatly refused to sign and waved us away saying, "You people are just trying to start something." Finally, the clerk of the Superior Court signed the forms, which certified our status as residents of the state of Georgia, but he said, "This doesn't mean that you are going to get in." As an afterthought, he added, "Course it doesn't mean you won't get in either."

All this talk made little sense to me. After all, I had gone to school with white students before. My family and I had lived in Alaska while my father was stationed there.

I recalled the first day I walked into class there. I was the only Negro student in the eighth grade, and except for a few smaller students in the first or second grades, the only Negro in the entire school. I thought about my first day in class in Alaska a long time after the clerk had left. The first person to speak to me that day had been a sixteen-year-old girl from Alabama. We became close friends from that day on.

There was a boy in the class, too, a Texan, who eagerly jumped at any opportunity to sing the praises of his native state and of Sam Rayburn, Speaker of the House—and, of course, a Texan.

The two years between the time when Hamp and I first applied and our eventual admittance to the campus at Athens were filled with official excuses and delays, legal hearings and conferences, rumors and counter rumors in the press and elsewhere. The net result always seemed to be to push us further from our goal.

So I had enrolled at Wayne State in Detroit to begin working toward the journalism major which the University of Georgia still denied me. Hamp enrolled at Morehouse and began his pre-med work there. As the lawyers argued back and forth and we became "temporary" students on our own respective campuses, there were times when I myself began to doubt that I would ever get my degree from Georgia rather than Wayne.

So it was on the afternoon of January 6, 1961, when I rushed into the dormitory at Wayne, grabbed my mail, and ran up to my room on the second floor, my only concern was getting into something comfortable before going to sorority meeting at five o'clock.

I had not been in my room ten minutes before I was called to answer the phone out in the hall. Expecting to hear one of my friends on the other end, I was surprised to hear instead an unfamiliar voice saying, "Congratulations!"

"For what?" I asked, completely in the dark.

The woman on the other end identified herself as a reporter for a New York paper. She told me that news had just come over the wires that Federal Judge [William] Bootle had ordered Hamp and me admitted to the University of Georgia.

By the time she managed to read the entire release to me, both of us were between laughter and tears. My caller brought both of us back to reality by pointing out that she had a story to write.

From that moment on there was no possibility of a moment of calm and quiet in which I could think about what was ahead. Downstairs the switchboard operator was soon swamped by calls. I grew even more confused as reporters seemed to be arriving by the carload.

In a way it was a relief to break away and rush off to sorority meeting. I arrived, bubbling over with elation, and began eagerly sharing the long-awaited news with my Delta sisters. But I found their reaction rather puzzling.

Instead of sharing in my jubilation, they became quiet and solemn.

It was not until thirty-six hours later, as I sat on the plane to Atlanta, that I began to realize what they had already seen. As I looked around the plane, wishing for someone with whom I could share my happiness, all the faces I saw were cold and unfamiliar. Gradually I began to realize what I had left behind, what might be ahead.

It was several days before the full impact of my friends' unspoken fears struck home. Hamp and I, struggling through throngs of reporters, photographers, and hostile or curious onlookers, managed to get registered for classes. Though not before we had been temporarily brought to a halt by a last-ditch injunction granted the lawyers for the state. We had begun to learn how to hear and not to hear harsh names, the threats, the jeering laughter, while being silently grateful for the occasional friendly greetings of a small minority and the fair-minded treatment of most of the university officials and faculty members.

It was uncomfortable to have to attend classes under guard, but we were already hopeful that this would soon be unnecessary. There had been crowds outside my dormitory on Tuesday night after my first full day of classes, but the firecrackers and the taunts had not prevented my going to sleep. After my classes on Wednesday, January 16, I came back to the dormitory prepared for more of the same, but almost totally unprepared for what was actually to happen.

It was about 2 p.m. when the detectives brought me back to my ground-floor room at Center Myers. There were crowds outside and in the lobby of the dormitory, but then there had been crowds since the first moment I arrived on campus. Mrs. Porter, the housemother, came down and told the girls not to stay too long because I was tired. She had advised me earlier that it would be best to have my dinner in my room that night. This, again, seemed only a normal precaution considering the circumstances.

It began getting dark around six o'clock. After the last of the girls had gone, everything became amazingly quiet inside the dorm. I picked up a book and tried to study, but then the firecrackers began popping outside as they had the night before. I decided there was nothing to do but go to bed, despite the racket outside. Mrs. Porter came in again to see if I had eaten and to ask how I was feeling. She suggested that I keep the blinds closed and stay away from the windows. "We expect some trouble," she said.

Later, as I went out into the hall for a drink of water, I caught a glimpse of the faculty members the students had named "The Baby-Sitting Crew." It seemed to me the group was larger than it had been the night before. I returned to my room. After a while the noise outside gradually grew louder and uglier.

Though I did not know it at the time, a hotly disputed basketball team last-minute defeat at the hands of Georgia Tech had helped to create anything but a mood of sweet reasonableness in the crowd that had marched from the gym to the dormitory.

Reading or sleeping was out of the question. I was in the first room of the duplex apartment. Suddenly there was a loud crash from the bedroom. Not stopping to think, I rushed in, only to be stopped in my tracks by another crash as a Coca-Cola bottle followed the brick which had ripped through the window a moment before. Jagged splinters of window glass and fragments of the bottle had spattered across my dress, slippers, and the skirts and blouses I had not yet had time to unpack.

Strangely enough I was not at all afraid at this moment. Instead I found myself thinking as I stood there in the middle of the wreckage, So this is how it is.

At this time I did not know that all of the lights in the dormitory had been turned out. With the rest of the building in darkness the three brightly lit windows of my apartment must have made a most inviting target for the mob out on the lawn.

I heard the dean's voice in the hall and called out to him, but he did not hear me. I met a campus patrolman in the hall and told him what had happened. As he went into my room to investigate I continued down the hall to the counselor's office a couple of doors away. There in the darkness I went to the window and looked out. All I could see was a moving mass, not a face that could be recognized as that of a separate person. Even the voices seemed to run together in one confusion of shouts and jeers.

Turning from the window, I saw that the partition between the counselor's room and the lobby was open. The crashing of glass and the screams of one girl on the floor above, who had been struck by a brick as she looked out of her window, had brought most of the girls into the lobby. Some of them passed back and forth, looking in to see how I was reacting to all this.

I realized it was nearing time for the eleven o'clock news and that my mother in Atlanta would be waiting up for it. I called her and told her that I was all right. Though I knew she could hear the noise in the background, she seemed relatively calm. But I could not get her to promise that she would go to bed at once, without waiting to look at the television news program.

After I hung up, one of the most genuine persons it has been my good luck to meet came down and began talking to me. Though it was clear that she herself was nervous, she did all she could under the circumstances to take my mind off what was going on.

This was anything but easy, since by now the hostility from outside was being echoed by some of those inside the dorm. Perhaps it was partially out of hysteria, or partially out of a reaction to the fact that the girl upstairs had been hurt. At any rate, a group of girls began tramping in a continuous circle, yelling insults first at me and then at the schoolmate who had come in to befriend me.

It was hard to sit there and listen to some of the things that were said about me without being able to answer. I was told I was about to become "a black martyr, getting fifty dollars a day for this"—a piece of news that would have considerably surprised my family.

The city police outside, after having waited in vain for the state patrol, finally resorted to tear gas and the crowd outside began to break up. The gas fumes began seeping into the dorm and the girls were told to change the linen on their beds. This prompted deliberately loud offers of a dime or quarter to "Charlayne" for changing the sheets of these same residents who professed to believe I was already being paid at a rate of over six dollars an hour, if figured on the basis of an eight-hour day.

My little friend was beginning to get drowsy, though she tried not to show it, and I suggested that she go to bed, assuring her that I would be all right. After she had left I wondered how many people, myself included, would have had the courage to do what she had done.

The housemother came in, looking worn from the ordeal of trying to console 150 overwrought girls. She gave me an orange. "It's a sweet orange," she said. "I think you might enjoy it."

Mrs. Porter left again as I began peeling the orange. Before I had finished, she was back again. This time she was serious and unsmiling.

Slowly, sympathetically, she told me that the dean had said I would have to leave. I was to be taken to Atlanta so that I would be safe—and so that the other girls in the building would also be safe.

I don't think I heard the rest of what she said. I suddenly felt totally sick and miserable. All I could think was I've failed, I've failed. I began to cry and, hard though I tried, I couldn't stop. Mrs. Porter reassuringly patted me on the arm and told me not to cry and not to worry. "Everything will be all right," she said. But, needless to say, I could not really believe this.

I packed quickly, not even bothering to remove the pieces of glass from my suitcase. Dean Williams came to my room and repeated what Mrs. Porter had said. Feeling totally empty inside, I followed him out of the room, stopping only to pick up my Madonna from the table beside the bed. Afterwards it bothered me to think that people looking at the pictures might mistakenly think I was crying because of fear. But at that moment I was too sick to care.

The girls were all quiet now. They were huddled together in the lobby as I came by. A few of them started to hiss, but they were immediately shushed into silence by the others.

The state troopers had finally arrived. As we came out into the chilly night air I saw the gray patrol cars parked at the curb. The husky, red-faced troopers in their gray uniforms and broad-brimmed hats were impassive and coolly official in speech and manner.

We stopped to pick up the dean of women at her residence. I remember saying something about being sorry to inconvenience her at that hour, to which she answered that she couldn't sleep from worrying about what was going on. When we arrived at the home at which Hamp was living, he was on the telephone, talking to Attorney Hollowell in Atlanta. Hamp wanted to drive his car home. I realized how near hysteria I was when I found myself insisting almost wildly that he leave his car and ride back with me in the patrol car.

As we sped along the often bumpy highway toward home, Hamp and I had little to say. Neither of us could get used to the idea that we had been "suspended." Yet what could we say or do about it?

I remember almost nothing of the trip itself. Before I knew it we were in Atlanta, turning into my block and pulling up in front of the porch where the man had stood so many long months ago telling me that I should give up the idea of trying to go to the University of Georgia.

The news of our coming had preceded us and a few close friends had gathered at the house. Most reassuring of all, my mother, her hair done up in braids, came out with open arms to welcome both Hamp and me and to take some of the sting out of our forced homecoming.

That night is behind me now, no more troublesome than any other bad dream remembered once in a while.

What I prefer remembering now are the court rulings that readmitted us, the decision not to close the university, the legislature's dropping of the state's segregation laws. But most of all I appreciate the courage of those faculty members, students, and citizens of Georgia who spoke out against mob rule and stood up for our right to attend classes in peace. It was because of all these things that there was no disturbance when I went into the cafeteria with three classmates the other day for my first meal in a university dining room.

Today as I walked from class, I met many students who nodded, or smiled, or greeted me in one way or another. I had watched one student as she approached from quite a distance. We smiled—and so did the little kitten she was carrying in the pocket of her sweater.

Later that day, back in the dorm, the housemother came down to bring me a letter which had a "postage due" on it. In her own sweet way, and with a charming smile, she inquired as to how my day had gone. Before long she was called to help one of "her girls" make a costume for a ball she was to attend that night. Assured that I was all right and not lonely, the dear lady went off to perform another of her thousand-and-one duties as mother to over 150 girls.

Just about that time there was a knock at the door and a tall, blonde, rather attractive girl came in with a bag of groceries in her arms. "Hi," she said, smiling. "Let's cook dinner. I'm starved."

Whatever sadness I felt was forgotten as we made a tossed salad. I began washing the lettuce, and she and another girl who had come along began slicing tomatoes and all sorts of vegetables that go to make up a tossed salad. We fried hamburgers too.

Dishes washed, food eaten, company gone, I was alone again. A little sad still, a little lonely. Perhaps. But at least I knew that I would not always be lonely. My friends at Wayne would always be my friends— though they'll graduate and go their various ways . . .

The room was a little too warm—it gets warm early in Georgia. So I went over and opened the window. New screens had replaced the ones through which the brick and Coke bottle ripped that night. There were no mobs on the lawn outside. No tear gas was in the air, nor patrol cars at the curb. Only beautifully landscaped grounds, green shrubbery, and, across the street, a lovely modernistic church whose steps— once crowded with onlookers, demonstrators, and cameramen—were deserted in the shadows of late afternoon. A couple strolled past, hand in hand, completely absorbed in each other.

Maybe I am poorly qualified to predict what tomorrow will be like—a tomorrow made up of days which may be weeks, months, and even years in coming . . . when Charlayne Hunter and Hamilton Holmes will be forgotten except by those who have come to know them as classmates or as friends.

But tomorrow, when some of the "problems" which complicate living together for human beings in Georgia, and the nation, have faded far into the background, not one, not two, but many Negro students will be able to walk through a Georgia corridor unnoticed except for their abilities or the impact of their individual personalities.

A Hundred-Fifteenth-Between-Lenox-and-Fifth

The New Yorker
FEBRUARY 20, 1965

I first knew exactly where I was going to spend the fifth summer of my life when my great-uncle, who had met my grandmother and me at Penn Station as we arrived from Georgia, said to the cabdriver, "A Hundred-Fifteenth-between-Lenox-and-Fifth." Through my mind ran the streets I knew back home—Brown Street, West Street, Short Street. And now, as we drove through green and winding Central Park, I could hear above the anxious conversation of my elders the strange staccato rhythm of "A Hundred-Fifteenth-between-Lenox-and-Fifth."

Central Park, a mass of tiny green patterns, reminded me of the country. About twenty miles below the little Georgia town where I lived lay acres of pine trees and apple, peach, plum, and pear orchards. In the summer, when my family went riding, we drove along red country roads, unpaved and dusty, where there were only distantly separated houses, and we would come upon clusters of plum bushes filled with tiny ripe yellow or red plums. We'd stop and fill bags with them and go on until we'd happen upon another such find. And we had to be careful of the little green snakes that lay in the road, happy until disturbed.

But in New York, once the green park gave way to the city, I saw nothing that reminded me of anything I'd ever seen before. All around me were tall buildings with expressionless faces and cold stone stoops. As far as I could see, there were no hills or sand or clay or grass. Nor were there blossoming dogwood trees—no trees at all to identify the season. It was June, and in Georgia the crops were flourishing in summer sun and rain. But when the wind blew cold on my face, I realized that summer came late to this place. It was definitely not a Georgia June day, on which I would begin the summer without shoes.

Later on, my impressions of 115th Street changed with the scene. My spirits lifted on the days when children my age played hopscotch, jumping in and out of chalk-drawn boxes on the sidewalk, or when they shot marbles that weren't really marbles but bottle tops weighted with candle wax. These children spoke a fast and musical foreign language that I did not understand, and even when they spoke English I often had to beg their pardon and ask them to repeat. Their names, instead of being Betty Jo and Mary Ruth and Sarah Ann—my friends back home—were Ana and Maria and Alaina. The boys were called Tonio and Mario and Felipe, instead of Jimmy and Eddie and Pete. In the summer, when it was hot, the neighborhood young cooled off in the water from fire hydrants opened by boys who appeared from around the corner and disappeared like wisps. The children also cooled off with the grape- and orange- and lemon-ice cones that had little effect and cost a nickel.

At home, we had no such havens from the heat. Instead, my friends and I crawled under houses, some of which were raised high off the ground by brick pillars, and looked for dust-covered bugs making their way in and out of the soft brown earth. We suffered from the heat only when there was nothing else to do, and when there was no one in the calaboose behind my house to go and talk to. We'd wander around the boxlike prison—altogether different from the red brick jail where the more dangerous criminals were held—trying to find some crack that would allow us to see inside. But the cracks were always too small, so we had to be content with voices from inside and a slither of light.

The icehouse, two blocks away, past the corner veterinarian's and up a dusty alley, was always a source of interest in hot weather. We were never allowed inside, so we only saw the huge blocks of ice being hauled out onto the ramp to be cut up and sold to individual purchasers, or to be carried away on trucks that had on their sides "ice" in dull-orange letters.

There were not many places to wander on 115th Street. The hallways leading into apartment buildings were darker and more forbidding than the calaboose back home. Absently, one day, I walked into a strange building and climbed the first flight of stairs, but when I looked behind me the doorway seemed small, and I was alone, so I left hastily. Above the street were always people in windows, looking down on me and everything that moved. On the street, out of the corner of my eye, I once saw a man sleeping in a basement cove. He was a stranger (nearly everyone was), and the children's squealing voices failed to wake him, but they gave me comfort.

The nights on 115th Street were more vivid than the days. In my great-uncle's house, part of the hallway casually became a closet and the part next to that a bedroom. The house was laid out like the train that had brought my grandmother and me there. As I lay in bed, the smell of leather luggage and mothballs made the night seem close around me. I missed the intimacy of the nights back home, where the soft and barely audible voices of my parents on the porch made something warm and lovely of the night, where a few dogs barked or howled, sounding far off and dreamlike. From my bedroom window there, I could see a dying mulberry tree, its strong trunk decaying after being struck by lightning, yet the tree remarkably bearing fruit for still another season; behind its sprawling limbs stood the old and rambling Emmanuel House, with one room after another being sealed off as its wonderful old people died. My grandmother grew up with the two Emmanuel sisters. Their father owned the barbershop where my grandfather worked. He also owned the town square. When Old Man Emmanuel died, the two sisters married and moved away and left my grandmother to take care of the house. The town square, populated by dozing old men, took care of itself.

The sirens on Lenox Avenue frightened me for a while, and would not let me sleep. One night, I tumbled out of bed and walked to the front of the house, where one window looked out. For as far as I could see, people were walking along the street or standing languidly around their stoops, careless of the night or the sounds it brought them. Near the corner, people, colored by red and green and orange and yellow neon lights, stood gesturing and laughing about some secret thing that I could never know. Somewhere along the street, a bell rang with predictable regularity. It was the ragman, who got little for his time. Perhaps the nights would have come easier for me and would have seemed more like home had there been more windows. At home, there were several windows in every room, and the houses next door were not too close. But the windows on 115th Street were blinded by the buildings next door—they were almost close enough to touch—so I could not see the stars.

Mornings came quietly to 115th Street, unlike those in my home, where, at daybreak, clucking hungry chickens and silent hungry rabbits had to be fed. Most of my mornings there—in fact, most of my days—I spent running. I cannot remember ever walking anywhere in summer. I remember occasionally sitting long enough to dress a paper doll, but my mother always made me come in just at early dark, so I had to run and run and run to stay ahead of the day.

When it came time to leave 115th Street, I had nearly forgotten what I'd left at home. Everything that I hadn't brought with me—bicycle, bottle dolls, tree swing—I had learned to do without. I had learned to make marbles out of bottle caps weighted with wax. It had not been a lonely summer. Maria and her friends and I promised to send cards at Christmas. Our parting wasn't sad. I left, promising to return the following summer.

I did not, however, keep that promise. My family moved, and also my great-uncle died. New discoveries and new impressions clouded even the clearest days in my memory. Despite an annual exchange of cards at Christmas that always began "Dear Friend," written in ink above the printed verse, I had all but forgotten my promise to come back until some seventeen years later, when, one warm evening, on

the way to a party on 138th Street, I passed a corner that looked familiar. One side of the street had changed; a row of brownstones had
been replaced by tall apartment buildings with a scattering of trees and
grass. On the left side of the street, the old buildings stood impassive.
The soft darkness, coming late in summer, made their lines look like
a Fauve pattern—blunt grays and reds and browns—against the sky.
Here was the point where, in my mind, Brown and West and Short
Streets, and 115th Street as well, all entertained children playing hopscotch or climbing a mulberry tree. I knew I was trying to unravel a
fusion of my childhood and the reality of the moment in which I stood.
I knew also that though my awareness of the world around me had increased with the years, I still held the memories and impressions of the
five-year-old I had been.

A Trip to Leverton

The New Yorker
APRIL 24, 1965

The sliding doors that led into my bedroom were difficult to open. One spring morning while I was at home in Georgia on a break from school, I was awakened by someone trying to open them, and when I called out, my grandmother answered. I was sleeping late, having the night before been with some friends from the local colleges who belonged to a student organization called the Committee on Appeal for Human Rights. They had worked late into the night preparing a manifesto, which they hoped would be printed in the next day's papers, stating the grievances, philosophy, intentions, and demands of the student movement. I had been in school in Michigan, a thousand miles away, when this phase of the social protest began with a sit-in in Greensboro, North Carolina, and I had kept up with the news of it because it was the first widely publicized movement by Negroes who were all of my generation. Soon after, however, I had become much more involved. My mother had called to tell me that first one, then another of my friends had been arrested and was in jail, refusing bond, for nonviolent protests. They were all students in one or another of the five small liberal arts colleges in the Atlanta University Center. I felt useless on my anonymous and detached campus. I remembered high school, especially two sisters from whom I was so inseparable that most people thought we were all three sisters. Together we attended every football game our team played. When we were not together, we kept in touch by phone, and what we talked about was of no special consequence to anyone but ourselves. We were taught that we were children of middle-class Americans, and although our parents were proud to be Negroes, the fact that we were Negroes was emphasized at school mainly during annual Negro History Week. Montgomery and Little Rock made some impression, though a brief one. But now, just one year after high school, the moment was theirs, with all its historic implications. The realities of the day transcended their comfortable surroundings, and I was not a part of their physical suffering. Our spring vacations did not coincide, and while I was home I tried to lend them support—mostly moral—wherever and whenever I could. And if my being with them late into the night didn't really help the movement, it nevertheless gave me a sense of participation. Through the rest of the night, I had tossed and turned, restless with excitement over the manifesto, and when my grandmother came in I was still caught up in the vigorous spirit of such sentences as "Today's youth will not sit by submissively while being denied all of the rights, privileges, and joys of life." So it was not hard for me to snap awake when she entered.

Sitting beside me on the bed, she said, "I know it's Saturday, but I thought maybe, while it's still early, you'd get up and drive me home. We could be back here before any of your friends are up."

By "home," she meant a place I shall call Leverton—the small Georgia city where she had met and married my grandfather and had reared their children. When he died, many years before I was born, he was buried there. Many of their old friends still lived in Leverton—widows and widowers for the most part. My own family had moved from Leverton ten years before, and my grandmother, who had always lived with us, halfheartedly came, too. But for years she found many reasons, many memories, to take her back to Leverton almost every weekend.

When we first moved away, she traveled the thirty-six miles by bus. She was independent and healthy, and preferred going alone so that she could have the time all to herself. In her younger days, she was tall and stout, with steel-gray eyes and long, thin hair that reached below her waist. Most of the time, she wore it in two braids wrapped around the back of her head in a bun. She was self-consciously a Negro, although anyone who didn't know her would have thought from her fair appearance that she was white. She traveled quite a bit, and during her days of fierce loyalty to the Brooklyn Dodgers she and I would sometimes come to New York in the summer to see them play at Ebbets Field. She never allowed herself to be bored.

When she went to Leverton, her day followed a pretty standard pattern. First, she usually went to visit an invalid friend, whose favorite fruit was kumquats, and because they were difficult to get in Leverton my grandmother would take her a pound or two. Later, my grandmother would walk halfway across the town to see Mr. William Long (Will to his friends), to whom she took the week's newspapers, which were in short supply in Leverton, and the Negro magazines, such as *Crisis* and *Ebony*, in equally short supply.

Black and smooth as an onyx, and always clad in Liberty Bell overalls, Mr. Will was soft-spoken and a man of very few words. But he was good-natured and generous, and a little more talkative than usual during my grandmother's brief visits. From his house, she would gradually make her way to her church, about six blocks away. She took flowers for the pulpit, and articles on Negro history for the Sunday school bulletin board. She also checked the board to find out which of the members were ill, and made mental notes to send cards if they lived too far away for her to get by to see them. If the minister, who lived out of town, was there, she would leave a contribution with him. If not, she'd leave it with one of the deacons. And every few weeks she would, near the end of her rounds, deposit at the bus station her shopping bag full of fresh vegetables from Mr. Will's garden, then walk from there to the edge of town, where a narrow, crooked path led into the cemetery.

She would pass the two or three family vaults and the hundreds of plain white, square Georgia-marble headstones—graves of former Leverton soldiers who had died either defending the Confederacy against the Yankees or defending the country against foreign enemies. She would walk past those graves on a single path through neatly laid-out plots to the end of the cemetery, where a thick row of hedges and un-contained growth distinctly cut off the main all-white cemetery and concealed from sight all that was behind it. Through a small opening in this thicket, my grandmother would make her way until she found another path, strewn with dead, brown grass and dry, severed tree branches that had been cut in the well-kept part of the cemetery and flung carelessly over the hedge border. This accumulation, along with spreading kudzu and other creeping things, had, over the years, com-pletely covered the unattended and sunken graves back there except for my grandmother's plot and one or two others.

For some years past, the green wilderness that grew on the far side of these graves had been too dense to see through, but in recent months that land had been cleared and houses had been built almost up to the graves. A thin, insubstantial wire fence with intermingling vines provided the only protection from intruders. My grandmother had, for some time, hired Mr. Will to keep the grass and hedges cut around her plot, and he had voluntarily erected a white picket fence around the square cubicle to set off its border of evergreens. He had also planted a sapling in the left-hand corner, just below the foot of my grandfather's grave.

Although Mr. Will was the only person who tended the plot, the city nevertheless billed my grandmother monthly for upkeep. She had never complained about this, and had paid the sum regularly. She had allowed my mother to buy money orders and to keep in a lockbox the money-order stubs, along with the deeds, insurance policies, and rec-ords of every monetary transaction she had ever carried out. I had no doubt whatever that no oversight in payment had occurred. Yet in the past, whenever my grandmother had visited the lot, it was in almost as bad shape as the other neglected graves. Finally, after many months, she had assumed that the city did not intend to clean the lot, and it was then that she had hired Mr. Will. The Friday before my grandmother asked me to take her to Leverton, she showed me a bill she had got from the city of Leverton for monthly ground maintenance of her cem-etery plot, along with a notice that unless the bill was paid the property would be seized by the city. It was to see about this whole matter that she wanted me to take her to Leverton.

Sometime before this, when my grandmother was about seventy-eight years old, the first signs of arteriosclerosis had appeared, in the form of brief memory lapses. During some of these lapses, my mother, who had been closer to her than anyone else since my grandfather died, became the object of her deep distrust and harsh verbal attacks. The doctor had warned my mother to expect this, and to expect not to be recognized for short—or even for long—periods of time. He explained that sometimes my grandmother's memory would be faultless and at other times the realities of life, if not completely abandoned, would be arranged in complicated fantasies, and that to try to reason with her then would be a frustrating and unhappy experience. Nevertheless, Mother always tried to make things clear to my grandmother, and was seldom quite able to accept completely her periods of irrationality.

The nights were harder on my grandmother than the days. Once, for several nights in succession she called out to my mother and, thinking she was someone else, told her that her daughter had taken her every night to a different house to sleep among strangers. "I sleep in a house like this, but it's not my own," she'd say. "I don't like it. I don't know anyone here. Please take me home." When she could not go back to sleep, she would ask for a small glass of bourbon, and, as my mother had cleared this with the doctor, she would give it to her. Sometimes it quieted her; other times my mother would have to sit with her until she fell asleep.

My grandmother had always handled money efficiently, but now she misplaced quite a lot of it. The doctor suggested that my mother take out guardianship papers, so that she would have entire charge of the money, but this idea didn't appeal to my mother, who felt that to do something that might in some way justify my grandmother's occasional accusations would be more than she could bear. So, in spite of the doctor's advice, my grandmother was allowed to keep her money. This often led us on wild searches for sums ranging from one dollar to one hundred. And because we were all suspect until we found it, we were all equally eager to locate it.

Oddly enough, the person who provided the most relief for us in this difficult situation was usually my grandmother herself. Often, she would come into a room a few minutes after telling us of something that had never really happened and say, "You know, I do the craziest things sometimes. I'm really losing my mind." And, speaking to my mother for perhaps the first time in three or four days, she would clear up the whole confusion, set the details in order, and laugh so hard at her previous fantasy as to make us all laugh with her in relief. Later, she would most likely send for the evening paper and read it from front to back, occasionally commenting quite lucidly on some item she thought was of interest. And so I was easily persuaded to take her to Leverton that Saturday, not only because my mother was fearful of her going out alone but also because my grandmother was more coherent than she had been in several days. I thought it would be good for her to have something to occupy her mind.

She had already read the Saturday morning paper when she came into my bedroom. "The paper predicts showers, but I don't see a single cloud," she said. And as we pulled out onto the freeway at a little after eleven, the sun was young and bright, and where it shone on dew-laden fields of green wheat or acres of red clover the reflection was almost blinding. Few cars were traveling in our direction. Most of them were coming from the small towns along the way, their drivers headed for a day's labor in the city. We passed red-and-white Burma-Shave signs with slogans we both knew from memory. The long, white, unobstructed stretches of highway led us along smoothly. Sometimes I played the radio and we would listen without talking. But about fifteen miles out of the city the reception became poor, and I had to turn it off.

"The cemetery lot was a gift," my grandmother suddenly said, speaking almost as if we had been having a conversation all along. "My mother was a slave before I was born, and the man whose farm she lived on, Mr. John Robert Henry, gave it to her just before he died.

Later, she was freed and the people on the farm knew about the gift. They didn't need to see any legal papers as long as Mr. John Robert Henry had given his word. And they knew he had. My mother gave me the land later on, and I plan to tell them at the City Building just how it all happened. I know I can work it all out," she concluded, full of confidence in the relationship between slave and master.

I was bothered by her story for many reasons, the chief of which was that I didn't have any respect for any slaveholder, dead or not, and to me his word meant nothing. But my grandmother seemed perfectly satisfied that her explanation would be acceptable to the authorities, so for the time being I let the matter rest.

Driving through the center of Leverton, I was reminded of the pictures on church fans in which a devout young white Christian family is shown walking hand in hand up a pebbled path to a little white church on a hill. The town was laid out in a perfect circle around a square that featured the most revered of its long-dead heroes, General Lever, posed in an oratorical gesture atop a pedestal overlooking gray pigeons and white spittoons. My grandmother had an easy acquaintance with all the townspeople, including the sheriff and the local politicians, who had all been patrons of my grandfather's barbershop. Though polite, and probably in most cases decent enough to their wives, these men had the annoying habit of addressing every Negro, regardless of age, by his or her first name, so, whenever possible, I tried to avoid them.

Farther along, we passed the Methodist church—a modest white edifice with four Doric columns on its porch. No Negro had ever seen the inside of it, not even to clean it, and doubtless none ever would. We passed a dead-end street that I had never seen before, and my grandmother told me that this was where the new City Building was. First, however, she wanted to go by the cemetery. I drove there, but as we came to the road that wound around it I saw that a deep washed-out gutter would make it impossible to reach the hedge border in the car. I stopped just short of the gutter, and my grandmother and I started to cross it on foot. She was already ahead of me, but she could not get across alone. I took her by the arm and, balancing myself against a fallen branch, boosted her forward, and in a moment we had gone in through the narrow entrance.

Nothing had changed since my last visit there. A cloud of red dust from the disturbed hedges enveloped us and settled in our noses and on our clothes, and the high, decumbent grass made our legs and arms itch and sting. Through the growth, we made our way to my grandfather's grave and found hardly a grain of sand out of its proper place. In the left-hand corner was a budding little tree, surrounded by neatly blocked hedges and green grass that looked like a carpet. The simple headstone that marked the grave was clean and white, and the mound of earth beneath it was neat and solid. In this peaceful space, one could momentarily shut out the ugly jungle that surrounded it, but the bark of a dog in an adjoining backyard was ferocious and wild as he thrust himself at us against the fence. The dust and heat rising around us and the dog's barking and lunging made me anxious and impatient, and I persuaded my grandmother to leave.

A few minutes later, driving again, we reached the dead-end street and drew up in front of a new, one-story red brick building surrounded by a gravel walkway. This was the place the bill and notice had come from. I had intended to remain in the car, but when my grandmother got out she turned as if she expected me to follow.

There was no one ahead of us inside. The only person in the room was the clerk, a young woman not much older than I.

"That's Ella Mae Stevens," my grandmother whispered to me. "I remember when she was born."

Ella Mae Stevens looked up from her desk, and my grandmother, pulling the city's letter from her handbag, said, "Good morning, Miss Stevens. I'm Frances Wilson, and I'd like to see someone about a notice I received from the city this week."

Without getting up, Ella Mae Stevens told my grandmother to be seated, and continued riffling through papers on her desk. After about fifteen minutes, in which neither my grandmother nor I spoke, Ella Mae Stevens went out of the room and in a few minutes came back carrying a manila folder. "Now, Frankie," she said, "let's see what your trouble is."

My grandmother gathered up her black handbag and gray gloves from her lap and started over to the counter that separated the office from the reception area. "I received this notice—" she began.

"Yes, I know," Ella Mae Stevens said. "Have you got your proof of ownership?"

"The man who gave my mother the property many years ago was Mr. John Robert Henry."

"You have any papers or anything like that?"

"The land was a gift," my grandmother said, "and no one has ever questioned us about it. Mr. John Robert Henry was well known in this town. His father—"

"Well, Frankie," Ella Mae Stevens drawled, shaking her head, "all I know is I'm supposed to tell you you're going to have to pay the city to keep this lot up, or you might have some trouble."

"But just this morning I went over there and the city hasn't done anything for my property," my grandmother said, raising her voice a little.

"Your lot's clean, isn't it?"

"Yes, but Mr. Will is the one who—"

"Well, I don't know about all that, but I do know that you're going to have to pay this bill and continue to pay the city as long as you claim to hold title to the property."

As I stood there, hardly able to contain myself, I thought I could see what the city was driving at through Ella Mae Stevens. After all, the other people who owned cemetery land behind the hedge border had allowed their property to decline. Most of the Negroes in Leverton could ill afford to pay even the small amount of money the city was asking to keep up the lots. Nor would they dare question the city fathers if, when the Negroes couldn't pay, their land was taken from them. It was obvious that the city wanted the land, possibly to expand the main cemetery for whites only, or possibly to make pleasanter backyards or convenient driveways for the people, the sheriff included, who owned newly built houses on the other side. At any rate, it was clear that the city wanted to do away with the graves behind the hedge border.

I was about to suggest that my grandmother come away with me and get a lawyer when I realized what the city of Leverton had to offer in that line—homegrown lawyers and magistrates, loyal to their constituents and to the people with whom they'd grown up. In addition to that, my grandmother had only the word of Mr. John Robert Henry, and, besides, she was not really up to any complicated legal involvement. I remained silent, knowing that if I interfered my grandmother would be upset. Yet how could I not explain that everything my friends, whom she had watched grow up—the ones she prayed for when they went on Freedom Rides, the ones she worried over when they marched on picket lines, the ones who daily faced the screaming, hostile crowds in front of stores with segregated lunch counters, the same people she recognized on television and in the newspapers as my friends—everything they stood for was being compromised as I stood there silent.

I watched my grandmother as she stood for a few minutes with her fingertips tensely planted on the edge of the counter. Finally, she turned to me and said, "I guess we'd better go."

Without looking at my grandmother, the clerk handed the bill back to her and said, "All right, Frankie, it's up to you."

As we turned to leave, my grandmother accidentally dropped her handbag on the floor. I stooped to pick it up, and she walked on. When I got to the door, she was having difficulty getting it open. I took her by the arm and helped her outside. From the narrow porch of the building, we could see the cemetery. The smell of freshly cut grass traveled easily through the soft morning air. We got back in the car, and I turned it around and headed for the road that led to Mr. Will's house.

"No, let's not go there today," my grandmother said. "I'm a little tired, and, besides, I think I'd like to go home."

I could think of nothing to say that would not have been an angry denunciation of the city and everything in it. But I knew that words like that would not have comforted my grandmother, who knew and loved every inch of the town and all the memories it held. I drove fast through Leverton, but a red traffic light brought me to a screeching halt in front of the courthouse. On the steps sat men whose posture and expression were all the same. They looked neither forward nor backward, and not even the sound of the screaming automobile tires stirred them from their poses.

I was well out of town before I looked at my grandmother, so silent and so old. I wanted to speak to her, but I did not want to intrude upon her thoughts, whatever and wherever they were. The day became quite warm. We stopped for gas and a Coke at a small filling station next to a wide field with grazing sheep—a rare sight in that area. I handed my grandmother her Coke, and she wrapped her white linen handkerchief around it because the ice-cold bottle chilled her thin hands. She looked out abstractedly at the sheep, but I was not sure whether she really saw them or not.

When we got home, we had a late lunch, and my grandmother went to take a nap—a luxury she had never allowed herself until recently. I took this time to tell my mother what had happened on our trip, sparing her none of the exhausting details of my own feelings. She didn't seem surprised, and I found her reassuringly sympathetic as I told her of my anguish over not having interceded at the City Building. "At any rate," she said, "you've satisfied your grandmother by taking her down there, and now that's all behind."

Later, when the day reached evening, I went out for an early edition of the Sunday paper. The governor was in the headlines. He had said that the students' manifesto had not been written by students in the Georgia school system—or even adults in this country, for that matter.

I had just gone back into the house and settled myself in the den along with my mother when I heard my grandmother coming down the hall to join us. Her steps were hard and sure, and when she entered the room she looked rested. "I've slept quite a long while," she said to us. "Longer than I intended. Guess I'll have to do it next week."

"Do what?" I asked.

"Well," she said, "I had planned to ask you to take me to Leverton to see about a bill the city sent me yesterday. But it's too late today. The City Building is surely already closed. Maybe next week. Early on Saturday morning we'll go. Yes, I think next week will do fine."

After Nine Years

A Homecoming for the First Black Girl
at the University of Georgia

New York Times
JANUARY 25, 1970

ATHENS, Ga.—Several days after Hamilton (Hamp) Holmes and I entered the University of Georgia in 1961 under court order as its first two black students, I sat in a world history class, fighting desperately to stay awake and avoid confirming the stereotype that all blacks are lazy. The drowsiness was the result of my first few days on campus when white students, protesting our admission, rioted outside my dormitory.

Shortly after a brick and bottle had shattered the window in my room, sending chunks of broken glass within a foot of where I was standing, Hamilton, who lived off campus, and I were suspended for our "own safety." Our lawyers got the judge who had ordered us in to order us readmitted, but the girls who lived above me—I was the sole resident on the first floor—continued for a long time to pound the floor, night after night, late into the night, and I suffered the physical and mental exhaustion of those first few days throughout the winter quarter.

Somehow, it was always in this midmorning history class that I would find myself embarrassed as my head drooped and eyes closed.

Almost nine years later, during my first visit to the campus since graduation, I entered that same classroom—this time wide awake, and found not a course in world history, but one in African history, part of a new black studies program; and not one exhausted black girl, but five outspoken black men and women among the students and a young black man, with a heavy Afro haircut and wearing a turtleneck sweater, teaching the course. By the end of the hour, as the white students sat quietly taking notes, the black instructor was acting as referee for two of the black students who were engaged in a vehement clash of opinion on the subject of pan-Africanism.

"You won't believe your eyes when you see the changes," a Georgia English professor had told me when I called her from New York to say that I was coming to Athens. Then the professor, who, when I was a student, had lived in an apartment directly across the street, which she offered as a refuge whenever I needed it, went on to issue a warning: "Come on down; just remember the stir you caused last time."

We both laughed. Nonetheless, as I stepped off the bus at the dingy little station a block from the campus, I felt a slight wave of anxiety sweep over me. But before I could dwell on that, I heard someone call my name. Looking around, I saw a familiar face, although I couldn't place it.

"I thought it was you," the man said, extending his hand. "I'm Pete Sasser from the journalism school." Pete had been a student there when I entered, and although I was a journalism major, I had little contact with the students when I was there, and have had almost none since I graduated. Pete said he was on the faculty now, and invited me over to see the new journalism school. I told him that I had heard that the dean had retired, but that I hadn't known that the old building had been retired, too. We settled on three o'clock, which would leave me time to have lunch with some professor friends and to get from them some suggestions about whom I should see this time around. I had my own ideas about whom I did *not* want to see.

Again, at lunch, I was told how impressed I would be with the changes. One of the group, my former classics professor, Ed Best, had just returned from the University of Alabama, where he had served as a judge in the Miss Homecoming contest. Among the contestants, he told me, were a Japanese girl and a black girl with an Afro, and they both finished in the top three, although Alabama was not ready for either one to reign as queen.

"You won't find anything like that here," Dr. Best said, "but I do think you'll find some things have changed."

After lunch, armed with a list of other names and places, I left the Holiday Inn and headed across the street to the first building I had ever set foot in at the university to have a talk with the new acting dean of student affairs, a young white Alabamian named O. Suthern Sims.

On my way over, I caught a glimpse of the Kappa Alpha house. It had been one of several trouble spots which I generally tried to avoid. The fraternity brothers of KA could always be counted on to yell at least one mouthful of obscenities if Hamp or I was passing by their house. Most of the time, we pretended to ignore them.

But every now and then, they would rile the normally calm, easy-going Hamp, and he would say, "Just look at the way they treat that flag they're supposed to love so much," referring to the Confederate flag. "They couldn't be serious the way they leave it out in all kinds of wind and rain." Even though it was a symbol of disgust to both of us, I think Hamp would have respected them a little more if they had shown some respect for what they were supposed to cherish. Now, there it was, tattered and rotting, but still flying.

Across the street and inside the academic building where Hamp and I had registered for our first classes, Dean Sims was a welcome change from the tight-jawed, closed-minded segregationists who preceded him. Tall and slender and articulate, he greeted me warmly and said he hoped I had so far found the university to be a lot different from what it had been when I first came. I smiled noncommittally because I had not yet talked with any of the black students on campus, and urged him, instead, to tell me if he thought it had.

"We've now moved almost 180 degrees in regard to the psychology of in loco parentis," he said, and proceeded to outline the liberalization that had taken place in rules for students, particularly women, which had prohibited them from living off campus, staying out past 11 p.m. and wearing slacks. I found all this interesting, since along with the loosening up had come an end to the offices of dean of men and dean of women—in my years as a student there, the very personification of in loco parentis, particularly for Hamp and me, their unwanted children.

When after two and a half years in one isolated room in a freshman dormitory, I had asked for a transfer to an upper-class dorm, it was the dean of women's office that said it couldn't be done—not because of segregation, but out of "consideration." Dean Edith Stallings told Calvin Trillin, a friend who helped me maintain my sanity while covering my entrance and who came back later to write a book about it: "We don't like to put any student in a position where she's not wanted. It's not race."

Her counterpart, Dean William E. Tate, took much of the credit for "protecting" Hamp and me during our stay there. I never had much to say to him, nor he to me, but he always seemed quite fond of Hamp. I was told that he often spoke of "Holmes," telling of Hamp's initiation into Phi Beta Kappa—an invitation which Tate himself extended by letter—as if he were his own.

By the end of this year, both will have been retired. "Tate has accepted this thing beautifully," Sims said. "He has a truly wonderful capacity to adapt."

And what about the capacity of the university to adapt to the presence of black students beyond the number of two, and without pressure from the courts?

Suthern Sims paused briefly, then said: "I think you can think of the integration of blacks into the university in two ways—legally and attitudinally. There is no question in terms of all the proper compliances. I do not believe you can find any forms of racial segregation that you can take any legal action against. I've looked for it, especially in student affairs. It's just not there."

He went on to outline the areas governed by federal compliance regulations: "We will not list an apartment or job unless a compliance form is signed. We don't have any black rooms like they once had. To the best of my knowledge that stopped in '67." (My mind flashed back to my senior year when I had wanted Donald Hollowell, our lawyer, to go back to court for an order to desegregate the dorms. At that time, he had so many civil rights cases pending, including some of Dr. Martin Luther King's, that he just didn't have the time and probably thought it wasn't worth it. I think the black students who eventually did have to push it five years later would have disagreed.)

In addition, Sims pointed out, of a total of two hundred resident advisers—young women who live in the dorms, are paid $650 a year, and offer nonprofessional guidance to their fellow students—five are black. "We hired every one that applied," Sims said, not altogether unconscious of the two ways in which the remark could be taken.

"As to attitude," Sims said, slowing down a little, "I can't measure it." Then he brought up the subject of the Black Student Union. In nine years, the university population has increased from about 7,200 students to about 18,000, with the number of blacks growing from two to "approximately 125" (no one admits to knowing for sure just how many black students there are). About 75 blacks are undergraduates, and of the total—including graduate students—about 30 belong to the BSU. For two consecutive years, the group has presented demands to the university administration.

"I think what they're really talking about is attitude, and this is a tough one," Sims said. "This might sound awfully inept, but I think it's improving. This current generation is the finest generation of college students that this country has ever seen. They've been more right about more issues than any before them. And here is where I think you'll find the meshing of legality and attitude."

He continued: "Our blacks come in and they're experiencing

disgust and hostility, and it becomes really a paradox—'You do something about it now,' they say. But we can't just unilaterally rule against attitude. That's a fascist state." Back to 1961, in my memory: the white students who vowed not to accept desegregation, despite the fact that it was "being shoved down our throats." "You can't legislate morality," they were fond of saying.

Sims's personal assessment of the BSU was, in general, favorable. He was but one of several administrators who conceded that without its pressure, some of the changes that were taking place within the university "probably wouldn't have happened so fast."

"I think I understand what they want," Sims said finally. "They want role models, not tokens." Then he pointed out what he considered gains in that area—blacks hold clerical positions throughout the university; there is even one in administration; there are black "public safety officers." There are the five resident advisers.

But there were some ideas proposed by the BSU that Dean Sims simply could not reconcile with his own personal code. He said they had asked for a separate dormitory and had refused to bring the organization officially on campus because they did not want to sign the compliance.

"They told me frankly that, if they signed the compliance, they'd have to let whites in, and they don't want that. I make no bones about it. I'm an integrationist, not a separatist, because if you buy the separatist bag in the South, you positively reinforce the white supremacists. And to buy that would be to step back seventy-five years."

Next day, I stopped by the office of the dean of arts and sciences. He was not in, so I talked briefly with his assistant, Dr. Charles Wynes. Dr. Wynes had been in the history department when I was a student; since then, he has written a book, *The Negro in America Since 1865*.

Dr. Wynes said that the university has really moved fast over the past few years. As evidence of the growth, he cited an appropriation by the state legislature to increase the faculty by more than five hundred, citing it as "a breakthrough for educational excellence."

As I stood to leave, it occurred to me to ask Dr. Wynes how many of the five hundred new faculty members were blacks. He said there was one, Dr. Richard Graham, a musical therapist.

My next stop was at the building where Dean Sims had told me I could find Ben Colebert, a young black who is also a kind of first. Although he is a graduate student in the art department, he is the first black admissions counselor, and it is his job to travel throughout the state to recruit black students.

A handsome medium brown, with a quiet Afro, Colebert, who is twenty-seven, moved with ease in what I was surprised to find was the office of M. O. Phelps. At the time Hamp and I were trying to get in, Phelps was freshman admissions counselor. I didn't have any problems with him in person, but he was one of a panel of three administrators who decided, on the basis of their interview with Hamp, that he was "not a suitable candidate" for admission.

In addition to the fact that he did not say "Sir," they said that he slumped in his chair, gave short answers to their questions, mumbled when he spoke, and left them with "some doubt about his truthfulness." Hamp had a slight speech impediment, which often caused him to stutter or hesitate before he spoke.

Colebert said Phelps "admitted he had some prejudices," but that among the many dinner invitations he and his wife had received was one from Phelps.

"They really smoked me over," Ben said when I asked how he got the job. "I think they wanted to see how militant I was, but right away knew I was the kind of nigger they wanted. In 1959, I did sit-ins, when I was an undergraduate at Savannah State. But that was a decade ago, and don't have my master's yet, so I made myself very attractive to them."

Ben and I are the same age, and when he was sitting in at lunch counters in Savannah, I had just applied to the university. By the time I was admitted, it was 1961, and Ben, like me, would have been a sophomore. But he told me during my visit that he was encountering among black high school students in the state the same problem he had had—as late as the year we graduated: "I simply didn't know the school existed, and neither do they."

Once they know, there is the problem of money. Even though the university is state supported, expenses for an on-campus student can be $2,000 a year or more. "It does cost a lot of money," Ben said, "but there's a lot in this institution that needs to be channeled into the black community. The black community pays taxes, and supports this school." He added that 80 percent of the black students at the university receive either work-study or graduate assistantships or federal aid. "If you have the guts to come here in the first place, then you got it made," he said.

(That wasn't necessarily so in my case, despite the rumor that the NAACP was paying me fifty dollars a day. If I had been in it for the money that would hardly have been enough, but the rumor was totally groundless. The NAACP Legal Defense and Educational Fund donated its talents to fight our legal battles—but its support ended there, as it should have. Carl Holman, my closest friend, now a vice president of the National Urban Coalition, who was then a professor at Clark College and the editor of the *Atlanta Inquirer*, managed each quarter through friends to wrangle some money from such groups as the Elks of Memphis, who paid the eighty-three dollars a quarter or thereabouts for my room in the dormitory. And sometimes I made money speaking, although most of those engagements were for church groups that paid with "Praise the Lord" and "God bless you."

It never occurred to me to apply for a job on campus, although I had worked at Wayne State University before I transferred. And I'm not sure that with all the other pressures at that time I would have been able to handle a job, too. Nor did I think of applying for any kind of loan or aid. Having had to force my way in, I guess I couldn't imagine their doing anything to help me stay.)

Admission requirements have stood in the way of black applicants, according to Ben Colebert. For starters, a combined score of 900 on the nationwide Scholastic Aptitude Test (SAT) is required, in addition to a B-plus average. "The black school system just hasn't been geared toward passing these tests," he explained. "In a dual school system, black kids don't usually even come out with a foreign language. These tests are geared for kids who go to white, middle-class high schools. If a black kid does succeed in making 900 on the SAT, you know he could have made 1,500 with the proper background."

Most white students are, in addition, more test-conscious than blacks, having prepared for at least a couple of years for the SAT by taking old tests and using books with prepared tests in them. My high school was one of the few black schools that did that when I was preparing for college. We had sessions for several weeks, on Saturday mornings, but my scores were still horrible. Fortunately, I never made below a B in any of my courses, and graduated third in my class. This, according to Colebert, would make a difference today, even with a low score.

At present, the mean score for the entire university for boys is 1,050, and for girls, about 1,060. "Less than half of one percent" of the black students, according to Colebert, have even a 900 score. Their presence is the result of an admissions committee's recommendations. "The university does make some concessions," Colebert said.

I asked him about the football players—whites, many of whom could barely speak English.

Surely they didn't have 900 SAT scores. Colebert laughed. "We don't get into that," he said.

Because of inferior preparation, many black students have difficulties with their courses, particularly English—a bane to most Southern freshmen, regardless of color. Many of them flunked out. The BSU demanded that they be readmitted, and that some special counseling program be set up. President Fred C. Davison responded in this way: "The admission and readmission policies of the university are conducted without regard to race. The proposal to readmit all black students who have flunked out of the university is not only educationally unsound but it, too, could be challenged on the grounds of racial discrimination. Moreover, such a policy would result in a serious impairment of academic standards of the university."

Ben does not think that the liberal grants to black students will

continue for long—"particularly if they get a lot of black students."
However, he plans to continue recruiting. "It is ironic," he said as I was
leaving, "that now that the University of Georgia is concerned with
admitting black students, comes the insurgence of pride in black institutions and black environments."

"How do you deal with that?" I asked.

"The only thing I tell them is that you get more awareness of being
black here than in a black institution where it's taken for granted." It
was a theme that I later heard expressed again and again by black students here.

Gradually, I made my way to the history department, which houses
the black studies program. I knew that there I would get not only some
idea about the program, but also would probably run into some of the
black students. Although 125 certainly increases the odds of coming
across a black student, they still manage to get lost on the sprawling
campus among 18,000 whites.

While waiting for Dr. David Foley, the young white professor
in charge of the program, I looked at the paper. That morning, the
Athens Daily News carried the headline: "Black Studies Panel Hears
Local Professor," with a story out of Atlanta, which began: "While
most speakers agreed Monday that more emphasis on black studies is
needed in the state's public schools, a University of Georgia department head said this might result in building 'feelings of superiority
among blacks.'" The man, who was quoted later in the story as saying
that Negro history taught distinctly "could backfire badly," is chairman
of the social studies department.

Dr. Foley, who taught for three years at the University of Sierra Le-
one, turned out to be pleasant, enthusiastic, and intensely pleased with
himself. "In most universities," he said, "whites ignore the existence
of black culture. They're not anti—they just spend their time saying,
'What a wonderful fellow I am.' This is more degrading than anything.
I don't know whether a black would like somebody to just come up and
whack 'im one or ignore him."

Foley feels that students "cannot understand the demands or aspirations of Afro Americans without an understanding of the black man as the inheritor of African culture." As for his own preparation, he said, "I'd like to think my two years in Africa helped me to rap here."

Downstairs, in an African history classroom, Anderson Williams, a young black graduate assistant who had just passed his PhD orals, was lecturing on the "strong indigenous civilization in Africa that began a thousand years before the Europeans came to the continent."

After the class ended, I introduced myself to the black students sitting in front of me, and invited them to have lunch with me. Anderson Williams joined us, and we drove to a steak house in town—one of many that did not serve black people when I graduated.

On the way out, Benny Roberson, a junior from Athens, majoring in anthropology, started to chuckle. "Charlayne Hunter. You know how I remember you so well? The day you entered Georgia and all that stuff was going on with you, I started getting ready to go to town, and my mamma said, Boy, you are not going nowhere near that town today. And I sat back down."

"When I first came here," said Joe Sales, a handsome senior from Columbus, Georgia, who reminded me of Hamp, "I knew every black student on the yard, but not now."

Russell Williams, a graduate student who had been at the university off and on, having started his freshman year when I was a senior, concurred, and added, "There are even some black students nobody knows."

They explained that, although they and about thirty other black students belonged to the BSU, the majority did not. And while, they said, many of those who were not members sympathized, there were others who would not have anything to do with them.

Then Joe said: "You see, there's a basic division between those students who come from predominantly black schools and people who went to a white high school. The ones who went to a white high school are more willing to relate."

"Still," Russell interjected, "even those who participate are, at best, being tolerated. Those are the ones who catch it from both ends." It was clear that my luncheon companions had no plans to get involved in university life or activities. I asked why. They all started to speak at once. Joe, who emerged strongest, said, "We tried it, but after all this time, we still feel like aliens in a strange land."

They explained that the BSU was formed in 1967 because of that. "At first," Joe continued, "it just provided a social outlet—black-oriented functions. We would all meet at Bob Benham's house and party. It got to be known as 'the Black House.'"

Benham, now in his last year of law school, had been president of the BSU when it presented a list of twenty-two demands to the university—the first step the BSU took after its members realized that "partying all the time wasn't going to lead to any change in our lives within the university."

"The first year, we were concerned with getting a fair break," Joe explained. "We asked for things like an end to discrimination in housing—black people always ended up in the same rooms—and an end to discrimination in employment—as usual, they try to token you to death. We asked for a wider range of things because the whole idea was not just to represent the militants, but to represent a wide range of political opinion. Like, I'm not interested in fraternities, but the brother here is."

In that connection they asked for a ban on racist fraternities—specifically KA. "There are still incidents in front of that house," they told me. "Black women are constantly subjected to all kinds of verbal abuse and getting things thrown at them."

During the next year, an expanded set of demands was presented to the university—some in the same vein as the previous year, but some more militant. Some of their optimism had waned. A young freshman from Atlanta, James Hurley, had gone out for football. He made the freshman team, the Bullpups, but as the year wore on and he began looking with anticipation toward playing with the Bulldogs, a sympathetic coach called him aside one day and told him that Georgia would probably dress him, but that if he was really serious about playing football, he'd better look elsewhere. (Subsequently, Vanderbilt offered him a scholarship—and a chance to play—and he took it.)

Among the new demands that year was one for the establishment of a black dormitory. "If asking for an end to discrimination in housing one year, and a black dormitory the next sounds contradictory, it's not," Joe said. Then, talking all at once, they said that the demand was the logical next step to take with a university that says one thing, but does another.

Earlier, Ben Colebert had said it bothered him that some black students would want to request such a thing, but added, "The university should spend less of its energies condemning it, and more trying to find out why they want it." One indication of why might be revealed in the letter President Davison wrote to Benham in response to the demands. The letter, dated March 8, 1969, stated, in part:

> As for the recruitment of athletes, Athletic Director Evans has advised all coaches by memorandum that the university would recruit regardless of race, creed, or color. A Negro student has been designated to receive a tuition and books scholarship in the spring quarter if he is academically eligible to compete. To date, six Negro athletes have been offered full scholarships (three in football, two in track, and one in basketball) or would have been had they been academically eligible.

This sounded vaguely reminiscent of the series of technicalities on which Hamilton and I were denied admission to the university for a year and a half.

On KA, President Davison wrote: "Kappa Alpha is a duly constituted and recognized social fraternity and is in compliance with the provision of the department of student activities. The university cannot arbitrarily abolish such an organization."

It seemed almost as if the incidence of racism had risen in direct proportion to the number of blacks on campus. Joe put it this way: "To me racism is when you take English 101 and have to read *Heart of Darkness*, and point out that it's racist, just like *Othello*, and the teacher takes points off my essay for it. In short, when you're looking at things from a black perspective, they can't understand it."

Several students at different times told me of a psychology professor who, upon seeing two black girls in his class, launched into a discussion of the high incidence of crime, illegitimacy, syphilis, and gonorrhea among black people, and ended by saying that he knew of at least two people who were going to flunk the course. The girls withdrew from the class.

In some instances, escape was not so easy. One sociology major told me of a course required for a master's in his field. It was called "Community Reconnaissance." He was told he could not take the course that time around because it involved a field trip to Oglethorpe County, where the class was to survey community leaders on what they felt was wrong with their communities.

The student, Leonard Lester, called Pie by the other blacks, said that he suspected there weren't any black leaders in the area, but he demanded that he be allowed to take the course. When an alternative— not involving the community reconnaissance—was offered, Pie said: "The professor told me, 'I understand your problem, but sometimes you have to go in the back door.'"

Pie went on: "I blew my stack. Then I went to the head of the department and they finally found some Negroes for me in the county. One was a black school principal, who wouldn't consent to the interview until I shaved my beard off." Pie subsequently dropped out of the university. He said he "just couldn't take it anymore."

"The thing about segs," Bob Benham said to me later, "is that they're a lot more sophisticated than they used to be when you were a student. Last year, for instance, I belonged to the Demosthenian Society, and I was elected to the office of custodian. It was my duty to procure things for the organization, open up, and so on. One of the members was Albert Saye, a political science professor and one of the most notorious segs around. He responded by proposing that the custodian be paid a salary of twenty dollars a quarter."

Bob says he's given up "trying to get along with honkies." Last summer, he, along with several of his classmates, served as an intern in the office of Governor Lester Maddox. He says he enjoyed it, but he doesn't think he could do it again.

"Time was, when a guy slipped and said 'colored' you'd consider it an accident and let him slide."

Benham said, "You excused it even when you showed up for class in a shirt and tie and they responded by saying, 'Hi ya doin', preacher?' Or you'd try to study with them, and the first thing they're talking about was sex and how they'd like a black woman. Then you realize that their attitude toward blacks is still that the majority of them are low-life, slimy dogs, and I'm the exception. Their Booker T."

Although the black students say that what is called a black studies program this year is what the school already had, plus two new courses, and that it doesn't tell blacks anything they don't already know, they are at least partially responsible for that much of a beginning.

Also, they are responsible for the removal of the segregated bathroom signs. Penny Mickelbury, a striking dark-skinned girl from Atlanta with a Kathleen Cleaver–style Afro, said that she and "a group of the brothers and sisters" went into a university cafeteria "determined that those signs were going to come down." They walked to the head of the food lines, she said, and simply refused to move.

I marveled at the story, even up to this point, since this was a cafeteria frequented by many of the Bulldogs. In my day, Bulldogs were known for their pugnacious character.

At any rate, a few of these types, according to Penny, took exception, and although there's some question as to who actually landed the first blow, it wasn't long before the cafeteria was in an uproar. Most of the whites and a few of the blacks left. Penny and a "few of the brothers," including Pie, remained to do battle.

"I climbed up on top of a table and started throwing forks and knives and trays," she recalled. "Anything I could get my hands on. That's one of the reasons they leave us alone. They think we're crazy. Imagine. Thirty black kids got eighteen thousand honkies scared to death."

Because at least a few of the black students make no secret of their readiness to retaliate "much of the harassment," they say, "has all but disappeared." And despite the fact that the average black student does not participate in the BSU, many have benefited from their protests. Bendelle Love, a young resident adviser in an all-white dorm, is there as a result of BSU demands. She says she works nearly forty hours a week advising others on their problems and that, because of the time consumed between that and her studies, she just doesn't have time for meetings. Of her own situation, she says: "There's static."

Others, I think, feel there are some benefits. Pie and Floyd Williams, a graduate student in art, debated the point one evening. Pie said that all he wants to be is a soldier in the revolution. But Floyd argued that the revolution needs professionals—doctors, lawyers, technicians, even sociologists. The struggle, he said, benefits from those who know well their opposition.

But even the most militant of the black students say that things have improved "a little bit."

Some say that the number of whites they can talk to is increasing.

I was, of course, particularly curious about how the white students felt about the blacks. In my own time, I had felt that most of them were too preoccupied with fraternity and sorority parties really to concern themselves about us. And from what I was able to glean from various sources, this is still pretty much the case now.

Rebecca Leet, a junior from Atlanta and news editor of the *Red and Black*, said that she had talked to many white students who had come from integrated high schools, so that they did not consider Georgia's desegregation unusual. (High school desegregation began the year after my entrance at the university.) "I just sort of don't feel anything toward them," one freshman from a small Georgia town told her, adding: "But I don't feel anything against them." She said she saw "discrimination emanating, to some extent, from the way people talk about them and stuff."

A prelaw senior said that he had been disappointed last year when he tried to "get a human relations seminar started." He said it was "a shock to him" that black students wouldn't accept him as being sincerely interested. "What do you do when you're sitting there and you are sincere and he doesn't believe you? Where do you go?" he asked.

(I recalled the all-too-numerous occasions when I was expected to provide easy answers to such questions as "What can we do?" so that they could go out and say, "Negroes say they want . . .")

But charges made by the BSU are confirmed unintentionally in other circumstances by white students who are neither pro nor con. "I wouldn't be comfortable if I were black on this campus," one white student said. "There's an awful lot of discrimination. It's just the way people have been raised to feel about blacks," he said.

At the end of my visit, of all the people I talked with, Joe Sales, the student who reminded me of Hamp, and Andy Williams, the graduate instructor in the African history class, are on my mind. Both bright and articulate, and by no means crazy—by my standards, at least—they came to the university under no other pressure than the knowledge of their communities that one of theirs had made it to a white school.

Now, with most of that behind them, they are disillusioned. "You'd have a lot more militant black people if they attended schools like this," Joe said. He also said: "A lot of things have happened that made me develop negative attitudes about whites that will be with me the rest of my life.

"Nothing here balances out the things I lost—like the inability to keep up with the tempo of the black community. Like I go home now, and I don't feel the same sense of belonging."

Andy feels that way, too, but desperately wants to "return to a black environment." If offered a job at the university, he says, he wouldn't take it. "I just couldn't function, because I think of the question Malcolm X raised and answered: 'You know what they call a black PhD?'

"'Nigger.'"

It has been more than six years since I left the University of Georgia and the South, and I am still weighing the things I lost against the things I gained. At one point, I even spent six months in graduate school because I felt I needed to fill in the gaps from the education I received from Georgia. Yet, before the six months were over, I realized that the education I received outside the classroom more than made up for what was lost inside. And, maybe, Joe and Andy will experience this, too.

They were not "firsts" in the sense that Hamp and I were firsts. So they are not getting the positive attention that we received from throughout the world. I would be less than honest if I did not admit that many ways were paved for me, at least, because I was a first. (Hamp now has his medical degree and is serving as an army doctor in Germany.)

But they did come to the university out of the same backgrounds as Hamp and I, children of the black bourgeoisie, (mentally) or in fact, protected by the same system that discriminated against us. Joe and Andy are appalled at the treatment they are receiving at the University of Georgia because for the first time in their lives, they are feeling it personally. Discrimination through separate and unequal schooling is not something you feel personally.

I remember resenting to the point of being rude that almost my only visitors in my dormitory were the girls whom no man would look at twice, the wallflowers who came because they had no Saturday dates, the overweight, the bookworms, or the religious nuts. Not that there weren't exceptions—and some wonderful ones. But the former were the rule. And often, listening to records at night and dancing with the closet door, I would ignore their knocks because I found the whole charade disgusting.

And yet, I stayed, partly because I knew the world was watching. I think that, at that time, such a commitment was necessary. But the need is greater now, precisely because the world isn't watching. The move of black students to black colleges is fine for those who can afford it. But Benny Roberson lives here in Athens, where there is no black college, and he can't afford to go out of town. Things for blacks may improve now, not because the world is watching, but because there are more Benny Robersons.

The University of Georgia may not have prepared its black students for life in the orthodox way we have come to expect universities to do. But if they leave still unsatisfied with the treatment they received as blacks in a microcosmic white society, then I think the university will have succeeded far better than they may be able to realize now.

How the AME Church Helped Build My Armor of Values

The Root
JUNE 26, 2015

Even though I can't physically be at Mother Emanuel AME Church in Charleston, South Carolina, for Friday's funeral service, I am there in spirit—through a connection planted deep in my soul from an early age.

My father, Charles, and grandfather, known as Shep in an abbreviation of his middle name Shepherd, were both pastors at the AME Church. My grandfather was a presiding elder, who traveled South Carolina preaching and teaching preachers. Both of my grandmothers were saints who lived the church's teachings. My mother, Althea, who joined the AME Church after marrying my father, was also very spiritual and saw to it that I learned from those teachers, as well as her.

I was born in South Carolina in a town called Due West, a ways from Charleston. But we didn't live there long. My father was then an army chaplain and stationed in Riverside, California. So we soon left Due West so he could get to know his new baby girl.

My mother traveled not only with the fat, little, hairless infant that I was; she traveled with the values embraced by the black people of Due West and the African Methodist Episcopal Church. These values helped African Americans keep on keepin' on, despite the fact that the society around them every day and in every way tried to hold them down and enforce white superiority through Jim Crow laws and attitudes.

And while my father was serving his country, even in an army that segregated him and all those who looked like him, he wore the armor of values forged in the AME Church. This armor enabled him to tend the black soldiers dying in his arms on the bloody battlefields of World War II and Korea, fighting for a country that didn't recognize them as full citizens.

Yet they were able to give their lives, if necessary, because they understood better than those who segregated them the American promise of freedom and justice for all. And that enabled the ones who didn't die on the battlefield to return home and continue the fight for their rights at home. They were guided, as they were on the battlefield, by the values in their head, heart, and history.

It was those same values that my father and my mother and my grandparents and members of my segregated community used to create my suit of armor. They were values that spoke to the notion that all God's children were equal in his sight (though as I grew older, I wondered about that pronoun but dared not do so out loud in the AME Church).

They were values, principles by which we were taught how to live as good citizens, even as the larger society refused to recognize us as such. What the AME Church and its black families did was to give black children like me a first-class sense of ourselves.

Early on, as I read that the massacre took place in an AME church during a Bible study session, I was transported back to St. Augustine, Florida, and many other locations in that state where my grandfather had been stationed, where my mother used to send me when I was a little girl to get further steeped in these values and to be outfitted in more layers of moral armor.

My father's mother—my grandmother, Alberta Hunter—was a

mighty crafter of the mission. Every day at noon she walked the few feet from the parsonage, the preacher's home, to pray in the church.

Each day, despite my tomboyish efforts to elude her, she would eventually find me and make me learn a Bible verse. Her favorite was the 23rd Psalm, with its lines, "Yea though I walk through the valley of the shadow of death, I will fear no evil. Thy rod and thy staff they will comfort me all the days of my life."

As a nineteen-year-old entering under court order the previously all-white University of Georgia, I was confronted by a mob of people screaming and throwing rocks at my dormitory window and shouting for me to leave. They saw only their institution of white privilege, but I was shielded by my armor.

And as I read about twenty-six-year-old Tywanza Sanders, who last week in Charleston threw his body onto Susie Jackson, his eighty-seven-year-old aunt, to shield her from the demented assailant's bullets, I wondered if he, too, had been able to do that because he was clad in that moral armor, taught him during a Bible class at Mother Emanuel. It seemed so to me. And I hope as the victims perished, they felt the comfort of the rod and the staff they had been taught protected them.

Today, as I reach back to my history in the AME Church, I understand the forgiveness by those who have lost loved ones. It's about enveloping themselves in the armor of their values to heal the hurt in their own souls, as Nelson Mandela did when he forgave those who had imprisoned him for twenty-seven years and waged a brutal, vicious war on his people.

But that kind of forgiveness doesn't preclude seeking justice. As a child of the AME Church, I am sure that those who are in pain in Charleston will use their tears today and in the days to come to polish their armor so that they, like those of us who mourn with them, can endure and prosper like so many generations before.

Especially crucial are those teaching lessons in Bible study.

They are needed to help America meet its most enduring challenge: racism and its role in failing to help America keep its promise to all its citizens whose lives matter.

Lifting My Voice

AARP Magazine
SEPTEMBER/OCTOBER 2014

When I was a little girl, I sat at my grandmother's knee while she read the newspaper. Pigtailed and proper, I'd wait patiently until she finished and handed me the comic strips. My favorite was the one about the dashing blue-eyed redhead, Brenda Starr, reporter for the *New York Flash.* I loved Starr's life of adventure and romance—the fearless way she traveled the world, the clever way she figured things out. I dreamed of being a reporter like Brenda Starr, and one day told my mother so.

She didn't flinch.

"Well, if that's what you want to do," she said, in her soft-spoken voice.

It was a remarkable response from a black mother in Covington, Georgia, in the 1940s. In that small, segregated town, black people knew their places: in all-black neighborhoods, schools, and churches; in the one all-black movie theater, where whites like Tarzan were the featured heroes and blacks played *Gone with the Wind*–type "mammies" and butlers. In the white stores around the town's circle where we shopped, employees smiled, but that geniality ended at the cash register. And yet from some deep, historical reservoir, my mother knew the power of dreams.

She instinctively knew if I wanted it badly enough, I'd find my path.

And I did, but with challenges the fictitious reporter in my life could never have known.

My elementary school was one of those "separate but equal" schools the U.S. Supreme Court's 1954 *Brown v. Board of Education* decision exposed as a lie. Our books were hand-me-downs from the white schools, some with pages missing. When it rained, our dusty, red-clay playground turned to mud. For lunch, a stand in the cafeteria sold pig-ear sandwiches on white bread, or other parts of the pig, fried to a crisp, known as "skins." But still we learned, living proof of that African proverb: It takes a village to raise a child. And so, once a year, our black village helped overcome some of those deficits with a fundraiser. And the child of the family raising the most money was crowned king or queen. I got the crown one year, a "diamond" tiara. And for a time, I was insufferable to my classmates. Eventually, I stopped wearing the tiara. But the notion that I was a queen had taken up residence in my head and, years later, would help steady me during one of the most formidable tests of my life—desegregating the University of Georgia, a place that had been resolutely white for its entire 176-year history.

Until then, my only experience going to school with whites had been in 1955, in Alaska, where my father, an army chaplain, was stationed. I was the only black child in my class, but I made friends and was comfortable in my skin. Only when prom time came was I the only student who didn't have a date. I went anyway, and my two white gay male teachers saw to it that I got to dance. With them.

I didn't hold that against my white classmates, though, as I never developed much animosity toward whites, even growing up in Covington, where the very street we lived on—Brown Street—was named for a white man who fathered several black children, including my mother's father. I suppose my lack of animus came from being raised in a religious household and a churchgoing community that taught love, not hate. "Do unto others as you would have them do unto you" was the creed we lived by. It was also a layer in the armor that protected me as the years went by.

After a year in Alaska, I happily returned to my all-black high school, and blossomed with each successive year as I learned about people like Ida B. Wells, the muckraking black journalist, and Henry McNeal Turner, the activist "race man" for whom our school was named. The education philosophy of my teachers: if they couldn't give us first-class citizenship, they were going to ensure we got a first-class sense of ourselves. So in the final months of my senior year, after I wore still another crown as homecoming queen, two of Atlanta's progressive black leaders came to our school looking for students who might be interested in attending an all-white college—a test case five years after the *Brown* decision. Without hesitation, Hamilton Holmes and I, both top students, volunteered.

A year and a half later, when we finally showed up at the university under court order, hate-filled crowds greeted us with jeers of "Nigger, go home!" But I paid them no mind, for I was wearing my invisible tiara and knew they weren't yelling at the queen. Three nights later, though, hundreds of students rioted outside my dorm; one threw a brick through my window, forcing me to dig deeper into that arsenal of armor—this time for a Bible verse given to me by my other grandmother, with whom I spent many summers in Florida: "Yea, though I walk through the valley of the shadow of death, I will fear no evil."

I was escorted off campus that scary night, and Hamp and I were suspended under the ruse of "for our own safety," but we were soon re-admitted and lived the next two years in relative quiet. Determined not to be bound by limits, I made a few white friends, mostly journalism students, including one who later became my first husband. By then, young people across the South were sitting at lunch counters, marching in the streets, challenging segregation at the coal face. (Three years later, during the tide-turning Freedom Summer, hundreds from the North would join them in a "righteous crusade" to win black Mississippians' right to vote—a crusade that would lead to the passage of the Voting Rights Act of 1965.) So in quiet solidarity, I joined an upstart black newspaper headed by activist M. Carl Holman, with Julian Bond as managing editor, and spent weekends and holidays writing stories about Atlanta's often-jailed yet steadfast demonstrators.

Month after month I watched as my friends exposed themselves to palpable hate—and, sometimes, violence—but I refused to harbor anger. I knew that, like me, these students were wrapped in that familiar coat of armor and were simply doing what we were brought up to do: take control of our destiny—without ambivalence or fury or fear.

Upon graduation, I left for New York, where the late, great editor of the *New Yorker* magazine, William Shawn, had read about my case and my dream and invited me to join the staff, along with other young graduates from prestigious northern universities. Initially, like them, my job was typing rejection slips and story lineups, but before long I was promoted to reporter, the first black to be named to that position. I kept my eye on and my soul in what was going on in the civil rights movement, and wrote about black people in ways they were rarely portrayed anywhere in the media—in their full humanity. I continued this work at the *New York Times*, and in the decades since, never strayed, even as my reach widened to television, radio, and other media, and to the world beyond our borders—most notably South Africa during the days of apartheid. I always felt I had a responsibility to confront issues of race and racism, but in ways that narrow the divide and focus on the positives of difference, rather than the all-too-exploited negatives. It hasn't been without its challenges. Once, when I was working at *PBS NewsHour*, I surprised a white guest when he saw me sit down on the set to interview him.

"How long have you been doing this?" he asked after the show was over. And when I answered, "About thirty years," he responded, "Well, I guess it beats being a hairdresser."

I view unintentionally hurtful comments like that as coming from people who, if not ignorant, are uninformed. Unfortunately, expressions of racial insensitivity or hatred are still littering the landscape of our ever-elusive "more perfect union." And the reversal of some of the progress we made—sadly evident in the resegregation of our nation's schools and neighborhoods—is spurring scant public outrage, not even another righteous crusade. And so, wearing my invisible tiara, I continue to renew the commitment and the mantra of the civil rights movement: to "keep on keeping on," to use the values the village instilled in me all those years ago, to recite and write about our history and its relevance to our struggles today, to work at ensuring people are judged not by the color of their skin or the god they worship or the person they love, but by the content of their character—Martin Luther King Jr.'s dream of "the Beloved Community."

Oak Bluffs, More than a Region in My Mind

The Vineyard Gazette
JULY 5, 2012

Throughout my high school years in Atlanta, Georgia, in the 1950s, Oak Bluffs on Martha's Vineyard was a region in my mind. I can still remember the image I had of the island back then—an enchanted place with beautiful green grapevines gracefully covering a landscape with children roaming freely in and around them. One of those children was my classmate, Bobby Jackson, whose father was a prominent doctor in the city. Every summer Dr. Jackson took his family away from a South still segregated and limited in terms of where black people could play, to a place where they were free to be who they were: black and middle-class with all the aspirations of any middle-class family in America.

Those memories came flooding back to me a few days ago as I spotted a man standing in his backyard with his dog, looking like he was at peace with the world. The moment carried me back to high school. This was my friend Bobby. I remembered how our parties at the end of the school year were timed around when the Jacksons were leaving for Martha's Vineyard so Bobby could be included. Older now, his hair thinning but not quite as gray as mine, he has come back to a place that clearly, from the contemplative look on his face, is as magical as ever. I stop to say hello and he tells me his son will be here soon. Now Oak Bluffs for him, as for me, is the place we call home. After more than fifteen years of commuting some sixteen-plus hours from South Africa to Martha's Vineyard, my husband, Ronald, and I will be spreading the roots we have already put down here during summer breaks, tending them into fall and maybe a snatch of winter in the place we call home. This is the place we looked forward to coming back to every year to reconnect with friends both new and old—and not necessarily old in the sense of age, for our many friends are an intergenerational lot and we are stimulated by all of them. We love to peruse all manner of things with them, from art to politics, both high and low, to local news from their communities all across the country, sometimes with roots beyond our shores. Martin Luther King Jr., who once vacationed here, might refer to Oak Bluffs as the beloved community.

Many years after Bobby Jackson and I graduated from Turner High School, Martha's Vineyard and Oak Bluffs became more than a region in my mind, thanks to an invitation from Mike Sviridoff, then vice president of national affairs at the Ford Foundation and my husband's boss. I was so excited to finally be getting to this magical place. We landed at the old airport, with its tiny, aging one-room reception area filled with people unhappily departing, and others like ourselves, happily arriving. The place was standing-room only, generating a closeness among friends and strangers alike, some of whom became friends right then and there. This is where I experienced my first Vineyard magic. (I love the new airport, but . . .)

Our next stop was what was then Gay Head, with its mystical cliffs and dunes and fiercely compelling waves whose undertow once during our trip took my husband and Bill and Mimi Grinker a little too far out (they were rescued by two island teenagers on Styrofoam kickboards). My disappointment over my image of the vine-filled Vineyard was soon more than assuaged by the multifarious landscapes at every turn in the road after our visit with the Sviridoffs. Oak Bluffs was calling. So we rented a car and drove through the enchanting towns of Chilmark, West Tisbury, Vineyard Haven, and at last, Oak Bluffs.

I'd never been there but had heard about the more-than-century-old, black-owned Shearer Cottage. We immediately set out to find it and spent a night there before we began our Oak Bluffs exploration, which took us to places I had heard about from Bobby, including the Inkwell.

There I discovered (well, kind of like Christopher Columbus "discovered" America) one of the main arteries that was the heartbeat of Oak Bluffs: beautiful black bodies of all shapes, sizes, and ages frolicking freely in and out of the water they owned by virtue of years of occupancy.

I was so excited about what I was seeing that I immediately got my editor at the *New York Times* on the phone and convinced him to allow me to extend my vacation by a few days so I could tell the world about something many would find hard to conceive, since even then in 1970, after the Civil Rights Acts abolished the last of the "separate but equal" lie in the South, there were still places in both the North and the South that were not welcoming to people of color. And tell the world I did, on the second front of the *New York Times*, illustrated with a picture of longtime Vineyarder Teixiera Nash in a huge sun hat. By this time, we had met Dr. and Mrs. Leslie Hayling, who graciously invited us to stay with them in their home with a beautiful grand piano and copious amounts of great food.

Over the years and many more trips to the Vineyard with our children Suesan and Chuma and our friends and theirs who joined us, we put down roots—even though they were in the yards of other people. There was the legendary Lee Simmons, who knew (and would share) everybody's business because everybody found in her a sympathetic mother confessor. And there were longtime Vineyarders like Claudia Bowser, who lived next door to Jessica Harris, whom I came to know as a great culinary anthropologist who could cook as well as write about foods from all over the world, and her diminutive mother, Rhoda, who is long gone from us, but whose Wisdom in a Pouch cards still rest on a table in our home for all newcomers to learn from.

While others have decried the loss of Oak Bluffs landmarks that spoke to the so-called historic African American presence here, and while the name Inkwell is now debated among those who believe it carries unkind racial overtones and others who defend it, insisting the name derived from the many writers who waded there, the beach still beckons the older generations and their children. People like Skip and Karen Finley's daughter Kristin, who married Timothy Brown at that beach a couple of years ago and now lives in Oak Bluffs full-time.

It would be great to have a bookstore on Circuit Avenue featuring the history of black Oak Bluffs, but there is Zita Allen's Cousen Rose Gallery, which showcases current and past black history makers, and C'est la Vie, one of the few stores owned by a black man, Roger Schilling.

Thankfully it features artifacts that draw in black people looking for things that look like or feature them. So Roger and Zita are there and they represent! As do artists and writers like Jill Nelson and her brother, the award-winning documentarian Stanley Nelson, and Abigail McGrath, niece of Dorothy West, who holds writer's workshops that put an Oak Bluffs imprimatur on those who dream of following in her aunt's footsteps—and may in time.

Many Vineyarders whose history in Oak Bluffs long predates ours continue to nourish the roots they planted here generations ago and tend them as they spread. I have watched Colin Redd, son of Sharon and Frankie, grow into a handsome young man who no longer has time to play as he once did (at least in the daytime), busily dividing his time between work at Biscuits and the new Johnny Cupcakes on Circuit Avenue. Gretchen Tucker Underwood plays host and takes occasional stabs (or whacks) at being a disciplinarian to her growing grandchildren, seventeen-year-old Jason and thirteen-year-old Brandon, who come every summer. The other day I ran into Shayna, the daughter of Harry and Charlena Seymour of Oak Bluffs, down with her husband, Steve Carr, and their two-and-a-half-year-old son, Blake, who now have their own house in town. A television reporter in Boston, she had come to do a piece on historic Oak Bluffs. I suspect I will see Blake in a few years out on the tennis court, now abandoned by his grandmother, keeping the tradition alive and preparing for the historic Tucker Invitational. Or maybe they will be joined by those yet to come in the Finley household. Judy and Ron Davenport will make sure their huge stable of grandchildren, including the most recent entry of twins, will inherit their love of Oak Bluffs.

I even know some folks who spent years going to the Hamptons who have now discovered Oak Bluffs and are here to stay, soon with a brand-new grandchild in tow.

So I have no doubt that while some of the so-called historic memories of Oak Bluffs will fade, in their place others will be created by a multicolored, economically diverse crowd, and it will be up to all of us to ensure that Oak Bluffs continues to be a place we and our children, grandchildren, and generations to come will happily call home.

Taunts, Tear Gas, and Other College Memories

The New Yorker
NOVEMBER 13, 2015

Hearing about the indignities faced by students of color at the University of Missouri, I am taken back fifty-four years, to when Hamilton Holmes and I entered, and then matriculated, at the University of Georgia as its first two black students.

The initial response of many white students to our presence was overtly racist. One night, students and others gathered outside my dormitory and shouted, "Nigger go home." The town police threw around tear gas, ostensibly to disperse an already-thinning crowd. By the time the state troopers arrived, the protesters were long gone. The university suspended me for, they said, my own safety. (Hamilton, who lived with a black family a few blocks away, was also suspended.) As I left the dorm that night, a group of girls who had been told to change their sheets, so as not to be affected by the tear gas, formed a semicircle, and one threw a quarter at me and yelled, "Here, Charlayne, go and change my sheets." Although "nigger" was their preferred shout-out, the students would also use other words they thought would be hurtful.

They didn't realize they were complimenting me when they yelled out "Freedom Rider." And there were other, nonverbal incidents. Both Hamilton and I had our car tires flattened from time to time, and on at least one occasion the side of my little white Ford Falcon became a maze of knife scratches.

The first semester was the worst, and things died down after that. But what we might today call "microaggressions" were still evident: The time I went to see if I could work on the school newspaper and was welcomed by the editor, but never got an assignment. Or when professors went a whole term without addressing me in class. I never reacted to any of this publicly, but I spent a lot of time, especially early on, in the university infirmary with mysterious stomach pains. My one visitor was Hamilton, who was finding it difficult to make friends. Despite all the stress, he was elected to Phi Beta Kappa and went on to enroll as the first black student at Emory University School of Medicine. He became an orthopedic surgeon and, at one time, the medical director of Grady Memorial Hospital, the gargantuan public hospital in Atlanta. In 1995, he died, at the age of fifty-four. I read that they thought it was heart failure. Now that I know about PTSD, and as I cope with my own post-college problems with claustrophobia, I wonder if that didn't have something to do with it.

I still tear up when I speak of Hamilton, but have been comforted by the fact that the doors that were shut for so long to black students are now open. To be sure, many have come after me and are thriving, including on the football field where Hamilton was not allowed to play, despite his love of the game, because, so the argument went, either his teammates or the opposing team would try to hurt, if not kill, him. Today, the Georgia Bulldogs are a powerful force, impressive as teammates who accept each other for their prowess rather than for their color. As a team they send a powerful message, as do the football players at Missouri, who understood how to use their power off as well as on the field. But as I read this week the stories of young people at Missouri, I am struck by an awful déjà vu. My stomach hurts again, and this time the origin is not so mysterious.

I Desegregated the University of Georgia. History Is Still in the Making.

The New York Times

JANUARY 9, 2021

Sixty years ago, I walked onto the campus of the University of Georgia along with my high school classmate Hamilton Holmes.

Ordinarily this would have been a routine exercise, as it had been for students since the institution was established in 1785. Except in all that time, not one Black person had ever been allowed to attend the University of Georgia.

Hamilton and I wanted to change that, though not because we wanted to make history. We applied to UGA with the same kind of dreams and ambitions as every student there. Hamp, as he was widely known, wanted to be a doctor. I had wanted to be a journalist since I first read the comic strip *Brenda Starr, Reporter* when I was around five.

We were approached by an activist group of Black men in Atlanta known as the Atlanta Committee for Cooperative Action (ACCA), who wanted to put *Brown v. Board of Education* to the test. It had been five years since that 1954 Supreme Court decision; they believed it was time for action.

So they proposed that we apply to a local college in town. But to their surprise, we suggested an alternative: the University of Georgia. While it was some seventy or so miles from Atlanta, a journey riddled with KKK-inhabited towns along the way, we were not deterred.

The rest, as they say, is history.

Though, really, the rest was only the beginning. History is often defined as what happened in the past, and, as my journalism professor said on the first day of class, "We learn from history that we do not learn from history."

But this does not mean we should allow ourselves to forget. Sixty years after Hamilton and I desegregated the University of Georgia, I hope we can all remember and examine our country's history in its difficult entirety—at a time when the kind of division I experienced walking onto that campus on January 9, 1961, has reared its ugly head all over this country.

In my five decades as a journalist bearing witness to the cyclical nature of our country's history of racism and division, I've come to believe that my professor's sentiment was his way of challenging us to not only learn from our history, but also to use our craft as journalists to help the public know our past, because the duty to remember does not belong to journalists alone. It's only through this knowledge that we're all able to make informed decisions about our lives—decisions that, in turn, affect our neighbors near and far.

Indeed, knowing our history inspired Hamilton and me to make our own: we had attended a high school named for Henry McNeal Turner, a pioneering minister and politician who was elected to the Georgia legislature during Reconstruction, a brief time in the 1800s when newly freed slaves were granted full citizenship and could vote for the very first time. We were reminded of that history every day as we walked through the school doors.

A few months before we enrolled in college, six-year-old Ruby Bridges exercised her right to enroll in the all-white William Frantz Elementary School in New Orleans. Her walk, accompanied by federal marshals, was immortalized in the Norman Rockwell painting *The Problem We All Live With*. (The same painting formed a shadow in Bria Goeller's photo illustration of Kamala Harris after Ms. Harris became the first Black woman nominated by a major party for vice president of the United States.)

Hamilton and I were also empowered by the history of our people and the struggles they confronted and overcame, dating to their first steps off the slave ships and onto these shores in 1526. It took a village to teach us this legacy—the teachers in our segregated schools and churches; our neighbors and families.

And it took yet another village to help us play our own part in this history. Our lawyers Constance Baker Motley, Donald L. Hollowell, and Horace Ward were advocates for us, along with the newly minted young lawyer Vernon Jordan. Mr. Jordan helped lead us through the crowd of students yelling ugly racial epithets as we walked on campus to register for classes. And earlier, that village comprised the men of ACCA who encouraged us to apply to college in the first place.

It's because of this village that a Republican judge, William A. Bootle, gave his historic ruling ordering UGA to accept us. It's also because of this village that, forty years after we set foot on campus, former governor S. Ernest Vandiver of Georgia apologized in person at the university for having vowed, "No, not one"—not one person the color of Hamilton and me would ever be allowed to enter its hallowed halls.

With this history in my head and heart, my path forward includes working to ensure that the doors of my alma mater are open even wider to Black students who, along with their classmates of all colors, will embrace this stated UGA goal: "to foster the understanding of and respect for cultural differences necessary for an enlightened and educated citizenry."

We have many challenges ahead. There are times when, watching the news, I am brought to tears, not least when I see some of those I still think of as my fellow citizens, nevertheless exhibit awful behavior toward others who don't look like them—the latest in the despicable behavior at the Capitol.

It is in these moments that I wonder: Why have they not learned from history? Is it because not all of our history is being taught in many schools around the country? And why is there no embrace of respecting differences of opinion?

As we make sense of these questions, history will continue to echo itself. As Georgia elected its first Black senator, Raphael Warnock, I thought back to Henry McNeal Turner, my high school's namesake, and other Black officials freely elected to office during the brief period of Reconstruction over 150 years ago.

And so as I reflect on the sixtieth anniversary of my university's desegregation—as a Black person and a woman, as a wife and mother, as a sister, aunt, and citizen—remaining true to my calling as a journalist, I leave you with the question: what can we all do to keep working toward a more perfect union? Go Dogs!

PART VI

Honoring the Ancestors

I was brought up to respect my elders, never for a moment thinking that one day I would be one . . . until now. And one of the inevitabilities of aging is losing friends. But I was brought up in a religious household, and while tears were often shed when a loved one or close friend passed on, I was taught not to let sorrow linger, and among the consolations were songs sung at funerals. Songs like "In the Sweet By and By," which from an early age I learned, to wit:

> *There's a land that is fairer than day,*
> *And by faith we can see it afar;*
> *For the Father waits over the way*
> *To prepare us a dwelling place there.*
> *In the sweet by and by,*
> *We shall meet on that beautiful shore;*
> *In the sweet by and by,*
> *We shall meet on that beautiful shore.*

Later, when I moved to and began reporting from South Africa, among the many things I learned from its people early on in my seventeen years there was how they approached loss, including never using the word *death*. Instead, one who has passed on is referred to as having transitioned. And the term for one who has transitioned is *ancestor*, and when that ancestor is being remembered, you end with the phrase "Long live!" And so it was that spirit I tried to evoke when I had to write about people I knew or admired. I tried to share their lives and capture their spirit, those I knew like Julian Bond and William Haywood Burns, as well as the pioneering Dr. Kenneth Edelin, who was a brave and committed obstetrician/gynecologist, and the great poet Langston Hughes.

I never thought I would be writing a postscript about Julian Bond, for Julian and I were contemporaries, long before we became elders. We had been close friends since the early days of the civil rights movement in Atlanta in 1961, when I was attending the University of Georgia.

Julian was working with the Atlanta Student Movement as one of its main theoreticians and later as the managing editor of the *Atlanta Inquirer*. I continued to follow him in his various iterations with great interest, if not pride, including his service in elective office in Georgia, as well as when he moved on but not away from the causes he championed: freedom and justice for all . . . up until the day he joined like-minded ancestors who preceded him. So, as hard as it was for me emotionally, with Julian's spirit in my head and heart, I got it done. And while we have a new generation of conscious, activist young people who are drawing the world's attention to some of the same issues Julian fought for, I think they can learn from his example, not least his recalling the heritage of dissent going back to the creation of what he and all those who joined him were committed to. His is still relevant advice to those who are protesting, and that is to appreciate the need to carry their energy into work at the local level. Julian also gave another bit of advice, and with the exception of the new terminology for the race he was speaking about, he said: "Negroes must not forget race consciousness as long as they are victims of racism."

It was during this time that I also met another man who would become an ancestor far too early. So, on the fiftieth anniversary of Dr. Martin Luther King's death, I wanted to help in some small way to keep his dream alive. I wrote about the one time we met, and one of the things I learned that day that helped make him so very special—his humility.

I was not as close to another civil rights activist who, like Julian and Dr. King, was dedicated to achieving justice for all, and that is all, no matter their color. That was civil rights attorney William Haywood Burns. But I would see him occasionally at events like the fundraising dinners for civil rights causes, mostly in New York. I had followed him through his books like *The Voices of Negro Protest in America*, with a foreword by the great historian John Hope Franklin. It came out the year I graduated from UGA and went to work for the *New Yorker*, where I would later write about him.

Haywood became deeply involved in South Africa after meeting Nelson Mandela when the latter first visited New York in June 1990, four years before he became president of a new South Africa—one Haywood helped create, for in 1993, Haywood went on to become a legal advisor in the drafting of South Africa's interim constitution. Like so many of us who became attached to South Africa, not least because of the similarities between U.S. segregation and South Africa's apartheid, Haywood was drawn to the country and wanted to experience it firsthand. That, alas, was how it came to be that he was killed in a car accident in Cape Town, South Africa, in April 1996. Long live, William Haywood Burns. Long live!

The same joy was in evidence at Columbia University when seven months after the death of Langston Hughes, the university held a memorial service for him. I had never met the man, but as a passionate student of poetry like his, I felt like I knew him and was so excited to learn that Columbia was going to honor him, not least because Hughes was one of the poets our Black teachers used to inspire us in our segregated schools. His poem "The Negro Speaks of Rivers" had taken us to places we could only dream of, but nevertheless stimulated our imagination as well as "I, Too [Sing America]." Thus it was with fondness and anticipation that I attended the event that was not only a memorial, but an acknowledgment of Columbia's own racism in taking a step to try to repair what was broken.

To all, I continue to say: Long live!

A Love Affair That Lasted for Fifty-Six Years

The Vineyard Gazette
SEPTEMBER 19, 2013

When Lucy Durr was a high school junior in Montgomery, Alabama, her older first cousin, John, invited her to a party. There John introduced Lucy to his good friend Sheldon Hackney, a college junior.

"I fell in love with him immediately," Lucy told me recently, giggling like the schoolgirl she was at the time.

What was it about Sheldon that so captured her young heart and lasted for more than half a century?

"Well," Lucy said with a devilish grin, "for one thing he was tall."

A noted historian of the American South and past president of the University of Pennsylvania, Sheldon Hackney died September 12 at his Vineyard Haven home in the company of his children, grandchildren, and beloved wife of fifty-six years. Those who knew the Hackneys well say it is impossible to talk about one without the other, such was the strength of their partnership and bond of love.

"It's as though they had their own unique glue that kept them together," said Tess Bramhall, a longtime close friend. "Even when they came to our house for dinner parties, Lucy would always sit next to Sheldon. There was never a space between them."

Lucy, too, was tall. "I guess he thought I was good-looking," she told me this week.

So did many of the boys at Lucy's high school, according to her sister, Virginia Foster Durr, also known as Tilla.

"She was absolutely a honey," Tilla said, "and our yard was always full of Harleys. Until she met Sheldon."

Now seventy-six, Lucy still manages to look like a honey, hardly showing her age, except for strands of gray in her medium-long bobbed hair that sometimes blows in her eyes when she hits one of her mean forehands on the tennis court down the hill from their home.

The real beginning of Sheldon and Lucy's courtship started with a long-distance phone call from Birmingham, where Sheldon lived, and an invitation to a movie. Sheldon drove almost ninety-three miles to Montgomery, and while Lucy can't remember the movie, she remembers the end of the evening.

"He kissed me and I liked it," she said, smiling.

They stayed in touch—kind of—because while Sheldon was still at Vanderbilt University in Nashville, Lucy had graduated and was now miles and light-years away at Radcliffe College in Cambridge. This was before the internet or cell phones and long-distance calling was expensive, especially for a college student. But Sheldon had his eyes on the prize and would from time to time drive the one-thousand-plus miles, more than sixteen hours, to Cambridge to see Lucy.

"I thought that was pretty brave," Lucy recalled. "That was a long time in an old car."

By the time Lucy was a sophomore, Sheldon had graduated and joined the Navy. Lucy Myers, who along with Lucy cooked for a family in Cambridge to earn extra money for school, remembers they used to talk about Sheldon, and Lucy would always refer to him being "in the Med," meaning that he was stationed somewhere in the Mediterranean Sea. When he came back to the United States, Lucy drove the old car he had given her to Philadelphia to meet him. When he failed to appear three hours after she had expected him, although worried, she went to bed. Remembering it as if it were yesterday, Lucy recalled: "It was about ten o'clock when he finally got there, and of course I was in my pajamas. But I hear this 'beep, beep,' and I ran down in my pajamas and there he was, and he had this wonderful, loving look on his face and said right off:

"'Why don't we get married?'"

Lucy of course said yes, and immediately called Radcliffe to let them know that she would not be coming back.

Lucy's parents were happy about the upcoming union, but there were more miles to travel than the distance between Montgomery and Birmingham.

The Durrs were in the forefront of the dawning civil rights movement. Lucy's uncle was U.S. Supreme Court justice Hugo Black, who took part in the unanimous decision of *Brown v. Board of Education* to end racial segregation in public schools.

Rosa Parks, who famously refused to give up her seat to a white rider and move to the back of the bus, was a family friend. When she was arrested, it was Lucy's father, an attorney, who got her out of jail and Lucy's mother who picked her up from the jail and took her home.

Somewhat sheltered in his own segregated hometown, Sheldon had grown up being cared for by black people but was surprised, Lucy recalled, when he once visited and found Mrs. Parks sitting at the table having lunch with Lucy's mother. Both were part of a racially mixed group of women who met together and worked on civil rights issues. Sheldon had not seen anything like this back in Birmingham.

Back then, the racial atmosphere in the South was so poisonous that Lucy's cousin, who was to be one of her bridesmaids, decided not to attend the wedding after she learned writer Jessica Mitford would also be there. A member of the Communist Party and a well-known civil rights campaigner, Ms. Mitford's presence had the potential for provoking demonstrations or worse.

Mrs. Parks, "a fine seamstress," Lucy remembers, had made clothes for Lucy to take to Radcliffe and also worked on redoing a dress Lucy had been given to be married in. The dress turned out beautifully, Lucy recalled, sending me upstairs to see the picture of it on a wall covered with loving family photographs. And Mrs. Parks, as the Southern girl in Lucy still calls her, was also invited to the wedding. But the white Episcopal pastor who was to marry Lucy and Sheldon insisted she either sit in the church balcony or wear a white maid's uniform if she wanted to sit in the main church pews.

In the end, it was Mrs. Parks who made the decision not to go to the wedding. But even today, when Lucy tells the story, she gets a bit misty-eyed, as she says it was one of her only regrets about her wedding. It was also a wake-up call for the new husband.

The Hackneys' longtime friend Davis Weinstock put it this way: "Lucy left Radcliffe for him and he left that Alabama with her."

Indeed, Sheldon Hackney went on to become not just a historian, but one who would try to heal the nation's racial wounds in numerous ways. The *New York Times* said his award-winning book *Populism to Progressivism in Alabama*, written in 1969, "established him as one of the foremost historians of the post–Civil War South."

In the intervening years, as the Hackneys had three children— the first, Virginia, conceived two weeks after they got married—Lucy managed to go back to school, at Princeton, where Sheldon began his meteoric rise up the ladder of academia, ultimately becoming provost. Arising before 5 a.m. to get her homework done, then preparing her children for school and getting Sheldon off to work, Lucy—attending university part-time as only the second student allowed to do so— would eventually earn both a bachelor's and a law degree. But for much of that period, she would always be home in time to make dinner and help the children with their homework.

"Do we have to have hamburgers every night?" she recalled Fain, then a teenager, once asking.

Lucy says Sheldon always encouraged her educational pursuits, reading her papers and making positive and welcome suggestions for how to improve them, and eventually supporting her careers outside the home, which included working at the Children's Defense Fund and founding the Pennsylvania Partnerships for Children, a broad-based advocacy center for children. "But," she added with smile, "he was never very good around the house. And that was fine with me."

One of their greatest challenges related to their first child, Virginia, who was brain damaged during birth. Friends point to the strength of their bond as together they made the tough decision to let her go to a special school apart from them for a while, ultimately resulting in her being able to live independently here on the Vineyard. A popular figure on the Island, Virginia would always greet me with the question: "Are you behaving yourself?"

Virginia's death at age forty-nine was devastating to Lucy and Sheldon, but also "hugely binding," Davis Weinstock recalled. My daughter Suesan remembers that after Virginia's funeral service under a tent at the Hackney home, where she was asked to sing some of the karaoke songs that Virginia loved to sing at the Ritz in Oak Bluffs, she sang Virginia's favorite: "Girls Just Wanna Have Fun."

"I was so moved when Lucy turned to Sheldon and grabbed his hand, pulled him up from his chair, and started dancing," Suesan recalled.

Sheldon and Lucy's son, Fain Hackney, spoke of the equality of their partnership.

"My father did not give her expensive jewelry or flowers or gifts but she always knew that he loved her. They respected each other's opinions and judgment and intelligence. They consulted each other on issues big and small in their lives," he said. "They discussed politics and current events and, though they did not always agree, they always disagreed without being disagreeable, as someone once said."

Added daughter Elizabeth McBride: "I never in my entire life saw them argue. Well, maybe one time. But I've never seen him raise his voice."

Like so many of their friends who spoke of his selfless devotion to Lucy, Elizabeth remembers one of his final days when her father was struggling day and night with the debilitating disease that would eventually claim him.

"It was in the morning and when he saw me, he said, 'Your mother really had a hard time last night.'"

One of several poems found by the family after his passing includes these lines written by Sheldon in 2005. Called "Separations," the poem speaks volumes about his other gift: prescience.

> Like the universe, itself, our private worlds expand with age,
> But each horizon that we chase is matched by the one
>   disappearing. Marriage begins a new family and changes an
>   old one.
> Children draw our love and change our notion of the self. Then
>   children leave, and parents too; Nothing stays the same.
> Which is why we hope reunion waits beyond this world, and why
>   we dream of summers yet to come.

Black Muslim Temple Renamed for Malcolm X

The New York Times
FEBRUARY 2, 1976

The Black Muslims' Temple No. 7 in Harlem, which was destroyed eleven years ago after the assassination of Malcolm X and was later rebuilt, has been renamed in honor of the dissident Muslim who broke with the Nation of Islam in an acrimonious dispute that many felt ultimately led to his death.

The dramatic move was confirmed yesterday by Minister Abdul Farrakhan, national spokesman for Wallace D. Muhammad, the organization's leader, in a taping of *Black Journal*, to be telecast nationally on the Public Broadcasting System on February 15.

In response to a question from Tony Brown, the show's host, Mr. Farrakhan said that the temple was being renamed Malcolm Shabazz Temple No. 7 "in recognition of the great work that Malcolm X did when he was among the Nation of Islam."

The renaming of the temple, part of a complex of Muslim enterprises at 116th Street and Lenox Avenue, is one of a number of major changes instituted by Mr. Muhammad since he succeeded his father,

Elijah Muhammad, who died last February after serving as spiritual leader of the Chicago-based organization for forty-one years.

The renaming of the temple also comes at a time when several of the changes Malcolm X had urged on Elijah Muhammad and which led in part to his break with the organization are being promulgated by Wallace D. Muhammad as policy.

Since Malcolm X, thirty-nine years old, was assassinated in Harlem in 1965 by three men said to be Black Muslims, he has grown in stature among blacks and others all over the world.

This has been in marked contrast to his public treatment—or the lack of it—by the Nation of Islam, with which he broke partly because his positions increasingly differed from those of the religious movement, which was founded in the early 1930s.

Those differences centered on Malcolm's belief that the Nation of Islam's religious interpretations that excluded whites were too narrow, and that its policy of nonengagement in politics and civil rights was too restrictive.

He developed these attitudes following a pilgrimage to the Muslim Holy City of Mecca, where he met for the first time, and was impressed with, Muslims of all colors. It was at that time that he began to adopt more orthodox Islamic beliefs, as well as the Muslim name, El-Hajj Malik El-Shabazz.

But his troubles with the Nation of Islam, which until last year referred to whites as "blue-eyed devils," had begun before that, when Elijah Muhammad suspended him for saying that the assassination of President Kennedy was an example of "the chickens coming home to roost."

Mr. Farrakhan, who like Malcolm X was also at one time head of the Harlem mosque, the largest and most influential in New York City, said yesterday that the new recognition of the slain Muslim was not a "departure from previous teachings of the Nation of Islam."

"It is historically true and world-known that Minister Malcolm made great contributions to the Nation of Islam," Mr. Farrakhan said. "But when he departed from the Nation of Islam there was no mention of Malcolm's accomplishments.

"Now, since the Honorable Wallace D. Muhammad has taken over and his mind is a mind of balance and justice, he wants to give balance to the whole Nation of Islam."

Later, in an interview, Minister Farrakhan, who changed his name from Louis to Abdul under the new leadership, explained that the new recognition "had nothing to do with the rehabilitation of Malcolm."

Nor is there any softening on what the Muslims believe was a justifiable reason for Malcolm's suspension.

"Malcolm was instructed by his leader to remain silent and he disobeyed," he said. "This is a violation of the organization's discipline. Not that it [the statement on the Kennedy assassination] was not the truth.

"Punishment of him was wise, because it took the heat out of Malcolm's statement. Otherwise, the anger of blacks and whites who worshiped John Kennedy would have been misdirected at Malcolm and the Nation. And we would have been vamped on [attacked]."

Mr. Farrakhan said that Malcolm X's "mistake" was that he "knew where the Nation [of Islam] should go and would ultimately go, but as a leader he lacked the patience to wait for the development of the minds of the followers toward that direction."

In explaining why, for example, whites were now being permitted and encouraged to join, Mr. Farrakhan said that Elijah Muhammad had not been a strict separatist, but rather had believed that blacks had to develop a strong sense of "self" and of unity before joining with others.

The same, he said, applies to their entry into politics, which Elijah Muhammad had also barred.

What effect the change on Malcolm X's status, like all of the other sweeping policy changes being made, will have on the ranks of Muslims is impossible to assess at this time.

Minister Farrakhan said that with the naming of the temple for him Malcolm's "place in the history of Islam is assumed."

He added: "It forces the community to deal with it and think about it and assess this man unemotionally. It stimulates growth and development."

Columbia's Overdue Apology
to Langston Hughes

The New Yorker
DECEMBER 22, 1967

On a miserably wet evening seven months after the death of Langston Hughes, we sat, almost comfortably (except for our damp feet), in the cavernous Wollman Auditorium, at Columbia University, and listened to the low, bemused voice of Hughes on tape as, against a taped musical background, it sent his "Weary Blues" floating over a group of people who had assembled to pay tribute to him. The program, "A Langston Hughes Memorial Evening," was sponsored by the Forum, which is, in the words of its nineteen-year-old president, Bruce Kanze, "a student organization that brings to the university interesting people whom the university itself would never consider bringing, to discuss issues and topics that are important."

A few minutes after eight, when nearly every seat was filled, three men walked onto the stage: Leon Bibb, the actor and singer; Jonathan Kozol, author of *Death at an Early Age*; and Professor James P. Shenton, of Columbia. ("He teaches a course on Reconstruction—the closest thing to a course on Negro history at Columbia," Mr. Kanze told us later.) They were soon joined by Miss Viveca Lindfors, the actress, who was wearing a pale-gray fur coat but removed it as she was sitting down, and gracefully placed it over her mini-exposed knees.

Professor Shenton, who had to leave early, was introduced, and hurried to the microphone. "I am here partly as a way of saying for Columbia that we owe some apologies," he said solemnly. "For a while, there lived a poet down the street from Columbia, and Columbia never took the time to find out what he was about." The professor paused for a few seconds, and then continued, "For a while, there lived a poet down the street from Columbia, who even attended Columbia for a while, and yet he never received an honorary degree from here. When we buried him, then we gave him a memorial. But, after all, that's the experience of the black man down the street from Columbia."

Professor Shenton left the platform, and Mr. Kozol, a slim young man wearing rimless glasses, came to the microphone. In 1965, he was discharged from a ghetto school in Boston, in part because he read Langston Hughes' poem "Ballad of the Landlord" to his class:

> *Landlord, landlord,*
> *My roof has sprung a leak.*
> *Don't you 'member I told you about it*
> *Way last week? Landlord, landlord,*
> *These steps is broken down. When you come up yourself*
> *It's a wonder you don't fall down.*
> *Ten bucks you say I owe you? Ten bucks you say is due?*
> *Well, that's ten bucks more'n I'll pay you*
> *Till you fix this house up new.*
> *What? You gonna get eviction orders? You gonna cut off my heat?*
> *You gonna take my furniture and throw it in the street?*
> *Um-huh! You talking high and mighty. Talk on—till you get*
> *   through.*
> *You ain't gonna be able to say a word*
> *If I land my fist on you. Police! Police!*
> *Come and get this man!*

He's trying to ruin the government
and overturn the land!
Copper's whistle!
Patrol bell! Arrest.
Precinct station.
Iron cell.
Headlines in press:
MAN THREATENS LANDLORD TENANT HELD NO BAIL
JUDGE GIVES NEGRO 90 DAYS IN COUNTY JAIL

Mr. Kozol said that he might have avoided some of the trouble that eventually led to his firing if he had chosen to "restrict his reading and reference materials to the list of approved publications"—poetry, for instance, to be read from officially approved selections called "Memory Gems." He gave the Hughes audience a sample:

Dare to be right! Dare to be true:
The failings of others can never save you.
Stand by your conscience, your honor, your faith;
Stand like a hero, and battle till death.

And another:

There is beauty in the sunshine
An' clouds that roam the sky;
There is beauty in the Heavens,
An' the stars that shine on high.

Later, Mr. Kozol read from a paper that had been handed in by one of his fourth-grade students after he had asked the class to write about the kinds of things they saw around them:

In my school I see dirty boards and I see papers on the floor. I see an old browken window with a sign on it saying, Do not unlock this window are browken. And I see cracks in

the walls and I see old books with ink poure all over them
and I see old painting hanging on the walls. I see old al-
furbet letter hanging on one nail on the wal see a dirty fire
exit, I see a old closet with supplys for the class. I see pigons
flying all over the school. I see old freght trains throgh the
fence of the school yard

The young teacher spoke at length about his experiences in this
school, and then read a few paragraphs from a description of Africa in
a book called *Our Neighbors Near and Far*:

Yumbu and Minko are a black boy and a black girl who live
in this jungle village. Their skins are of so dark a brown
color that they look almost black. Their noses are large and
flat. Their lips are thick. Their eyes are black and shining,
and their hair is so curly that it seems like wool. They are
Negroes and they belong to the black race.

Two children in another area of the world were described this way:

Two Swiss children live in a farmhouse on the edge of town.
These children are handsome. Their eyes are blue. Their hair
is golden yellow. Their white skins are clear, and their cheeks
are as red as ripe, red apples.

Mr. Kozol said that he had never met Langston Hughes but that
a short while after his much-publicized firing he had received a new
collection of Hughes' "Simple" stories from the poet, with these words
written on the flyleaf: "I wish the rent / Was heaven sent."

Leon Bibb, in his turn, rose and thanked Mr. Hughes, whom he
called Lang, first by reading the James Weldon Johnson poem "O
Black and Unknown Bards" and then by giving a poignant rendering
of Mr. Hughes' poem "The Negro Speaks of Rivers" and the spiritual
"I've Been 'Buked and I've Been Scorned." He wound up by saying,
"Lang had the foresight to stand on his own words."

Soon Hughes' own words were being read by Miss Lindfors, who remained seated, and whose Swedish accent was lost in translation as she read from *The Panther and the Lash*, a recent Hughes collection, brought out by Knopf. She read about the "Junior Addict":

> *Yes, easier to get dope than to get a job—daytime or nighttime job,*
> *teen-age, pre-draft, pre-lifetime job.*
> *"Quick, sunrise, come!*
> *Sunrise out of Africa,*
> *Quick, come! Sunrise, please come! Come! Come!"*

And she read about the "Dream Deferred." And she read "Impasse":

> *I could tell you,*
> *If I wanted to,*
> *What makes me*
> *What I am.*
> *But I don't*
> *Really want to—*
> *And you don't*
> *Give a damn.*

Miss Lindfors also read the poem whose first line is "That Justice is a blind goddess" and the poem about "Birmingham Sunday"—September 15, 1963, when four little Negro girls were killed in Sunday school by a bomb thrown from outside the church. Miss Lindfors read several more poems—some bitterly humorous ones, and the one that asks, "What color / Is the face / Of war?" and one called "Peace," and, finally, "Down Where I Am":

> *Too many years*
> *Beatin' at the door—*
> *I done beat my*
> *Both fists sore.*
> *Too many years*

Tryin' to get up there—
Done broke my ankles down,
Got nowhere.
Too many years
Climbin' that hill,
'Bout out of breath.
I got my fill.
I'm gonna plant my feet
On solid ground.
If you want to see me,
Come down.

The memorial to Langston Hughes ended as it had begun, with Langston Hughes' low, bemused voice—this time telling about how he came from the Midwest to Columbia to go to school, and caused great consternation when he presented himself at Hartley Hall. That was in 1921, and no one of African descent, he says, had ever lived in a dormitory at Columbia. "There are many barriers people try to break down," he told an audience (which had also been a Columbia audience) when the tape was made, in 1964. "I try to do it with poetry."

Remembering John Lewis and the Significance of Freedom Rides

The Palm Beach Post
AUGUST 2, 2020

Being only two years younger than John Lewis, even now I well remember his early years when he took the first blow for freedom, stepping off a bus during an effort to test the Supreme Court's ruling against segregation on interstate bus routes and toilets.

It was a case that came to be known as the Boynton decision, bearing the name of Bruce Boynton, a Black college student discriminated against on an interstate bus route.

There was no social media and only three television networks, none with any people of color. But that seminal moment in our history lit up the country and the world to the challenges America faced on the road to freedom and justice for all, regardless of race, creed, color, or national origin.

And before that journey began, John and a group of thirteen Blacks and whites signed their wills. As John wrote: "We were prepared to die. Some of us signed letters and wills. We didn't know if we'd return."

In Rock Hill, South Carolina, they encountered their first violent resistance. As I wrote in *To the Mountaintop*, a book for younger readers whose parents weren't even born then:

> A group of white toughs who frequented the bus station's pinball machines were not waiting on the Freedom Riders, but when John Lewis stepped off the Greyhound bus and attempted to enter through the white entrance, one of the whites directed him to the colored entrance. Lewis responded: "I have a right to go in there on the grounds of the Supreme Court decision in the Boynton case."
>
> One of the white youths spat out a profanity, and when Lewis ignored it and started in through the door a young white man punched him in the mouth, thus giving Lewis the dubious (but dare I say today, honorable) distinction of taking the first blow to a Freedom Rider.
>
> When other attackers proceeded to beat Lewis, Albert Bigelow, a white Freedom Rider, stepped in between them and was beaten to the ground. So was Genevieve Hughes, a female Freedom Rider. But beaten, bruised, and bleeding, they all got up and refused to press charges against their attackers.

The next day, the group stopped only once, and briefly, in Athens, Georgia. What is most significant about that moment to me is that a few blocks from where they stopped, I sat alone in my dormitory, segregated on the first floor, away from all the other female students on the second floor—the University of Georgia's (UGA) way of resisting the law they couldn't legally resist to desegregate.

But while I didn't know about the Freedom Riders' stop at that time, I did know about those who were engaged in the struggle for justice—as they were only seventy-three miles away in Atlanta, my hometown. On weekends, I used to travel there to practice what would ultimately become my lifelong profession as I helped out on the *Atlanta Inquirer*, a small newspaper started to accurately cover the Atlanta Student Movement, which the all-white newspaper in the city didn't do and which the Black newspaper didn't do fully, due to constraints by its white advertisers.

One of two editors on the *Inquirer* was Julian Bond, a local student from the all-Black Morehouse College who later teamed up with John to push for voting rights; and an English professor, M. Carl Holman, from the all-Black Clark College.

Julian divided his time between getting out the paper and working with the Atlanta students, including helping write their manifesto called the Committee on Appeal for Human Rights. They swore to go to jail without bail until their demands were met. And some did, in fact, go to jail, along with Martin Luther King Jr., who had joined them.

Like today, the young ones had ideas of their own about how to confront injustice, but respect for elders in the movement and the road they had traveled led to a coalition of the generations that ultimately proved successful.

That decade is where the passing of John Lewis took me to. For while Hamilton Holmes and I were alone as Black students on the UGA campus, part of our ability to survive that lonely and sometimes challenging journey was the example of people like John Lewis and Julian Bond and so many others who were confronting violence—beyond the silent violence we were being exposed to daily and being the horrified victims of it—all to make America live up to its promise and to understand its potential greatness.

And while these protests were aimed at achieving equality for people who looked like me—darker or lighter—and were led by people my age and even younger, they were joined by people of all ages, races, creeds, and colors who were on board with the ultimate goal of freedom for all.

John Lewis and his moral crusade continued until he became our latest ancestor last week. We all have an obligation to ensure his life was not in vain. How do we do that, in a nation so divided that we can't even agree on how to protect ourselves and each other from this latest pandemic?

We need to figure out how to share our history, especially with our young, because there is evidence that some 85 percent of our schools are not teaching all of it. On my *PBS NewsHour* Race Matters series, author Margaret Hagerman told me this:

> I think that the most important thing that white parents can do is embrace the idea that all children are worthy of their consideration and that we should care about our community. We should think about the collective good. We should focus on how we can help everyone, rather than just focusing on our own child.

Even when our segregated schools had to depend on hand-me-down textbooks from the white schools, often with pages missing, when our people couldn't give us first-class citizenship, they gave us a first-class sense of ourselves. So many of us today are trying to hold on to that important message.

Now, in this current moment of twin pandemics—COVID-19 and injustice—I return to John Lewis and his now immortal words, most recently remembered by his civil rights colleague, Andrew Young: that we need to learn to "disagree without being disagreeable."

With my history and John's in my head and heart, I agree.

Mandela's Birthday and
Trayvon Martin's Loss

The New Yorker
JULY 18, 2013

The convergence of outrage over the verdict in the Trayvon Martin case in Florida, where I live, and the celebrations of Nelson Mandela's ninety-fifth birthday in South Africa, my home for many years, brought me back to a story from a time in Mandela's life when he was on the run.

It was 1961. Mandela and other members of the African National Congress had just declared war on the unjust system of apartheid. He had organized the ANC's underground wing Umkhonto we Sizwe (Spear of the Nation)—resorting to violent force after, he insisted, all peaceful means of trying to achieve freedom and first-class citizenship for the black majority in South Africa had failed. He was being sought by the police, moving from place to place. On this occasion, he had taken refuge in the home of Wolfie Kodesh, a white supporter.

One day, Kodesh got up at 5 a.m. to find that Mandela, a fitness buff from his early days, was dressed in a tracksuit and getting ready to go running. Mandela wrote about it later, simply saying that he "annoyed Wolfie every morning, for I would wake up at five, change into my running clothes, and run on the spot for more than an hour."

But there was more to it. When Kodesh got up for the first time and saw Mandela preparing to run, according to the South African journalist Max du Preez, "He told him that a black man running around a white suburb would look very suspicious and refused to give him the key to the door."

Mandela might give his great-grandchildren the same advice today—even fifty-two years later, and even under different political circumstances—in most of the country's suburbs, which remain predominantly white. In an article from South Africa entitled "From Trayvon Martin to Andries Tatane: Cognitive Dissonance and the Black Male Body," the writer Gillian Schutte reports what I have heard from many other South Africans—that the Trayvon Martin case has resonance there and that there is "shock and anger" over the not-guilty verdict. "We commiserate about our own black sons and how unsafe they would be in the United States," Schutte writes. But then she goes to cite instances when black men and boys in South Africa have recently met fates parallel to Trayvon Martin's—including the case of Andries Tatane, who was "beaten by police and shot in the chest at close range with rubber bullets." Continuing, Schutte writes, "And somehow in all of this we fail to make the connection with the continued violence towards the black male body in South Africa."

Schutte asks the question that many people in the United States— black and white—are also asking: When is this going to change? How much longer must we watch young black boys and men die?

And the questions come as the world—almost as one—prays for the man who was once warned not to go running in a suburb, Nelson Mandela. Statements from his African National Congress party ask everyone to reflect on his life, and say that this day "most importantly . . . provides an opportunity to emulate this life well lived."

These are appropriate words for the South African nation, including the ANC, which many believe sometimes sends mixed signals about its commitment to those ideals. But they also resonate for those living in the United States in troubled times like these. In a few days, another case will be heard, in Wisconsin, involving a white man killing an unarmed black thirteen-year-old, in which three of four black people in the jury pool have been removed by the defense.

One of my nieces wrote to me saying that she was so angry about the verdict in the Trayvon Martin case and asking me, "Auntie, what can I do?" She is of the age that South Africans call "born frees"— those born long after Nelson Mandela went to prison. I will tell her to honor his birthday today and channel her anger by studying (maybe anew or reviewing) his history and that of the people in this country who fought and made sacrifices for freedom. And maybe she and her generation (and members of mine who need reminding) will come away understanding that it takes more than a few days of protest and momentary righteous anger to redress wrongs. I will write and ask my niece: how long are you prepared to fight for what's right?

I will also suggest, if she plans to post a birthday greeting to Nelson Mandela on her Facebook page or elsewhere, that she might do so with the words that he and his fellow freedom fighters often used when they spoke about freedom and those who fought for it—here and there: "Long live!"

Postscript: Julian Bond

The New Yorker
AUGUST 17, 2015

The opening lyric from that old civil rights song—"Woke up this morning with my mind stayed on freedom"—may not have been written with Julian Bond in mind, but he personified it. As a member of the Georgia House of Representatives and the Georgia Senate, as a leader of the NAACP and the Southern Poverty Law Center, as an activist and a professor and a friend, he answered the call of justice every day. Julian passed away over the weekend, at the age of seventy-five. I will miss him terribly. He and I were children of the civil rights movement and, in a way, grew up in it together.

I first met Julian in the summer of 1960, at one of the informal gatherings of the burgeoning Atlanta Student Movement. (Well, it might have been a party, which was one of the ways that the demonstrators de-stressed.) I was home in Atlanta, waiting for my desegregation lawsuit against the University of Georgia to work its way through the courts, and Julian was a rising senior at Morehouse College. Even then, his style of writing and thinking was evident in his work. In March of that year, he had helped draft an article called "An Appeal for Human Rights," which ran as a full-page advertisement in several Atlanta-area newspapers. The document was forthright, elegant, powerful. "Today's youth will not sit by submissively while being denied all the rights and privileges and joys of life," it read. "We do not intend to wait placidly for those rights which are legally and morally ours to be meted out to us one at a time." Segregation, it concluded, was "robbing not only the segregated but the segregator of his human dignity." (As Julian made clear in 1967, when I interviewed him for "Talk of the Town," he didn't have much patience for embellishment. One of the hardest things about serving in the Georgia legislature, he told me then, "was getting used to the flowery language.")

Although Julian's main brief was as a theoretician and tactician, he also spent time on the front lines. He took to heart the teachings of Ella Baker, a leader from the older generation of black activists, who, in 1960, convened the meeting from which the Student Nonviolent Coordinating Committee (SNCC) emerged, with Julian as a cofounder. Baker's invocation address, called "Bigger than a Hamburger," set the tone for the organization: its task was "to rid America of the scourge of racial segregation and discrimination—not only at lunch counters but in every aspect of life." The group was more militant, more in-your-face than the Southern Christian Leadership Conference and the NAACP; Julian and his fellow activists became known as the movement's shock troops.

Julian left Morehouse halfway through his senior year to devote himself more fully to SNCC. (He was the son of a college president and came from a long line of educated black folks, and eventually he went back and got his degree.) That year, he became the managing editor of the *Atlanta Inquirer*, an upstart protest weekly, which was created to do what none of the white-owned papers or the more conservative black-owned ones would—tell the story of the Atlanta Student Movement in all its manifestations. By that point, I and my fellow plaintiff in the University of Georgia case, Hamilton Holmes, had won, becoming the first African American students to enroll there. I began working with Julian at the *Inquirer* on otherwise relaxing weekends home from the still tense UGA campus.

We settled into a predictable rhythm: the student protesters would stage their demonstrations in the morning, get arrested, make bail, and then come tell their stories to Julian, me, and the editor in chief,

M. Carl Holman, a professor of English at Clark College. We took turns writing up the narratives as news stories, although I sometimes did my own reporting. I spent one Saturday, for instance, at Atlanta's public hospital, Grady Memorial—where Hamilton later became the chairman of the orthopedic unit—chronicling the chaos in the emergency room. At one point, one of the young doctors showed me the path of a bullet that had gone through a man's head by sliding an instrument into it. Julian loved that story. He was a patient mentor, just as Ella Baker had been to him, and he had a quiet sense of humor. He wasn't the most energetic dancer, but at one of our parties, getting into the spirit of things, he wrote a poem:

> See that girl
> Shake that thing.
> We can't all be
> Martin Luther King.

(He remembered it when I mentioned it to him during a visit, almost fifty years later.)

In 1965, Julian was elected to the Georgia House of Representatives. His colleagues, however, refused to seat him, because of his opposition to the Vietnam War, and he didn't assume office until 1967. He was twenty-eight years old. He continued to campaign around the country, not only for civil rights but also for human rights, not only at home but also in the global community. When Julian came to New York to give a talk to the Southern Conference Educational Fund, one of the oldest interracial civil rights organizations in the country, I went to cover it for the *New Yorker*. In his address, Julian discussed the trajectory of the movement and how the passage of the Civil Rights Act, in 1964, had changed its tenor, making people complacent, making them think that the victory had been won. In his soft-spoken but firm and confident way, he went on to suggest that this apparent victory had sapped the movement's support. "Lack of interest is more killing than lack of money," he said. "Negroes must not forget race consciousness as long as they are victims of racism."

Up until the day he left us, Julian never forgot that consciousness. He served as president of the Southern Poverty Law Center when it was founded and, in 1998, was elected chairman of the NAACP, a post that he never could have imagined occupying during his years with SNCC. And his consciousness went beyond race—he also became a climate change activist and an advocate for marriage equality. Julian Bond's legacy surely lies in the fact that he steadfastly followed the movement's dictum: keep on keepin' on.

The Death of a Friend Inspires Reflections on Mortality

The Root

JANUARY 27, 2014

Something there is about the death of a friend or colleague close to your own age that makes you contemplate your own mortality. It happened to me several years ago when my good friend Ed Bradley passed, and it seems to be happening more frequently now as I am fully ensconced in my seventies.

On a slightly chilly Sarasota, Florida, morning this past weekend, my husband, Ronald, and I headed to a deeply frigid Boston to join friends, colleagues, and family in memorializing the most recent of our friends to pass: Dr. Kenneth C. Edelin, who had left us a few weeks before at age seventy-four after what seemed like a very brief illness and a determined will to live.

I often smile as I find myself imitating my late grandmother, who turned first to the obituary page when she opened the morning paper. I never knew until now why she did that. And I am not totally sure why I do—except, almost on a weekly basis, I find people I knew or knew about, who are a few years younger or a few years older than I am.

People like Julius Chambers, once head of the NAACP Legal

Defense and Educational Fund; the poet Amiri Baraka; and John Dotson Jr., who was one of the few black leaders in the newspaper industry. Like Ken Edelin, he died of a rare, aggressive cancer. And there are many more who, when I read of their passing, cause me to confront my own mortality—although for now, with the exception of a few arthritic joints, my health is good.

But it is a time of life when I look at the "things" I've accumulated—including a closetful of shoes that would make Imelda Marcos jealous—and I find myself thinking about getting my house in order so that my survivors won't have too big a burden once I'm gone. Even my husband, a great physical specimen who is obsessive about his weight and otherwise diligent about his health, wondered aloud as we were driving somewhere recently why it seemed to him that more men were passing and leaving behind women who suddenly had to manage alone. Women like our dear friend Barbara Edelin, who was steadfast in her support of her husband of thirty-six years through each debilitating state of his health and who, along with him, planned the service to which we were now flying.

So as I sat in the chapel waiting for the service to begin, I thought about the things I had begun to think about—silly things like what would become of my closetful of shoes, but more seriously, how I should live what days I have left that will leave something for which to be remembered.

But before I could go there again, the service began, and for the next two hours, elevating, as well as instructive, reflections came from friends who knew Edelin in all of his incarnations.

Deval Patrick, the boyish-looking governor of Massachusetts, was the first to give reflections. He remembered a man who was subjected to what he called "a nasty prosecution" in 1975 over a late-term abortion that he performed on a seventeen-year-old that eventually led to an acquittal and a landmark ruling on reproductive rights—and Edelin's designation as a hero of the women's movement.

Giving a brief summary of Edelin's pioneering career, the governor recalled that Edelin was the first black chief of obstetrics and gynecology at Boston City Hospital, the chair of the obstetrics and gynecology department at the Boston University School of Medicine, gynecologist in chief at Boston University Hospital, a dean at Boston University, a crusader against health disparities when we had few, and a mentor for a generation of health care professionals who learned from his work and his example. The governor went on to speak of a man with a "twinkle in his eye, as if he was anticipating, or even hoping for, some mischief, and that warm, almost shy smile. Ken was a loving man—as a husband, father, grandfather, friend . . . and leader."

But in his closing line, the governor set a tone and a theme that was to be repeated by those who followed, summarizing the essential core of a life well lived, saying of Edelin: "He was a man of justice, importantly—not because he had set out on a crusade, but because justice is what love looks like out in the open."

Each speaker—from the president of Planned Parenthood to the NAACP LDF executives who spoke of Edelin's commitment to the board—inspired with words that grabbed at the heart and the mind.

And there was a little bit of Marvin Gaye's "What's Going On," with words that had as much meaning, in a different way, as they had when Gaye himself sang, "Brother, brother, brother. There's far too many of you dying." Hmm, I thought, as I swayed in my seat to the music.

There was Dr. Robert Rusher, a Kaiser Permanente pulmonary physician and Boston University School of Medicine alum, who stood in the pulpit wearing his white doctor's coat and a red tie because Dr. Ken Edelin had insisted that the interns always keep their red ties on.

Dr. Edgar—aka Eddie—Mandeville, chief of obstetrics and gynecology at Harlem Hospital, spoke of Edelin's courage in the face of the illness that finally took his life. "We all saw it on display during the trial," he said, referring to the abortion case of 1975. "Last year," he went on, "Ken underwent a pelvic exenteration, which, without being specific, is one of the most devastating surgical procedures we offer. It robs one of great chunks not only of your anatomy but of your personhood. Most of our medical colleagues who I told of Ken's decision stated that they would have thrown in the towel, but Ken never blinked or whined."

Deborah C. Jackson, president of Cambridge College and a long-time friend of the family, spoke also of how "Ken did not go gently into that good night." Several of Edelin's eight grandchildren stood in the pulpit as sixteen-year-old Kendall read a letter she wrote to God, asking why He took her grandfather, but ending with the uplifting "I'll see you later."

It was Jeh Charles Johnson, the secretary of homeland security and Edelin's nephew, who spoke of the impetus for Edelin's decision to become a doctor when "he helplessly watched his mother die when he was twelve years old." And these, Edelin's own words in his powerful book, *Broken Justice*:

> She was only 46. Through the loneliness of being a moth-
> erless child, shuttled from relative to relative through the
> turmoil of adolescence and rebellion, I became all the more
> determined to be a doctor—a woman's doctor—to save lives
> and perhaps spare some other woman's son the anguish I
> had to go through.

And finally, the Reverend Liz Walker delivered the eulogy. The former television anchor spoke movingly about the support she got from Edelin, her obstetrician, twenty-something years ago when she was being publicly vilified for being public, pregnant, and unwed. Dr. Edelin, she said, gave her the inspiration and support to face the criticism without shame.

In her softly soaring voice, she went on to tell the hushed and crowded chapel at Boston University, "He probed the most profound depths of life [and] he confronted his own mortality, something few of us are able to do." She concluded with a few words about the many ways people used power, but also of the proper way Edelin used his, saying, "Power at its best is love implementing the demands of justice, and justice at its best is power correcting everything that stands against love."

But the most powerful words of all came from Edelin himself—not the caring crusader, healer and teacher, but a poet, whose prescient words in the poem "The Labyrinth of Life," written a year before he transitioned, adorned the last page of the memorial program:

Remember what you learned each day,
Use those things to find your way.
Exercise your hard-won choice,
Give your inner self a voice
Walk through the dawn, run through the night.
Don't be paralyzed by fright.
The journey's course will set you free,
This journey is your life, you see.
Now I'm at my journey's end.
There is one gift to give again.

By the end of the service, I was no longer thinking about my own mortality but Ken's, which left me and so many others with a challenge and a road map to navigate this mortal life.

When I Met Dr. King

The New Yorker
APRIL 4, 2018

My one and only encounter with Martin Luther King Jr. was during a chance meeting on what was then called "Sweet Auburn Avenue," the prosperous hub of black-owned businesses in Atlanta. It was the summer of 1961, when King had earned the love and respect of the city's young civil rights demonstrators with whom he had marched. I was working as a reporter for the *Atlanta Inquirer*, an independent black newspaper covering the city's ongoing segregation, writing stories that mainstream newspapers chose to ignore.

By the time I met King, he and a group of local students had triumphed in their effort to end the racist practice of separate and unequal in local restaurants, shops, and schools. King had joined them on the picket line, at sit-ins, and in jail. The attorney Donald Hollowell represented the students in court. The experience would inspire the young people to add a new mantra to their freedom slogans: "King is our leader, Hollowell is our lawyer, and we shall not be moved."

King's support for the demonstrators in Atlanta led to one of the worst experiences of his career. When the students were released after merchants agreed to desegregate, King was forced to remain in jail and was transported to a prison miles away from Atlanta. He was made to lie in the back of a police vehicle with a dog snarling at him the entire way there. Even after his release, challenges remained throughout the South.

I met King many months after his release on a bright, sunny day, when I happened to be on Sweet Auburn Avenue with a colleague, who suddenly turned to me and said, "There's Dr. King." I was awed by this chance meeting with a man who, at that point, was already the icon of the civil rights movement.

I ran up to him, prepared to introduce myself and to lavish praise on him for all that he had done for Atlanta and the students, and for his sacrifices on behalf of black Americans. As I started to introduce myself—before I could get past my name—he reached for my hand, energetically shaking it, while telling me he was proud to meet me. "You are doing a such magnificent job down there," he said, a reference to my enrollment at the all-white University of Georgia, where Hamilton Holmes and I were the first African American students to attend earlier that year. As I recalled, in a book I wrote years later, King told me that education "was the key to our freedom, and then he generously thanked me again and wished me success."

Before I could tell him how proud of him I was, he was mobbed by other admirers, which prevented him from seeing the tears rolling down my cheeks. I will always remember that moment and what it taught me about King and one of his core values: humility. Over the next several years, I watched King with admiration as I tried to find my way in journalism. In 1963, while sitting at my desk at the *New Yorker*, I watched the March on Washington, which he and other civil rights activists organized, and shed more tears as King talked about his dream of living in a country where his four children would not be judged by the color of their skin but by the content of their character. In the speech, he displayed the humility as well as the strength of his convictions that I had seen in Atlanta, before hundreds of thousands of Americans.

King's assassination fifty years ago caused me to leave a special fellowship for "new journalism" I had at Washington University, in St. Louis. By then there were riots in the streets all over the country, and I didn't think the classroom was where I needed to be.

I went to Washington to cover, for *Transaction* magazine, the Poor People's Campaign and the next phase of the civil rights movement, focusing on human rights and economic justice. Thousands traveled to the nation's capital to spend their days in tents, undeterred by the pouring rain that left the Mall a muddy mess.

They made their way, each and every day, for six weeks, to the grounds and halls of Congress to make their demands heard, undeterred by nature or by human resistance. And while King was no longer physically among them, surely they were motivated by his spirit and his determination for all of God's children to be free at last.

Nelson Mandela, the Father

The New Yorker
MAY 3, 2013

To the very end, Nelson Rolihlahla Mandela, though frail and somewhat forgetful, remained the Father of the Nation for South Africans. It could even be said that, in the several trips he's made to the hospital over the past two years, he was, in his own way, preparing his family—biological and extended—for his final return home. The renowned South African writer Zakes Mda once told me, "In our indigenous languages, we reserved the equivalent words of 'death' only for animals. For humans, we say 'she has left us,' 'He had passed,' 'she's gone home,' 'He's gone to join the ancestors.'" It seemed as if Madiba—that is Mandela's Xhosa clan name—had delayed his departure long past that of many of his contemporaries and comrades-in-arms so that his family, both near and national, could simply mourn him, without the sense that his loss might throw the country into a crisis.

Fathers can make themselves felt through their absence; Mandela did, by walking away from power after his term as president was up. Mandela's own father passed away from tuberculosis when Mandela was nine. And yet, Mandela has written, "I defined myself through my

father." By that he meant that his father possessed "a proud rebellious-
ness, a stubborn sense of fairness, that I recognize in myself."

Mandela would be the first to admit that he did a lousy job as
the biological father of six children, by two different wives. He was
married first and foremost to the movement—to the liberation of his
people from the vicious, stifling bondage of a white minority who saw
themselves as superior, who forcibly removed blacks and other people
of color to isolated townships that often lacked running water and in-
door plumbing, and which the regime could easily encircle in case of
trouble. Mandela wrote about the difficulties of his first marriage, to
Evelyn Mase, in his autobiography, *Long Walk to Freedom*:

> My devotion to the ANC and the struggle was unremitting.
> This disturbed Evelyn. . . . I patiently explained to her that
> politics was not a distraction but my lifework, that it was an
> essential and fundamental part of my being.

The aftermath of the separation from Evelyn was not pleasant.
Soon, however, Mandela, by then a young, successful lawyer, met and
married a beautiful social worker named Nomzamo Winfreda Madik-
izela. Winnie, whose first name, Nomzamo, means, appropriately in
retrospect, "she who undergoes trials," also demonstrated against the
white regime and paid for it with imprisonment, once almost losing
the child she was carrying; she spent 491 days in solitary confinement.
She rarely saw her husband. When Winnie's second child, Zindzi, was
born, Mandela was miles away, visiting his ailing son by Evelyn, itself a
rare act on his part. Mandela even remained outside, in the car, when a
comrade came into their house and asked Winnie to pack some clothes
for him, because he was going away, to an unspecified place, for an
unspecified amount of time. It was almost three decades.

Knowing Mandela meant getting used to his absences. He had
come into his political consciousness after leaving his rural home, in
the Eastern Cape, where he was born, in 1918, and, after his father's
death, was reared in the house of the powerful Thembu acting regent,

a member of the Xhosa nation. By the time Mandela got to college, his innate moral compass and the traits he had inherited from his father had begun to define him; he prematurely left Fort Hare, a prestigious black college, after a protest about the poor quality of food ended in a compromise he couldn't accept.

After that, Mandela headed to Johannesburg, the fast-paced city known to South Africans as Egoli—the City of Gold. There, despite living in bleak quarters, studying by candlelight, and often going hungry, Mandela, who wanted to become a lawyer, met the people whose guidance put him on the path that joined his history with his country's. Men like Walter Sisulu and Oliver Tambo and Gaur Radebe got him involved in his first public demonstration, a bus boycott in the Alexandra township; others provided his first introduction to the African National Congress. He rapidly became one of its leaders, organizing peaceful protests. All this extracurricular activity meant that it took Mandela longer than usual—about seven years—to qualify as an attorney. He finally managed it, just as the white-controlled government introduced the apartheid system, in 1948. In 1952, Mandela opened the first black law firm in Johannesburg with Tambo, defending mostly poor black people—for little or no money—who would, no doubt, not have had legal representation otherwise; and, for the first time, he got to know Indian South Africans, who were also victims of the system, as well as whites, although for a time he was distant from both. And he continued his work for the ANC.

On March 21, 1960, police opened fire on a group of black South Africans who were peacefully protesting laws requiring blacks to carry passes that restricted their movement. The police killed sixty-nine people, in what became known as the Sharpeville massacre. Shortly afterward, the regime declared a state of emergency and banned the ANC. Sharpeville persuaded Mandela that peaceful protests wouldn't be enough. Already facing treason charges, he went underground as a leader of the ANC's new guerrilla wing, Umkhonto we Sizwe ("Spear of the Nation").

Dressed in different disguises—a gardener, a chef, a soldier—he popped up around the country, and then disappeared again. His exploits earned him a nickname: the Black Pimpernel.

As Mandela said, in a statement released in June, 1961:

I have had to separate myself from my dear wife and children, from my mother and sisters, to live as an outlaw in my own land. I have had to close my business, to abandon my profession, and live in poverty and misery, as many of my people are doing.

He was posing as a chauffeur when he was finally caught and arrested (thanks, it is widely believed, to information that the CIA or MI6 intelligence agents gave to South African authorities). In court, Mandela defiantly wore the traditional outfit of a Xhosa chief—a leopardskin kaross with one bare shoulder exposed, and beads around his neck. This time, he was charged with inciting workers to strike and with leaving the country illegally. He was faithful to his movement marriage. He accused the government of "behav[ing] in a way no civilized government should dare behave when faced with a peaceful, disciplined, sensible, and democratic expression of the views of its own population." The South African political journalist Max du Preez wrote, of Mandela's goodbye to Winnie, "There were no tears, no clinging to each other; he gave her advice—almost like a father figure—on how to conduct herself in his absence, and gave her a letter of love and encouragement written earlier."

Seven months later, he and nine others were brought back to court, this time charged under the all-encompassing Suppression of Communism Act, as well as the Sabotage Act, in what became known as the Rivonia Trial. They faced the death penalty.

Mandela, known as Accused No. 1, was undeterred. Given a chance to address the court, he spoke for four hours, talking passionately about the desire of the black majority to have "a just share in the whole of South Africa," as well as "equal political rights." He insisted that "the violence we chose to adopt was not terrorism," and that the ANC was committed to "nonviolence and negotiations."

And then he spoke words that captured the attention not only of those in the courtroom but of people all over the world. They remain to this day among his most memorable—and are the only words of his captured on audio for almost three decades:

> During my lifetime, I have dedicated myself to this struggle of the African people. I have fought against white domination, and I have fought against black domination. I have cherished the ideal of a democratic and free society in which all persons live together in harmony and with equal opportunity. It is an ideal which I hope to live for and to achieve. But if needs be, it is an ideal for which I am prepared to die.

The sentence was not death but life in prison.

For the next two and a half decades, Mandela was the invisible man. He and other political prisoners were first confined on Robben Island, two square miles of land surrounded by the waters off Cape Town. While they managed to create an atmosphere that was referred to as Mandela University, where the younger prisoners were encouraged to study, prison life took its toll. Mandela was forced to dig in a lime quarry, day in and day out, without protection for his eyes from the sun and dust, and suffered such lasting damage to them that, even after his release, he could not abide the flashing lights from journalists' cameras. In time, he also developed tuberculosis, which made him vulnerable to problems with his lungs that continued until his death.

After eighteen years, he was moved, along with Walter Sisulu, Raymond Mhlaba, and Andrew Mlangeni, to Pollsmoor Prison, near Cape Town, which is where he was when I first went to South Africa, in 1985, when the country was in yet another state of emergency. Mandela, I had been told, busied himself with a garden he had planted. I stood on a nearby hillside and tried in vain to catch a glimpse of it or of him, but I had been followed by security police and so couldn't linger long.

I found that children in every black township knew his name, and not only his. One day, walking up to a small group of teenagers dancing in a circle and singing in Zulu, I asked what the words meant, and they told me breathlessly, "We want Mandela to be released, and Walter Sisulu, Raymond Mhlaba, Andrew Mlangeni, Govan Mbeki, and all the other political prisoners."

Mandela's marriage to the movement had produced children like these. But his daughter Zindzi was only eighteen months old when her father was sent to prison, and, along with her mother and sister, Zenani, endured night raids from security forces, along with banishment to a remote town. In 1985, young Zindzi stood before a crowd of thousands at Jabulani Stadium, in Soweto, and read a letter from her father that had been smuggled out of prison, his first public statement in twenty-one years. She began, "My father says . . ." and went on to read his refusal of an offer of conditional release that involved renouncing violence. It ended with the resounding words "Only free men can negotiate. Prisoners cannot enter into contracts. . . . Your freedom and mine cannot be separated. I will return."

The speech invigorated the movement. But in time, and on his own, Mandela began discussions with the apartheid regime about how to bring about a peaceful transition. Five years and a day later, on February 11, 1990, to the surprise of even his comrades, both inside and outside the country, Mandela was released. He was seventy-one. He had been in prison for twenty-seven years.

In the ensuing months, before he actually became president of the country, he spent time not only embracing the children of the movement but extending an olive branch to the whites who had never reached out to them or to him. He seemed to many to go out of his way to reassure whites that he believed in the words he had long ago spoken—that South Africa belongs to all who live in it, black and white. It wasn't obvious to everyone in his own ranks that he should be so welcoming, so inclusive. It was obvious to Mandela. It also earned him and the Afrikaner president who freed him, F. W. de Klerk, the Nobel Peace Prize, in 1993, the year before Mandela replaced de Klerk.

Mandela further solidified his credentials as Father of the Nation, the whole nation, when he pitched up at a rugby match wearing the team cap. The Springboks team had been all-white, and blacks associated them with apartheid, but when the game was over, and the team had won the 1995 Rugby World Cup, a broadly smiling Mandela walked onto the field, shook the team captain's hand, and encouraged the entire nation to "get behind our boys."

He had another nasty divorce, from Winnie, in the interim, though they eventually reconciled. When his eldest son died of an AIDS-related illness, the country saw Mandela as a grieving father, one who also stood up and told the nation—his nation—that there was no shame in being HIV-infected, and that people living with HIV should not be stigmatized. It was a dramatic departure from the position of Thabo Mbeki, his successor and the president at the time, who had dismissed the connection between HIV and AIDS.

In his autobiography, *Long Walk to Freedom*, published in 1994, the year he assumed the presidency, Mandela wrote: "To be the father of a nation is a great honor, but to be the father of a family is a greater joy. But it was a joy I had far too little of."

And so Mandela wasted no time in trying to locate the father he had not been to his biological children, their children, and those of his third wife, Graça Machel.

I interviewed Mandela in 1994, a few days before he was to be sworn in as president of the Republic of South Africa. I apologized to him for not being able to be at the inauguration itself, explaining that there was hardly anything on earth that would make me miss that historic occasion, but that my son Chuma was graduating from Emory University, in Atlanta, on the same day. And I needed to fly back for it. At that, Mandela relaxed his stiff, about-to-be-interviewed posture, leaned forward slightly in his chair, and smiled, with an enveloping warmth.

"Of course you have to be there. You can always interview me," he said.

I found myself responding, "Thank you, Tata"—just what a child of Mandela would have called him.

Now I am reminded of something else I learned during my years in the country—which is probably why South Africans, though sad now that the Father of the Nation has closed his eyes forever, will not be desolate. It is the tradition that takes South Africans to the grave site of a departed one to speak about whatever problems they may be having, in the belief that wisdom will come from one who is now an ancestor, and who lives forever.

Epilogue

Reasons for Hope amid America's Racial Unrest

PBS NewsHour
JULY 1, 2020

Charlayne Hunter-Gault:

Despite the unity seen in Black Lives Matter protests, Americans have often been portrayed as being woefully divided on most major subjects.

But David Brooks, a *New York Times* columnist, has been insisting even before recent events that this country is more united than divided.

You surely know David from the *NewsHour*'s weekly "Shields and Brooks" segment each Friday.

But, in another role, he's been reaching out to Americans of all stripes to understand how they're feeling in these uncertain times.

David Brooks, thank you so much for joining us.

David Brooks:

Oh, it's so great to be with you.

Charlayne Hunter-Gault:

You know, you have written columns in the past few months saying that the country is more united than divided.

Who were you talking to, and what was leading you to that conclusion, that we're more united than divided?

David Brooks:

I put out a plea to my readers, and 6,500 sent me essays about how they were doing.

And a lot of them were in bad shape. And yet, when I spoke to them over the weeks and over the months, they were super impressed by how their neighbors were showing up for each other. And the things they talked about over and over again was: My local restaurant is now giving away food. My local church is now a soup kitchen. My neighbors are showing up for me.

And there was a sense that the country was actually acting for each other.

And so I think there was a feeling—especially in the first few weeks of the pandemic, a feeling of common action and common purpose and common vulnerability.

Charlayne Hunter-Gault:

Has there been anything else, as a result of the pandemic, that has made people come closer together or realize they were more united than they thought?

David Brooks:

The reaction to the Floyd murder has been, on the whole, a very good news story.

I look at the marches, and there was some violence in the beginning, but the violence has gone down now. They were not a Black uprising. They were an American uprising.

Charlayne Hunter-Gault:

What's the solution to making the unity last?

David Brooks:

I think the first thing we have to do is learn from each other and talk to each other.

My rule is—the more uncomfortable the conversation is, the more I learn from it. And so I'm hoping the first thing we do is make use of this moment of useful discomfort to face realities in our country and to face each other.

And that's the shift in consciousness that needs to take—you know, personal transformation and social transformation happen together. But then it has to be institutionalized with action.

And one of the things that needs to be happening is, because of redlining and segregation and prejudice, we have areas of concentrated poverty all across this country. To me, this won't be fixed until the school I visited in Detroit a few months ago, which was all African American, where three percent of kids were reading on grade level, this won't be fixed until that's fixed.

And so getting involved in the things that join us together, the things we love together. We love our kids. And if we can focus on African American education, education for poor people, that's part of the solution, not just police reform.

We love our work. If we can give common work, so there's a little more economic equality in this country. And then we love our neighborhoods. The people who are doing the best work are in the neighborhood.

I was talking about Watts recently. And there's an organization there, Sisters of Watts. And they have been living in Watts their whole lives. They know what Watts needs. Outside groups don't know what Watts needs. But if we got money to them, and resources and power to them, they actually know what to do.

And so getting money right to the grass roots, to the people who can't write grants because they're too busy, that, to me, is how you build up a neighborhood. And the neighborhood is the unit of change here.

Charlayne Hunter-Gault:

Tell me about the Weavers and how they fit into your solution for unity.

David Brooks:

Yes.

So, for years and years, it seemed like, every problem, every column I was writing and every appearance I did with Mark [Shields] was about social isolation, social disconnection, and polarization.

And I realized—this is a problem underlying a lot of other problems. But it's also being solved at the local level by community builders, who I call Weavers. And they're creating connection. They're bridging divides. They're creating a better country, and they're finding a better way to live.

So, for example, in Chicago, in a neighborhood called Englewood, which is a tough neighborhood, there's a woman who lives there named Asiaha Butler. And Asiaha was going to move out of Englewood because she had a daughter and she was afraid for her safety. And she was going to go to Atlanta.

And she had booked the moving company and everything. On the day before she was going to move out, she looked across the street at an empty lot, and there was a little girl in a pink dress playing with broken bottles.

And she turns to her husband and says, "We're not moving out. We're not going to be just another family that left this behind."

And so she googled "volunteer in Englewood." And now she runs

RAGE, which is the big community organization in Englewood. They have cleaned up the lots. They have created connections within the community.

Now, if you go there, there's some stores. And when stores are open, they sell T-shirts, "Proud Daughter of Englewood," "Proud Son of Englewood."

And so the community begins to get turned around by Weavers. And I find Weavers everywhere. We drop into a place, Wilkes, North Carolina. We ask around: Who makes a difference here? Who's trusted here?

And we found seventy-five people doing amazing stuff. And so Weavers are—I think, are leading us into a better future.

Charlayne Hunter-Gault:

Are you hopeful, based on what you have seen, that the solutions you have seen working are going to continue? And how do you make them continue for the benefit of all of us?

David Brooks:

When I look at the marches, when I look at the people I speak to through the Weave Project, when I look at the people I interview through my journalism, I just see such a desire for just a new era, and such a sense that this is a portal to a different future.

And I have faith in that.

Acknowledgments

When I think back over my sixty years of reporting on My People, one of the things that comes to mind is a song I first heard in 1954 when I was in eighth grade and which has stayed with me until this day: "You'll Never Walk Alone." To be sure, while I sat alone at my computer writing about My People, I never walked alone. And for that I want to express my deepest appreciation to all who supported my journey. Many of those supporters, like my mother, Althea, and Grandmother Frances, are now Ancestors; as is M. Carl Holman, my very first editor at the *Atlanta Inquirer*, which, unlike any other local papers, fully covered the Atlanta Student Movement and its goal to end segregation in Atlanta. Over the years, I have had encouragement and support from far too many to list here, but I hope they will know how deeply grateful I am that they allowed me to walk with them. And that brings me to those who walked with me as I assembled this collection: my husband, Ronald, and my children, Suesan and Chuma—always available to read and react, as only loving Family members can; my agents at Aevitas Creative Management: David Kuhn, Nate Muscato, and Arlie Johannson; Kelsey Coffey, my fellow Georgia Dawg, '21, now a blossoming reporter and upcoming anchor who never grew weary of helping me dig deep and kept detailed records of all she managed to unearth . . . and finally Sarah Ried, my editor at HarperCollins, whose gentle but authoritative, ever-present guidance helped me "walk on with hope in my heart," enabling me to produce *My People*.

About the Author

CHARLAYNE HUNTER-GAULT is an Emmy-winning journalist who has been in the field for more than five decades. After starting her career at the *New Yorker*, Hunter-Gault joined the *New York Times*, where she established the Harlem Bureau, the first of its kind, and eventually joined *PBS NewsHour* as its first substitute anchor and national correspondent. The author of four previous books, Hunter-Gault lives in Florida and on Martha's Vineyard.